THE EVERYTHING

DATING BOOK

How to meet new people, where to go
and what to say—make the most of every date!

Leah and Elina Furman

Adams Media Corporation
Holbrook, Massachusetts

To Faivel

Acknowledgments

We'd like to thank everyone who helped make this project possible, including Pam Liflander, our editor, for all her hard work, and our mother, Mira, for her unwavering support. John Nikkah's assistance in gathering interviews, as well as his input as the Date Doctor, has been invaluable. Thank you to everyone who so kindly contributed their thoughts and experiences to the pages of this book.

An Everything Series Book.
The Everything Series is a trademark of Adams Media Corporation.

Published by Adams Media Corporation
260 Center Street, Holbrook, MA 02343

ISBN: 1-58062-185-6

Printed in the United States of America.

J I H G F E D C B A

Library of Congress Cataloging-in-Publication Data
Furman, Leah.
The everything dating book/Leah and Elina Furman.
p.   cm.
Includes index.
ISBN 1-58062-185-6
1. Dating (Social customs) 2. Man-woman relationships. 3. Single people—Psychology.
4. Courtship. I. Furman, Elina. II. Title.
HQ801.F88   1999
646.7'7—dc21   99-32098
CIP

Illustrations by Barry Littmann

This book is available at quantity discounts for bulk purchases.
For information, call 1-800-872-5627.

Visit our home page at http://www.adamsmedia.com

Contents

Introduction: Looking for Love

Why is it that so many people cower in horror of the dating circuit? Married couples complacently sympathize with the plight of the bachelor/ette. Single people are no better. Ceaselessly looking to find the "one" with every romantic encounter, many singles are more interested in putting their player days to an end than in having a good time by simply playing the game. Whatever happened to "it's not whether you win or lose...?"

Okay, so love is a many splendored thing and all that jazz, but is the search for love any less wonderful? The new people, the mystery, and the repartee alone are worth the effort, never mind the sumptuous dinners, the funny movies, and the sexually charged evenings, which may or may not factor into any given date. Mmmm, we get goosebumps just thinking about it—and so should you.

We wrote this book to allay the anxiety that accompanies the dating process of elimination. Because without the all-too-common impatience and fear of rejection, dating would be a happy ending in itself. And as all good things must come to a close, your free-wheeling lifestyle will also peter out eventually. Yes, you too will settle down. But instead of feeling relief, you may find yourself grappling with cold-footed reluctance.

The trick lies in acquiring a taste for being single. Start by considering how much less predictable life is when you're flying sans copilot. You can meet a worthy date on the street, bus, corner pub, or local dance club. And when you do, you can expect a fun-filled evening of activity and conversation (at least half of which should be about you!). Always on the edge, never knowing what's around the corner, that's the essence of a life worth living.

Not that there isn't something to be said for security. When you can imagine enjoying yourself with one person for the rest of your life, it's time to incinerate your little black book. But to settle for less just to quit the swinging scene is nothing short of a self-punishment. There's nothing exceptionally pretty about wedded bliss, so the first step to appreciating your life is to admit that your single days are about as good as it gets. Go ahead and say it aloud: "I'm dating and I'm proud."

This book was conceived and written as a response to the vilification of the single life. Although you'll find plenty of practical methods and advice contained within the following pages, don't look at this book as simply a "how-to." Look at it as a celebration of the joys of dating. Ideally, it should help you come to love your party-of-one existence, and if you can benefit from a few tips along the way, all the better.

Finally, while we, the primary writers, happen to be female, we did not want to overlook the seldom heard male POV. For this reason, we enlisted the help of our friend, John Nikkah, a seasoned (if not professional) dater and a self-proclaimed dating expert. You'll find him voicing his opinions on a variety of date-related issues throughout the book under the moniker of the Date Doctor. You'll also find first-hand experiences from a variety of daters past and present. With so many people pitching in their two cents, even the most hapless of dategoers is bound to walk away with a wealth of newfound wisdom.

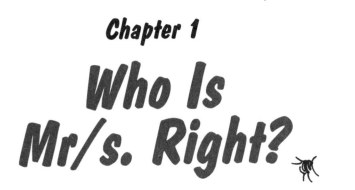

Chapter 1
Who Is Mr/s. Right?

Before you plunge into the inviting waters of the dating pool, you must first figure out what you're diving for. What is your definition of a sunken treasure trove? Ideally, you should be looking for someone with whom you can get on famously. Someone who not only agrees with you on critical matters, such as religion and family, but is also different enough to spice up your romance. So if a match is what you're after, there's no better place to start than compatibility.

Finding a partner who suits your needs is important, whether you're looking for a long-term relationship or just a satisfying fling. Opening up your heart or even your daily planner for someone takes an awful lot of energy—the last thing you need is to waste your efforts on the unworthy. After all, your poor nerves can only take so much. If you end up with someone who is constantly irritating you, you're likely to get caught in the downward spiral of a dating dry spell in no time. But if you meet a person who is well-suited to your values and personality, you'll be left wondering how you ever managed without them.

A Personal Inventory

The question of who is right for you can prove impossible to answer should you not have a strong sense of who "you" are. If your personality and activity roster change drastically with every passing romance, you'll need to unearth your true identity before you can conjure up an idea of Mr/s. Right. And while you do have to account for certain variables—such as your continuing personal development—which may bring about a new you come new year, you'll have a much easier time choosing your dates if you're armed with some notion of who you are right *now*.

It's a fact: People with scant self-knowledge have a sorry time of it on the dating scene. Going out with anyone who asks and doing anything that's suggested has never been the *modus operandi* of a happy swinger. The cool, calm, collected, and in-demand dategoers always know exactly what they want to do and with whom they want to do it. While such certitude may seem daunting at first, it makes the dating process much simpler. Think back to how many times you've had to sit through a lengthy pre-date brainstorm of the "What do you want to do?" "I don't know. What do you want to do?" variety. Such indecision doesn't sit well with either you or your potential beloved.

You can make most unnecessary date slip-ups disappear by getting friendly with yourself. After all, if you can't respect and admire yourself enough to spend some time getting to know you, who can? Self-exploration is your first step to going on fun dates with great people—no two ways about it.

"I Want to Be Alone"

Greta Garbo didn't have the last word on solitude. Plenty of people take time to get away from the undue influence of relationships. After all, spending too much time with others is bound to alter your opinions and point of view to some extent.

The time you invest in getting to know yourself will prove time well spent in the long run. Look at it as a great investment with a tiny window of opportunity. Once you're in a relationship, you'll find nary a moment of peace and quiet, much less quality time alone.

Out and About

Sitting at home with a giant bag of chips and the Classic Sports Network is not the type of solitary pursuit we have in mind. You are to get out of the house. And we're not talking about a jaunt to the market (for more chips) and back. Leaving the confines of your cozy pad will do you no good unless you stay out for at least two to three hours at a time. Better still, forget about your Timex and just go with the flow. Agoraphobia is no excuse, nor is the fear of leaving your couch. And don't even try to factor in the many hours you spend making a living. Your forty-hour work week has nothing to do with getting out of the house.

If you've forgotten what going it alone feels like, you'll be pleasantly surprised at how interesting your company can be. Once you're outdoors, the sky is the limit. With nothing but time and cab fare to sustain you, a great experience is sure to follow.

Write It Down

Your unchaperoned adventures deserve to be documented. But there's no need to lay the checking account on the line for a Camcorder when plain old pen and paper will do just fine. Even if you've never been the journal-keeping type, we recommend you give it a shot before branding the practice "strictly high school."

The World Is Your Jungle Gym

You'll feel invigorated the second you step outdoors. There's a whole world out there just waiting to be had. You can:

1. Find a sidewalk café and observe the flow of foot traffic
2. Hit the shopping district and window shop 'til you drop
3. Take in a matinee
4. Explore new neighborhoods
5. Get a psychic reading
6. Haggle with antique shop owners
7. Play with homeless cats and dogs at the anti-cruelty society
8. Secure a park bench and do what comes naturally (read, get a tan, feed the pigeons)
9. Ransack the magazine stand at your local bookstore
10. Just cruise the streets

Committing your life to memoir form has many advantages over simply taking snapshots or making home movies. First of all, the ritual of writing in a journal every day can act as a stress buster. Chances are, once you jot your worries and frustrations down on paper they will cease to seem insurmountable.

A journal will also allow you to explore the inner workings of your mind. In our fast-paced world, we rarely have enough time to stop and examine our feelings and reactions. Keeping a journal will draw a connection between your opinions, your experiences, and the many possibilities still waiting to be explored. You'll gain a stronger sense of self and emerge a more centered and confident person.

The beauty of a journal is that you can revisit it any time. You'll be able to gauge your growth process by simply rereading past entries. This record of your blossoming personality will keep you focused on what's truly important—your self. And no matter who comes into your life, you'll never forget who you really are.

Treat Yourself

Just because you don't have a boy/girlfriend telling you how fabulous you are right now doesn't mean that you have to lead a loveless existence. You've got to prove your love to yourself before you can believe anyone else who tells you those three little words. And while you can intone all manner of self-affirmations, actions will always speak louder than words.

Begin by behaving towards yourself as you would towards a visiting dignitary. If you had Margaret Thatcher staying at your house, you would probably try to impress her with your culinary prowess. Go ahead and do the same for yourself. Start creating wonderful lunches and dinners just for you. Also, as much as we hate to sound like your parents, it's best to keep your house clean. Not because you have company coming over, but simply because you shouldn't have to look at a messy place every day.

Once you've got the basics of high self-maintenance down pat, you can enter the advanced stages of self-adulation. Go to an expensive hair stylist, take a meeting with a masseuse, call in sick on a Wednesday, go to a group therapy session and spill all of your problems before the unsuspecting members. All these actions will serve to reinforce your VIP feeling.

The last aspect of treating yourself like British royalty involves the way you talk to yourself. Again, this is not in any way, shape, or form

WEEKEND TO DO LIST:
- Get up and go to gym
- Do a home facial
- RSVP to gallery opening downtown
- Get a cappuccino at Luigi's
- Walk through City Garden, write in Journal
- 12-5: Volunteer at children's museum
- Night: basketball game sports bar with roommates

PRIORITIES | Notes

a testimonial to daily affirmations. We're talking about basic protocol. If you silently barrage yourself with every name in the book, for whatever reason, you must immediately show contrition. Name calling is no way to treat yourself. Should you act in a way deserving of censure, sit down and ponder the error of your ways. Instead of making yourself feel awful, you'll wind up learning from the experience.

> *When my wife and I divorced after four years of marriage, dating was the last thing on my mind. While I was lonely, I wasn't ready for a new relationship. Getting used to being alone took some doing. But soon, I came to enjoy the feeling that I was in sole and complete control over my life. I began pursuing my long-time interest of studying graphic design. Then, I took a course in gourmet cuisine. Slowly but surely, I came to a new appreciation of myself and my life as a bachelor. Now, I'm enjoying dating. I know that I'll fall in love again eventually, but with my new attitude on life, I see no reason to rush into anything.*
>
> —JASON, 32, EDITOR

Give and Ye Shall Receive

Only after you've engaged in complete, unadulterated self-absorption can you begin to appreciate yourself through helping others. Random acts of kindness will gratify you like no spa treatment ever could.

Good will towards man is more than just a check to your favorite charity. While money goes a long way towards helping the less fortunate, aside from allaying your over-privileged guilt, what does that donation do for you? If a tax deduction is all you take away from your philanthropic endeavors, it's time to roll up your sleeves and get to work.

Friendly Inter-Faces

Your friends are key resources in the quest for a complete personal inventory. These people can bring out characteristics that often lie dormant during solitude. Take a good, hard look at the people you call your nearest and dearest. What about them do you like? What about yourself do you like when you're with them? These are

The Loner Mystique

If you think being alone is synonymous with terms like "desperate" and "dowdy," then think again. For decades, the idea of the mysterious loner has captivated and seduced the imaginations of millions. Think rebel, intrigue, excitement. The following list of loners will help you take pride in your single status.

- James Dean
- Greta Garbo
- The Lone Ranger
- Batman
- Marlon Brando
- Ally McBeal
- Jack Nicholson

Volunteering

The Corporation for National Service
http://www.cns.gov

The Corporation for National Service is a federal institution that matches people with volunteer opportunities serving the community and the nation. Their website offers a massive state-by-state listing of challenging positions nationwide.

VolunteerAmerica!
http://www.volunteeramerica.com

VolunteerAmerica! matches people with hundreds of volunteer opportunities—parks, forests, historic sites, or campgrounds—on public land all across the country. There are walking and hiking clubs, riding clubs, trail building organizations, and other volunteer groups.

United Way
http://www.unitedway.org

The United Way raises lots and lots of money for innumerable community needs nationwide.

Their goal is to use contribution money as effectively as possible to directly help the various local organizations and causes they support. Much of their work is done by volunteers, and they have chapters everywhere.

PBS
http://www.pbs.org

Whether it's Sesame Street, Antiques Roadshow, or Ken Burns you're into, there's something on PBS for just about everyone. Volunteering at PBS-affiliate auctions and fund drives is a great way to meet other people who prefer the fighting on Washington Week in Review to that on The Jerry Springer Show; what's more, you may wind up meeting your dream date, who's watched as many episodes of Sister Wendy's Story of Painting as you have.

PEN is a national organization for published writers. Even if you're not a card-carrying member of the literati and have not a single National Book Award to your name, you can join your regional branch of PEN as an associate member. This entitles you to attend their parties, readings, awards ceremonies, pub nights, and other fun events, and connects you to volunteer opportunities from literacy campaigns to political and human rights-oriented "Freedom to Write" groups.

Alumnae Fund Raising—You'll have something fundamental in common with anyone you meet at alumnae shindigs and fundraisers; perhaps you'll even rekindle an old flame! Most colleges and universities (not to mention private schools of any level) regularly have cocktail parties and fund drives all across the country. So raise a little money, have some fun, and enjoy lively conversation over free canapés.

important questions to answer if you plan to find an appropriate companion. Your behavior around your friends is an indication of how you will behave in a romantic relationship.

Most of us take our best qualities completely for granted, thereby paving the way for others to do likewise. We burn the midnight oil listening to our friends whine about their love lives (or lack thereof), we jump at the chance to lug boxes laden with personal effects during a pal's moving day, we go off club hopping at a moment's notice, but how often do we stop to consider what our actions say about us? The point is that whether you're a good listener, a fascinating conversationalist, or the life of the party, you've got something that someone out there needs. Learning to respect and admire your own personality isn't easy. After all, you've been with yourself since day one—chances are you're not surprised by anything that you have to offer. But once you look at yourself from a different perspective, you'll see there's a lot more to you than initially meets the eye.

Risky Business

There's nothing like conquering your fears to get you on the road to well-being. Our fears are what keep us from looking up to ourselves. Sure, we have role models whom we try to emulate. Some of us look up to entertainers because we admire their moxie, others look up to political figures because we wish we had their leadership abilities. But if you want to become your own role model, as well as someone else's, you're going to have to start saying yes to risk.

It's all too easy to go through the drive-thru of life with a "no thanks" attitude. But as the old saying goes, nothing ventured, nothing gained. Start by overcoming small fears, such as the fear that no one will show up at your party. Go ahead and invite a bunch of people for a "small get-together." If only a few show up, you lose nothing. If you end up the proud host of an out and out rave, all the better. With time, you'll be able to face even the most harrowing nightmares with some semblance of *savoir-faire*. In the meantime, do one thing that scares you every day and in a month's time you'll be a regular super hero.

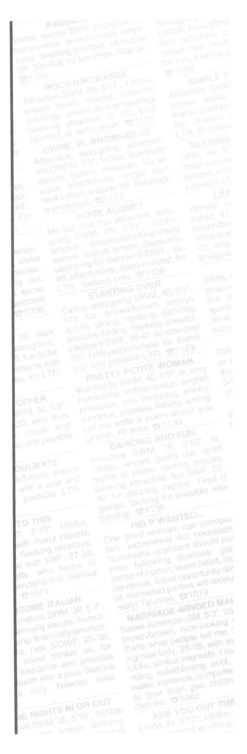

The Shopping List

An old joke has it that a father once said to his son, "Go to the store and tell me what they have."

"What do you want?" asked the son.

"Depends on what they've got," answered the dad.

Needless to say, what this anecdote lacks in humor, it makes up for in its suitability to our intents and purposes. The moral of the story is that this is no way to shop, much less to date. If you don't know what you want, you're vastly better off biding your time until you have some inkling.

People are a varied lot. Your choices are limitless. Just like the products at a supermarket, the ones that look best may not always be the best for you, and the ones that are good for you may induce an allergic reaction. If you don't want to come home empty-handed, you'll need to whittle down your options to a list of general criteria.

The Aisles of Personality

Before you can create a mental image of your ideal find, you'll need to weigh all of your options. Because most individual personalities are so complex, this task will require some drastic oversimplification.

The Age Old Aisle

Age comes before beauty when you're in the market for love. Nowadays, there's a formula for just about anything, be it a bra fitting or weight gain. We've even come up with the basic formula for settling upon an age which best suit your needs. All you do is take your age and multiply it by one. Voila! The result (plus or minus ten years) is your ideal age range.

While many of you may be looking for a Mama or Papa Bear to make up for a lack of parental affection during your childhood, your time may be better spent in therapy. This pattern will prove detrimental in a relationship. Cases of May–December romance are best left to the big screen because only a precious few have what it takes to survive the rigors of the real world.

The Appearances Aisle

Beautiful people can be found in the least accessible corner of the left-hand side; the rest are readily available all around them. Yes, lovely lads and lasses are hard to come by. Accounting for a whopping five percent of the population (and that's a generous estimate), the faces of this world are not always the best bet.

By narrowing your search to the *crème de la crème* of physical endowments, you may very well be short-changing yourself in other equally, if not more, critical departments. Sure, a specimen of aesthetic perfection may possess other positive attributes, but the chances that you'll find a good dose of dry humor in this paltry five percent are bleak.

We never said that finding a match would be easy. We only promised you a good time while cruising the market. You can try your hand at beauty all you want, and should you realize it's not all it's hyped up to be, you can steer your cart over to...

The Brains Aisle

Forget about the stereotypes, you'll find much more than pocket protectors and knee socks in this eclectic realm. While you may want to leave the Mensa quality brains to the intellect parade section, there's no reason to dig into the "Former Jerry Springer Guests" bargain bin either. Whether you want a challenge or a protégé to rival *My Fair Lady*, you're likely to find it when your first priority is the mind.

Again, a match is not guaranteed. Plenty of quick-witted prospects are liable to land smack dab in the "just friends" category. But then again, you never can be too popular.

The Lifestyles Aisle

Bohemians, accountants, jet setters, hermits, players, homeboys and girls, athletes, cyber fanatics, overgrown club kids; they're all here. You'd better figure out which turn your stomach before pairing off.

Sure, you can try to change your honey-bunny's lifestyle, but you won't succeed for long. The way a person conducts their life is indicative of their values. While your newfound Lothario may be only too happy to turn his reserved seat by the beer keg in for a Blockbuster membership in the first stages of your romance, once the honeymoon is over, you and *Sleepless in Seattle* are on your own.

What's Your Sign? Romance According to the Zodiac

Aries

Watch out! Romance with an Aries is an experience you don't quickly forget. Man or woman, these people are all passion and fire. They often form impulsive, rash attachments, but they don't hold back emotionally. They need to know, however, that they're appreciated and loved in return.

Romance with an Aries means movement, activity, and being on the go to museums, movies, midnight walks by the ocean, good food in good restaurants, and more exotic things like hang gliding, parachuting, or rock climbing. Remember that these people are fearless and they bring that courage to their relationships.

PASS...
Stable, secure SWM, young 55,... homeowner, professionally empl- oyed. Seeking younger, attractive SF, 30s-40s, for fun times. Kids ok. ☎1183

ROCK-N-ROMANCE
Attractive SWM, 26, 5'11", 180lbs, enjoys music, movies, romantic evenings, adventure and traveling. Seeking attractive, fit SF, kind- hearted, to settle down. ☎1176

DWPM, 45, BROWN/BLUE
Attractive, easygoing, affection- ate DWPM, 5'9", 170lbs, financially secure, builder, musician, ivy le- ague, Middleboro, single dad, seeks short, shapely SF. Race/age unimportant. ☎1122

HOME ALONE?
Me too! Call this attractive, easy- going DWM, 49, 5'11", 190lbs, smoker, emotionally/financially secure, enjoys simple pleasures, searching for slender S/DWF, 39- 49, affectionate, open-minded, for LTR. Serious only. ☎1126

STARTING OVER
Caring, easygoing, DWM, 40, 5'5", 175 lbs, brown/brown, enjoys sports, dining, cooking, dancing, and bike ridding. Seeking cheerful, intelligent SWF, 35-40, no one over 5'6", H/W proportionate, for friend- ship and possible LTR. ☎1129

PRETTY PETITE WOMAN
Wanted by SWM, 40, 5'9", fit, very handsome, entrepreneur, english professor, into shopping, poetry, romance, sunrises, fishing, writing. Let me write a poem about you. Lincoln RI area. ☎1130

DANCING AND FUN
Attractive SWM, 26, 5'10", fit 190lbs, enjoys going out, quiet nights at home, renting movies. Seeking attractive, fun SWF, 20- 30, for dancing, movies. Tired of games, looking for possible rela- tionship. ☎1138

HELP WANTED
One good woman, age unimpor- tant, experience not necessary. Successful applicant should pos- sess following qualities: gre... sense of humor, warm heart, ind... pendence. Equal opportunity da... all interested parties will recei... reply! Taunton. ☎1079

MARRIAGE-MINDED MA...
Native American SM, 6'3", 25... brown/brown, nice-looking, that's what people tell me... ing nice lady, 25-35, with s... looks, similar interests. I lo... nding, rollerblading, pool,... walks, romance, computer... ily type man, two childr... dleboro ☎1082

ARE YOU OUT THE...
...DWM, 44, 5'10", 190lbs...

Easygo...
160lbs, brown/bro... door activities,... neous trips. Seek... for fun, friends... ☎1058

SIMPLE P...
Attractive SWM... brown, seeks... enjoys quiet tim... trip, outdoor... LTR. Brockto...

SEEKING...
SPM, 49, 5'... cially secure... sincere, ...
possible L...

LET...
Honest, lo... SWM, 47,... brown/bro... attractive... 40, who... Bridgew...

SWM,... down-... live ... sports... 30-40... com...

DW... of ti... thi... S...

The Cash Station

Today, nearly every market comes equipped with a cash station. Thus, it stands to reason that some people are just in the market for cash, while others are shopping with a quick pit stop at the ATM in mind, and still others have all the money they need. Before you hit the mart, you've got to decide which category you're in.

On the dating scene, and in the market, you'll need an ATM card to receive cold, hard moolah. In dating, you must often trade all of your other requirements in for just one such cash card. Forget looking for physical attraction, a fun lifestyle, or anything else you may have fancied. With cash on the brain, that's all you'll get.

Of course, most people are in the market for more than just money. Men and women look for partners who are not only suc- cessful but also fit a variety of other needs. Some people don't care about finances at all. This last category often stops just short of dating the fry kids at McD's, thereby vastly increasing the possibility of interesting and unusual dates.

Staples of a Good Love Life

Once you've mulled over your many options, it's high time you learn to distinguish between your needs and your wants. If you've ever restricted yourself to a budget, you should have absolutely no trouble making such a distinction. Your needs are the bare necessi- ties without which there can be no relationship. Your wants are all those little extras that go a long way towards improving the quality of life.

People have been known to spend a lifetime treading the dating waters without ever encountering that ultimate wave of romance. Luckily, where dating is concerned, you don't have to save yourself. As long as someone meets your primary needs, you are free and clear to make beautiful music together. No commitment, no expecta- tions, no strings attached—that there, folks, is what the joy of dating is all about. The following considerations are just a few of the building blocks of solid love connections.

Background Checks

Ever date someone for a few months only to be confronted with the eerie "who is this person?" question? That can send chills up any old spine. Many of us choose to date people with similar backgrounds

The Three-Minute
Getting-to-Know-Me Quiz

Time to synchronize our watches. Can you answer the following questions in under three minutes? If not, you still need a good dose of solitude.

1. What's your favorite restaurant?
2. Who has had the biggest influence on your life?
3. Which public figure do you most admire?
4. What is your favorite activity?
5. What's your favorite book?
6. Where do you most want to vacation?
7. What is your favorite food?
8. What do you dislike most about other people?
9. What do you wish you could change about yourself?
10. Are you a Democrat or a Republican?
11. Of what achievement are you most proud?
12. Which celebrity would you most like to meet?
13. If you won the lottery, what would you do first?
14. What are your three favorite bands/musicians?
15. What would be your dream job?
16. What are you most cynical about?
17. What is your primary talent?
18. Death penalty: Pro or con?
19. Do you want your MTV, or would you rather pull the plug?
20. Why did the chicken cross the road?

The Date Doctor Is In

Q: Do guys care what women think? One of my friends said that it makes no difference to them.

A: *It definitely does make a difference when you're thinking about them, specifically concerning the long term. Guys also care a lot about what women think about them. Your friend has probably been slighted by an ex, so be careful not to apply this generalization to all men. Although it is probably true that men care less about their partner's thoughts than they care about their own—mainly because they are often thinking about sex—if you do find a guy who does listen to you and cares about what you have to say, you know he may be a keeper.*

simply to avoid the horrible truth that we never really know anyone, especially after a mere couple of months acquaintance.

If you can face the existential reality that posits every individual's eternal alienation from the rest of humanity, you can happily throw aside the basic need for a parallel upbringing. Otherwise, try not to give your dates third degree burns while grilling them over dinner.

True Values

When you first lay eyes upon a fine-boned specimen of the opposite sex, admit it, values are the last thing on your mind. But values, or our most cherished ideas and possessions, have the power to solder two people together or tear them apart.

Before you begin to size up your paramour for long-term commitment, you had better try to get a handle on their values. Listen intently and ask probing questions to find out what is nearest and dearest to your date's heart. Is it family, work, art, friendship, money, the environment, religion, or social status? Whatever you discover, be prepared to cut the whirlwind short if you can't respect your consort's beliefs.

It Don't Mean a Thing If It Ain't Got that Schwiiing!

While you may not need the likes of Naomi Campbell or Brad Pitt to get you in the mood, don't discount the importance of sex appeal in a relationship. To be physically attracted to your dates is your basic human right, ranking right up there with the pursuit of happiness.

Often, people accept their strictly platonic feelings, hoping that romantic love will arrive with time. The fact is that physical attraction is either there right from the beginning or not at all. So bear in mind that while physical perfection is not essential, physical attraction is—so listen to what it tells you.

Dumb and Dumber?

A match-up between looks and brains may seem like the makings of a dynamic duo, but it usually ends up with resentment, condescension, and the misuse of power. Intellectual inequality in a romance is a major pitfall that should be avoided at all costs (just consider the entire Woody Allen *oeuvre*).

People often fall for the less educated in hopes of changing or improving the other person. Sometimes, when the protégé surpasses

his or her mentor's abilities and moves on to brighter pastures, the plan works all too well. On the flip side, the reform strategies may not work at all and the relationship ends because of the intellectual superior's growing frustration. Either way, this type of scenario may make for a great film, but it won't make for a great relationship.

Remember: Relationships with only one mastermind are doomed to failure. Only a shallow and superficial few can sustain interest in situations devoid of all mental stimulation. And without this strong psychological pull, physical attraction often falls by the wayside.

Fortune Telling

When you look into the crystal ball, do you share your partner's vision of the future? In the early stages of relationships, most of us care more about the *Sports Illustrated* swimsuit issue than about what our beau/belle wants out of life. But since this aspect will become more and more important as time goes by, it may be wise to figure out where your love interest stands on the future issue.

As you start probing, try not to be too obvious. The wrong impression can spell disaster for a blossoming relationship. Steer clear of questions that include the words "aspirations" (when gauging ambition levels) and "marriage" (when probing for commitment potential). Act casual, but get the goods on your would-be guy/gal. The last thing you need is to fall head over heels for a person who will never agree to the ten children you've had your heart set on.

Luxury Items

While it's the fundamentals, such as physical attraction and shared dreams, that make relationships possible, it is the perks that make it all worthwhile. Of course, added benefits such as a mutual interest in frequent travel, a shared fear of crumbs on the linoleum tile, a common passion for camping and the great outdoors, a clean shave/naturally blond hair, and so forth (we can all go on ad infinitum), aren't relationship deal-breakers. Nonetheless, a person who displays all of your fave traits is still the most long-lasting aphrodisiac on the market. We'll call him/her "The One."

Again, it behooves us to underscore that dating need not be confined to people who fit "The One" criteria. Especially considering that we often don't know exactly what we want until we see it.

Psychic Dating Strategies

That Clicking Sound
Aside from all the obvious, quantifiable qualities capable of fueling or snuffing out a budding romance, you've also got the X factor, also known as chemistry, to worry about. Two people can be perfect for each other in every way, but if their personalities don't click, all relationship potential is lost.

As many as 90 percent of all dates end on this sad note. Unfortunate though it may be, nothing—not money, not beauty, not even brains—can save a chemistry-free relationship from tedium's death grip. You either have chemistry or you don't, so trust your instincts on this one.

Bad Apples

Few experiences can rival the disappointment of finding that ideal someone only to discover that their personality is flawed beyond repair. It's worse than going into debt for a car that ends up body-shop-ridden six months out of the year, worse than spending hours over the hot stove and then burning your dinner. It's a sheer travesty is what it is. But since it happens all the time, you must learn how to deal with it.

Denial is a common first reaction. Many people dismiss warning signs and continue to indulge their fantasies of a great future in couplehood.

To combat this pitfall, we suggest you begin digging for dirt from the very beginning. Don't be so quick to concentrate on your date's good qualities; remember, everyone is on their best behavior at first. Try to decipher signals of the real personality shining through the many layers of manners and etiquette. This way you won't let a nice facade lull you into a false sense of security.

> *I had been dating Jim for two months before we had our first fight. We were out at a bar with some of his friends. Everyone was drinking and having a good time. As we were getting ready to leave, a fight broke out. Neither Jim nor anyone from our party were involved, but Jim jumped in nonetheless. I had never seen this aggressive side of him before. I was horrified, and told him as much. This first fight was also our last. I just couldn't picture myself dating such a violent person.*
>
> —CAROLINE, 24, RETAIL SALES

Are You Asking Too Much?

We all know one or two people whose dates must meet a mile-long list of requirements before they can gain admission to the love-interest department. These folks refuse to lower their lofty standards and, worse yet, affect a high-maintenance, God's-gift-to-the-opposite-sex attitude. While some of these people may actually believe their own hype, most are simply suffering from a debilitating fear of intimacy and a deep-seated insecurity.

Quiz: What Kind of Date Are You Looking For?

A. A wealthy, single acquaintance of yours, twenty-five years older and interested in you, invites you to a lavish fund-raiser. You:
1. Accept—you'll have an unconventional romance and live the good life at the same time
2. Accept, even if unsure about your feelings
3. Decline politely—though you like this person, you're not interested in a romance, and misleading suitors isn't your style

B. You meet a good-looking, intelligent professional at a local workshop for people in your line of work. When you go out for a drink after the workshop, your new acquaintance repeatedly says how attractive you are, squeezes your hand, caresses your arm, and suggests that you take a moonlit drive out of the city. You:
1. Accept eagerly
2. Suggest that you meet for lunch later in the week, despite your feeling that the person is unnervingly overeager
3. Make a respectful but quick exit

C. This Friday night, you have two options: to go to the bar where you and your crowd always hang out, or to go to a party with a hip, intelligent co-worker who really wants you to meet her group of friends. You:
1. Go to the bar—you don't want to miss out on fun that your friends are having, and besides, the unattainable babe you've had a crush on for years will be there
2. Go to the party but plan to leave early enough so that you can still go to the bar and relax with the usual crowd
3. Go to the party—what a great opportunity!

D. At a party, you have an engaging chat with a witty, confident member of the opposite sex who is a bit gangly and has a naive sense of fashion. Though not your usual type, you find your new acquaintance appealing. You:
1. Forget it—this just isn't the kind of person you normally date
2. Exchange phone numbers and suggest that you get together—in a dimly-lit restaurant in another town
3. Pursue a date wholeheartedly

E. You're an administrator at a fast-paced tech firm; your blind date is a well-pierced professional snowboarder who plays in a rock band. Your feeling about this is:
1. My date's rebel allure is cool and will make me cooler by association
2. Our different lifestyles may be too much to overcome
3. Character is essential, width of pants is not. What's my date like on the inside?

F. Your date is intelligent, attractive, and fun to be around—except for the road rage, the screaming at other drivers, and the lack of interest in slowing down for pedestrians.
1. Who cares? I'm an aggressive driver myself.
2. Everyone has a few flaws. Let's wait and see.
3. Wait until the car stops, then get out and vow never to see the person again.

Scoring:
Give yourself 1 point for every A you chose, 2 points for B, and 3 points for C.

15-18 points: Right on! You're cautious, sensible, and open-minded. You know who you are, what you want, and how to navigate dating territory confidently.

11-14 points: You're on the right track, but you have a tendency to be wishy-washy. Refine your dating instincts and build your self-esteem.

6-10 points: You need to watch out. You're overeager, all too willing to overlook character flaws for superficial perks; meanwhile, you may be passing up great opportunities because you don't want to venture outside your usual territory. It's a good idea to rethink your priorities here.

There are others who only ask for one thing—that a relationship make them happy. Not too much to ask? Think again. Mostly found in people who are in love with the idea of love, this attitude is a surefire way to end up miserable and alone. When all is said and done, other people can never make you happy. You alone have the power to do that.

If you're not relating to either of the above categories, chances are you have a healthy attitude towards love. Still, every so often, you too must undergo an expectations reality check.

Do You Fit Your Criteria?

Before you start applying your guidelines to every potential dinner date, take a good hard look at what you're bringing to the table. Would you pass your own test? If the answer is "no way," take that as an indication that you need to pare down your list.

Of course, we don't mean that you should lower your standards and settle for just anyone with a solid 401(k). No, all you need to do is prioritize your demands. Some people get so carried away that they actually compose long lists of traits that "The One" would possess. But this tactic will get you nowhere.

You've got to take into account how much weight each trait carries. They can't all be equally important. You'll be able to dispense with some desires altogether once you realize that they're not all that crucial. After all, you wouldn't throw a great-looking, funny, and spontaneous person out of your house for using the wrong fork, or would you? It's your call to make.

The Role of Delayed Gratification

Wouldn't it be great if you could meet someone who possessed all the qualities you seek and so richly deserve? A person with whom you could find no fault whatsoever—now that's what most people would call a soul mate. Laboring under such an illusion, it's a wonder how anyone finds a soul mate at all.

In our fast-food saturated culture, we want our every whim satisfied without a second's delay. Today's highly competitive markets have accustomed consumers to the royal treatment. Unfortunately, this principle does not apply when shopping for love.

The truth is that we can't make the right decision about our date's long-term suitability based on hard facts alone. Consider your own personal development. Just as you've matured and changed over the years, so have your suitors. In fact, both of you will continue to grow and develop as time goes by. Don't write anyone off for what they're lacking today if you see great potential for tomorrow. Looking for a partner is a lot like house hunting—if you don't see the possibilities of the space, you may just end up losing out on a great rehab opportunity.

Upward Mobility

Individuals often become frustrated by their respective partners' lack of ambition or lowly careers. Everything else may be platinum—the personality, the intelligence, the sex appeal—yet whenever the check comes, this wonderful creature is nowhere to be found.

Looking towards the future, people tend to write off such a person as a loser. But, Mr./Ms. Present Day Pauper can turn into a Prince/ess overnight. We've all been in a rut. Your mission as a serious dater is to figure out if your otherwise ideal date is suffering from a temporary lack of funds or if this is a chronic situation.

Pay attention to personality characteristics rather than to the immediate circumstances. Your gal may be saving money for med school. And that cheapskate date may have just sunk all his funds into a business start-up. You never know, and if you don't take the time to find out, you never will.

Brain Dead or Just Out to Lunch?

Intelligence figures prominently on most people's list of romantic priorities. Yet few people can agree upon exactly what it is that makes someone smart. Some claim that an advanced degree is proof positive of intelligent life others stress the key role of interpersonal skills, and still others profess the importance of emotional intelligence. Clearly, there is no one right answer to this puzzle.

But while each person has to decide the intelligence question for themselves, the best indicator of a sharp mind is still aptitude. All too many of us choose to focus on an individual's acquired knowledge and pay no mind to their ability and willingness to learn. But whether you choose to believe it or not, many of the world's greatest men and women have benefited from mentors who recognized their potential early on.

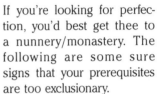

How to Tell if Your Demands Are Unreasonable

If you're looking for perfection, you'd best get thee to a nunnery/monastery. The following are some sure signs that your prerequisites are too exclusionary.

1. You can't count them on your fingers and toes
2. You've yet to meet anyone who meets them
3. "Likes to cook" figures prominently on your list
4. Your friends nod off while listening to it
5. You've been adding to it for the last five years

More Things Change...Still More Stay the Same

It's a fact: Some traits are more resistant to change than others. If a particular characteristic is embedded deep enough, you'll have an easier time pulling teeth with your bare hands than ridding your love interest of the offending quality. Save yourself from yet another exercise in futility—the following are sure signs that your main squeeze isn't budging:

1. **Defensive:** S/he responds to your criticism by telling you that you're not all that perfect yourself, and then launching into an hour-long rant about all of your faults.
2. **The Patriot:** S/he tells you to love it or leave it.
3. **Popeye:** "I am who I am" is your paramour's motto.
4. **Passive/Aggressive:** Despite your many comments, there's been no improvement.
5. **The Dictator:** Your suggestions for change are met with "It's my way or the highway!"

After our first date, I had absolutely no interest in seeing Bob again. He had little to say, and wasn't at all intellectual. Hardly what I'd call a turn on. Luckily, I didn't let my initial impression keep me from going on a second date. While he wasn't exactly a different person, Bob was much more talkative and self-assured. After a month of dating, he began to share his hobbies and interests, which made him more engaging. We broke up about a year ago but if I hadn't given him a shot, I would have missed out on some truly great times.

—LIZ, 31, PUBLIC RELATIONS ACCOUNT EXECUTIVE

A Pound of Cure

We all have a preferred body type that gets our engines all hot and bothered. There's nothing wrong with looking for that ideal physical form as long as you don't overlook people who stray from the straight and narrow (or the curvaceous and round for that matter). Relationships are about much more than the numbers on the scale. While physical perfection is temporary, trust, mutual respect, and shared values are the ties that bind forever.

NPA (Nit-Pickers Anonymous)

Many of us have a major relationship-impeding problem. You may have seen one of our spokespeople on a little TV show called *Seinfeld*. This man, Jerry Seinfeld, would careen from one woman to the next at the speed of light. This turbulence was due mostly to infinitesimally small flaws that somehow managed to drive Jerry to distraction. Jerry never did overcome his problem, but then he'd never associated with the NPA.

In order to beat Nit-Picker's Syndrome, you must first recognize that you have a problem. Here's how card-carrying members of NPA diagnose the syndrome:

1. Ask yourself why your last three relationships or dates went nowhere.
2. Try to pinpoint what exactly bothered you about these castaways.
3. Do you qualify the flaws you identified in question two as fundamental or superficial?

Quiz

If you're having difficulty making the diagnosis whether you suffer from Nit-Picker's Syndrome, take the following definitive quiz.

Answer True or False:

1. My relationships never last longer than a few months. _____

2. Someone who lasts three dates with me should be commended—they're one in a million. _____

3. My ideal mate must never annoy me. _____

4. It's the little things that count most in a burgeoning relationship. _____

5. Spinach in the teeth is grounds for permanent separation. _____

If you marked just two of the above statements as true, you are in the throes of Nit-Picker's Syndrome. The only known cure to this illness is extensive self-examination. As your problem stems mainly from a deep-rooted fear of intimacy, you must dig deep within yourself to overcome your feelings of unworthiness. Once you believe that you too are entitled to happiness, you can begin to build a healthy relationship.

Hilly and I met at a bus stop. She was wearing some baggy sweater and jeans number—it looked all wrong. Still, she was very friendly and outgoing. I had just been brutally rejected by a certain woman at my office, so I ended up asking Hilly out just to nurse my ego. She was nice and always had a lot to say. We dated for a couple of months. But for me, a good sense of style is important in a woman. Hilly dressed so bad, it became embarrassing. I even tried to take her shopping, but she just didn't get it. The second time I saw her in acid-washed jeans, I knew it was over.

—SAM, 27, DEPARTMENT STORE BUYER

The Whole Is Greater than the Sum of Its Parts

Once you know more or less what it is that you want out of your partner, you may find yourself disappointed. Fewer and fewer prospects may present themselves to you and you may even be having less fun. This is all to be expected if you stick too close to your list.

Don't forget that your "Dreamboat Requirements" are just guidelines. They're not carved in stone, nor should they be. You've got to experiment with your dates. Go ahead and set up a date with that leather-clad Hell's Angel-looking guy/gal. This person may surprise you, broadening your horizons and dispelling your stereotypes in the process.

Fun and Compromise

Because every date does not have to lead to long-term commitment, you can forget about your list when accepting gentlemen and lady callers. This is what's known as "kicking it"—putting aside your list of ingredients for husband/wife material and just having a good time.

Many wonderful relationships start off on just such a casual footing. When you first meet someone you may think, "No way. He talked about his screenplay all night!" or "She hardly spoke two words the entire night, what a bore." But before you know it, you're overlooking the initially repellent qualities and having a ball. The fun may last well into your twilight years. But even if it only lasts a few weeks, it's still better than nothing. That's what compromise and fun is all about.

A Human Masterpiece

DaVinci created perfection with the Mona Lisa, Michelangelo did it with David, but no set of parents to date have been able to produce the perfect person. Feel free to breathe that sigh of relief. Imagine actually coming across someone who matches all of your criteria to a T. That's what people call good to a fault.

Yes, one can be too good. You don't want some Stepford boy/girlfriend, a simple "Yes Dear" automaton to call your own. Ugh! Just think how abysmally dull that would be. Relationships thrive on moderate amounts of flaws, arguments, and reconciliations, so don't worry if everything doesn't always go your way.

Warning, Warning, Red Alert

Sometimes it's tempting to chuck your painstakingly compiled list altogether. This is especially true when infatuation kicks into high gear. All of a sudden it's, "I don't care if she's mean and nasty...I must see her." Or, "He's distant and emotionally unavailable...but he will be mine." Tsk. Tsk. Tsk. You're letting chemistry have its way with you.

This is a red alert situation. While you shouldn't go strictly by the list, you should never forget about it completely. If someone doesn't possess any of the qualities your reason tells you are important, he or she's not a keeper, no matter how good the chemistry is. Use the list you compiled before meeting this person as your guide while you're overcome by this frenzy of emotion. Infatuation may muddle your thinking, but if you rely on your rational, pre-crush self, you should get through this time with your heart intact.

The Date Doctor Is In

Q: Every time I meet someone I like, I discover that they have a major flaw that I can't live with. Why does this keep happening to me?

A: *This is probably happening to you for one of two reasons. First, it may be that you're a perfectionist with a slight case of obsessive-compulsive disorder; in that case you'll probably never find someone and you'll always be alone unless you get some serious therapy.*

A second, less pessimistic, reason may be that you're just not ready for a committed relationship and are looking for these flaws to give yourself a way out without having to cop to your fear of commitment.

Chapter 2
Hot Pursuit

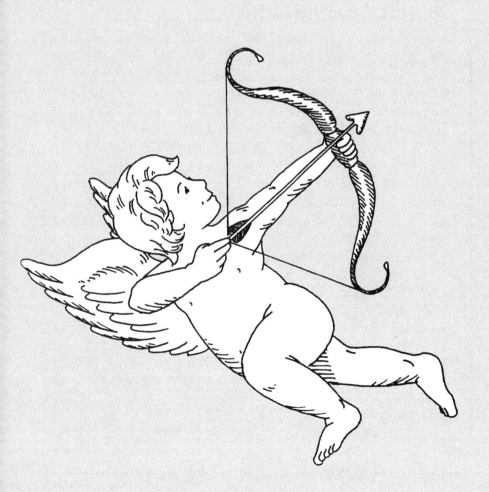

America isn't called the land of opportunity for nothing. In this, our great US of A, we have one of the highest single-to-married ratios in the entire world. Whether it's because we're concentrating on our careers, avoiding responsibility, or staving off old age, more and more of us are in no great hurry to take the vows. Contrary to the popular "man shortage" myth, people of all genders are staying single well into their thirties and often longer.

With all those wallflowers out there just waiting to be wooed, you should have no trouble filling your Rolodex with numbers galore. Once you know where to find them, getting dates isn't all that hard. When surrounded by potential consorts, you can start spreading your magic around the room. You're sure to run across a few people who fall for your particular brand of charm. After all, it's all about being in the right place at the right time.

Singles' Playgrounds

If there is but one certainty in life, it's that you're not going to meet the person of your dreams watching TV. Sure, you may see dozens who fit your description, but, reality check, they're not real. Love is a two-way street, so any feelings you may harbor for the cast of *ER*, no matter how intense, are strictly unrequited—and may even get you arrested should you attempt to act on them.

You have to put forth some serious effort if your date prospecting is to prove fruitful. That means looking through the paper for fun activities and stepping out of the house when all you want to do is curl up and nap. There's no shortage of ways to see and be seen. With the advent of the Internet, you can even interact and exchange photos with any number of fine men and women without ever leaving the house.

Forget about that old "looking for love in all the wrong places" refrain. In this day and age, the only places barren of romantic possibility are the gynecologist's office and the sperm bank. Still, some hunting grounds are more rewarding than others. To get you off on the right foot, we've racked our brains and asked around. The following are some great places to strike up an acquaintance. But don't stop here; the good times are only limited by the boundaries of your imagination.

The Intelligentsia's Playgrounds

You'll not find these ladies and gents queuing up for Susan Lucci's autograph. If you want to date a highbrow, you're going to have to wade on over to the deep end of the dating pool.

The Literati and the Philosophes

Many people think they'll land themselves a genius just by scouring the bookstores. Big mistake. Regular bookstore-goers run the gamut from intellectuals to milk-and-cookie enthusiasts. In fact, you're likely to come across more of the latter if you confine your search to the major bookstore chains (ever notice how crowded those bookstore cafés get?). If you truly want to meet a clever Al or Alice, your best bet is to search at small, independent bookstores. The people who show up at these stores have a real love for books and reading.

If there are no independent bookstores near you, all is still not lost. Next time you hit the Barnes and Noble, forget about camping out in the Young Adults section (try your best to put those cute Sweet Valley twins out of your mind), and shun the *Cliffs Notes* aisle like the plague. You'll find erudites aplenty in the literature section, and all manner of mental giants in the ever-stimulating philosophy aisle.

I remember coming home from work feeling terribly exhausted. All I wanted to do was veg out. Unfortunately, it was the last day I had to return a book before the return policy expired. When I got to the store, I stopped for coffee in their café. On my way to a table I saw this cute guy reading Wittgenstein. But I didn't know how to approach him. I ended up waiting until he left the store and following him. Outside, I knew that it was now or never and I figured there was nothing to lose. If he said no, I'd probably never see him again. So I approached him. It was awkward at first, but we're still together so I guess it was worth it.

—Janice, 33, Magazine Editor

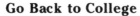

Go Back to College

You don't have to apply for admission to a university if all you want is to prowl the campus. Think about it—what better place to find a member of the intellectual elite than at one of our country's fine bastions of learning?

Swarming with graduate students and professors, college campuses provide the perfect opportunity to meet eligible scholars. You can attend a lecture, warm a bar stool at the alumni watering hole, or just hang out on the campus quad. Whatever you decide to do, chances are you'll come across an enlightened being while doing it.

Author Tour Groupie

Libraries and bookstores often invite well-known authors to do readings from their work. Usually, the people who show up for such spectacles are hard-core fans. But you don't have to be a fanatic to check out these earnest audience members.

The best place to find out about author tours is through your local newspaper. If you're having trouble locating the elusive Schedule of Events department, think nothing of calling the libraries and bookstores to find out first hand.

The Professionals' Playgrounds

White-collar workers congregate in their own highly specialized habitats. Next time the hankering for a computer programmer or a lawyer strikes, just follow it all the way to...

The Bank

Whether you're making a deposit or a withdrawal, you're sure to see crowds of people coming in to deposit their wages. You'll come across more working men and women if you go to a bank that's located in the hub of a large business district. Pick a busy time to go, like the lunch hour. While you'll have to wait in line to make your transaction, you never know what manner of well-tailored loveliness will be waiting alongside you.

Better yet, you can request to speak with a personal banker. Some of these eager cross-sellers are as cute as they come. And don't worry, just because they can assess your financial status with the push of a button doesn't mean they won't take a shine to you.

But keep in mind that a truly lowly balance (and here we're talking three figures or less) may work against you.

Happy Hour

Yuppies are a predictable lot. Once that quitting-time whistle blows, packs of professionals, young and old alike, drift towards the nearest tavern for after-work mai tais.

This is a great opportunity to connect with businesspeople on a social basis. What's more, as they leave their offices, these work-horses have their guards down and are looking for a good time. Snag a spot at one such after-work haven and watch the suits come stumbling in. Make sure you have a good view of the door and be prepared to discuss office politics.

Join the Club

Many career-oriented professionals would never consider an inter-office love life, yet remain interested in dating people in their field. If you count yourself among this group, you're in luck. Professional associations provide the perfect opportunity for networking with thousands of like-minded professionals. At just one such function you can pick up enough business cards to last you a lifetime and never risk sullying your workplace reputation.

But you don't have to check out associations strictly within your field of expertise. Today, you can't find a profession that doesn't have an association to call its own. Everyone from accountants to zoologists belongs to a group. To meet new dating prospects you can head to the *Encyclopedia of Associations*. Pick out one you like and call to find out about any programs or seminars they may have to offer.

Open Your Eyes

If you work in a large office building, you need only open your eyes to see countless available careerists. You'll see them in the lobby, in the elevator, and in the halls. As long as they don't work at your company or do business with it, they are fair game.

While you don't have to keep your eyes peeled for great lookers at all times, you must be ready to engage in a flirting session should the situation arise. You can talk about the building's crummy mail delivery system, the time the elevator broke down, and the weird people in suite 204. Before you know it, you'll be scheduling your lunch breaks together.

The Date Doctor Is In

Q: I like this guy at work, but I'm worried about getting involved. I'm very attracted to him. Should I pass or try to pursue a relationship?

A: *I have strong feelings about this one. You should pass. Unless this guy is your one and only chance at true relationship happiness, odds are it will eventually fail. Once this happens I can think of nothing worse than having to see your ex every day involuntarily. This will definitely hamper your pursuit of closure, especially if the relationship should be a long one. Best thing to do is to separate your love life from your work life. Spending all your time together, at work and at play, is never healthy.*

Information Goldmines

Bored with the same old same old? Looking for something new to do? The following on-line city guides are bound to get your new and exciting activity roster underway.

1. City Quest@www.citiquest.com

2. Sidewalk@www.<u>enter your city name here.</u> sidewalk.com

3. City.Net@www.city.net

4. CityInsights@www.cityinsights.com

5. Digital City@www.digitalcity.com

6. IntelliPages@www.intellipages.com

7. Metroville@www.metroville.com

8. Weekend Events.com @www.weekendevents.com

I've always been one of those guys who makes it his business to know what's going on in my office building. Call me crazy, but if there's a beautiful woman working within two flights of stairs from me, I want to know about it. Take it from me, there's someone attractive in every office building. Once you target the person, all you have to do is learn their patterns; are they smokers, what time do they go to lunch, and so forth. Once you have this stuff down, you have your point of entry. You can pick and choose when to ask this person out on a date. If you're rejected, simple, use your schedule to avoid meeting this person. This system has worked for me, and for many of my friends.

—RON, 41, ACCOUNT SUPERVISOR

Commuter Train

Public transportation is great for meeting the fully employed, but only if you use it at the right times. At midday hours, the only people you'll find riding the rails are the subway performers headed for their next gig. If you're not used to getting up at the crack of dawn, then you should wait until the clock strikes five before you hop the bus or train.

Of course, we're not suggesting that you ride the bus for the romantic potential alone. That would be going too far. But should you have an errand to run, do it at around five o'clock and, by all means, eschew the cab. Not only is the Transit Authority cheaper, it's also much more social.

The Playgrounds of the Physically Fit

So you think of your body as a temple, do you? Well, you're not going to meet anyone who shares your ideology spending happy hour at the neighborhood pub. It's time to leave the barflies behind and get physical at...

Health Clubs

Forget about sweating it out within the comfort of your own home if meeting people is the name of the game. Health clubs are packed with scantily clad bodies that you can ogle to your heart's content. And while some of these establishments will charge you big bucks for full gawk-fest privileges, others are quite reasonable.

What's more, thousands of fitness buffs share your ulterior motives. You should have no trouble spotting them once you set foot into the gym. They're usually the ones sporting the brightest workout gear and perpetually flexing their abdominals. And if you're worried about that Soloflex you bought last year getting lonely, it's time to face the music: It's either you or the machine—now which is it going to be?

Life's a Beach

Women wearing string bikinis and men going completely topless are about as good as it gets for anyone who takes the mind-body connection literally. And where are going to find such a uniform dress code but at the beach?

With nothing but heat and sand around them, people become very laid-back. Many of the sun's disciples also tend to get bored and are amenable to conversation while soaking up those rays. You can play volleyball, toss a Frisbee, swim laps, or just relax and enjoy the sun and the surf while you wait for the right gal/guy to spring into view. In case you're not into UV-B rays, bring your SPF 30,000 sunblock and an umbrella.

Happy Trails

Bike trails aren't just for die-hard bikers anymore. You can find rollerbladers and joggers navigating those bike paths at all hours. If you're ready to get a workout, you can meet plenty of shapely exercise buffs on these picturesque little roads.

As long as you don't make them stop what they're doing, meeting joggers and rollerbladers in their tight-fitting Spandex shouldn't pose too tough a task. Many people take to the trails alone because they couldn't talk a friend into tagging along. Such individuals would welcome a partner to push them the extra mile. Just stay away from anyone who looks like they're training for the marathon— a look of blind determination and lightning fast speed is your best cue to steer clear.

The Culture Lovers' Playgrounds

You don't have to take out an ad to find someone who shares your enthusiasm for Puccini's operas, Beethoven's symphonies, Miller's plays, Bergman's films, and Kandinsky's paintings. But if it seems as though you do, chances are you're looking in the wrong places. People equally heady with the pursuit of culture can be found at...

Museums and Art Galleries

While you can go to the theatre and the opera to meet dates, you're more likely to meet people *on* dates at these venues. Not so at museums and art galleries. Art lovers are notorious for popping up at exhibits unaccompanied. Which is not to say that they aren't open to your friendly advances.

The best thing about scoping out the art scene is that it comes with ready-made conversation pieces. Whether you're at a gallery or a museum, their walls are dense with topics of discussion. After you begin to discourse, you can adjourn to a cocktail lounge for more of the same.

Poetry Readings

You know the time to release pent-up energy at an open mike is upon you when you feel the stirrings of your restless inner beatnik. If you're not altogether confident about your way with words, there's no rule that says you must step up to the stage. Give listening a try. Your self-assurance will make great strides once you hear what others are willing to say before an audience.

It's easy to break into the type of crowd that goes in for poetry. These hep cats are suckers for new and interesting experiences. All you have to do is think of something clever to say. "Hello, my name is Joe/Jane. Do you mind if I have a seat?" should do the trick.

Appreciation Classes

Anyone with a casual interest in the humanities and a yen to fill up their datebook can kill two mosquitoes with one slap by joining a general survey class. Enlisting in a course will allow you to expand your fine arts acumen while coming into contact with dozens of study partners.

Outdoors Activities and Clubs

City, country, or suburbs: no matter where you live, you're sure to be amazed at the variety and number of nearby outdoor activity clubs in your area. Whether it's hiking, bicycling, mountain climbing, rafting, or cave exploring you're after, the great outdoors are exceptional places to relax, have fun, and meet vigorous, charismatic people. Here are some sample organizations to contact:

Hiking

http://www.americanhiking.org

Hiking's a great way to get to know people—hikes involve long, invigorating hours exploring nature, and since you're walking, you can talk as much as you want. The American Hiking Society, a national organization of hikers and trail conservationists, has more than 130 clubs all over the country and is sure to have one in your area.

Mountain climbing

http://www.outdoors.org

Founded in 1876, the Appalachian Mountain Club is America's oldest conservation and recreation organization. Though this particular club is located in the northeast, there are hundreds of similar clubs all over the country.

Bicycling

http://www.worldbicycle.com

Are you a bike nut? The World Bicycle Association is for you. It's a great source of information about bicycle-related events, the best bike trails anywhere, and great rides to try all across the world. Visit their website to learn more about bike clubs in your area; then strap on your helmet and pedal your way to paradise!

Whitewater rafting

http://www.awa.org

For you true adventurers out there, whitewater rafting is unparalleled for challenge, beauty, and excitement. American Whitewater, a national organization, boats a membership of nearly 8,000 whitewater boating enthusiasts and over 160 local clubs. If your idea of excitement is rushing water, tiny boats, and strong biceps, find your nearest club and get paddling.

Caving

http://www.caves.org

Caving, you ask? Yes, caving. Besides having an aura of mystery and adventure rarely found in our increasingly industrialized world, caving is great fun and a fascinating way to view geology in action. It also takes you to little-known places all over your region, and puts you in dimly-lit spaces with potential Indiana Joneses. The National Speleological Society, at the website listed above, has affiliate groups all over the country. And a warning to the uninitiated: veteran cavers don't like the term "spelunking." Also: look out for bats.

Just think, in no time at all you can be cramming for pop quizzes with the classmate of your choice. Once the course is over, you can sign up for another class together or just burn up the telephone wires discussing into the wee hours what you've learned. If you're the proactive sort, you can even start your own weekly discussion group and watch your circle of potential dates grow to mammoth proportions.

The Activists' Playgrounds

Looking for a mate with a good cause? No problem. You can do good deeds and meet other humanitarians in the process. Here's how:

Go Door to Door

Organizations such as Greenpeace, the Sierra Club and Save the (*enter name of endangered species here*) have programs that require volunteers to go house to house asking for donations. If you don't mind the rejection, this could be your golden opportunity to spend time with a special someone who is also dedicated to proselytizing the general populace.

Since the volunteers can opt to take the word to the street in groups of two, you can arrange to spread the message with a viable partner. The two of you can bond as you overcome the rigors of countless slammed doors and an uncaring society. Once you're done, you can look for solace at the bottom of a beer mug together. Just don't forget to exchange numbers at day's end.

Hit the Campaign Trail

Those who want to make an impact in the political arena need not look far to find eligible men and women (and no, we're not talking about the candidates). You have two options when working in politics—you can either back a candidate or lobby for a cause. Whichever you decide to pursue, you'll find that the passion of the volunteers creates a magnetic atmosphere.

The kinetic environment of a campaign office or a political lobby can ignite sparks of romance. If you don't believe that pots of coffee, late night pizza parties, and long hours are the makings of love, it's clear that you've never gotten sucked into the whirlwind of politics before.

Join a Philanthropic Organization

If you're neither politically oriented nor in the mood for pounding the pavement, you can still contribute your time to a cause that's near and dear to your heart, and meet people in the process. Not-for-profit organizations such as the Junior League and United Way all stand to profit from your help. You and many others will be involved in planning benefits and fundraising campaigns.

This is the time to take matters into your own hands and volunteer your house as the site for the next meeting. Make sure to invite the member(s) you fancy. Once you have home court advantage, you can make all the right moves and score a date for the next benefit dance.

Co-Ed Fun

Of course, you don't always have to engage in extensive planning to achieve romantic results. Daily life often presents us with a vast array of tenable date partners. But strokes of luck won't come if you don't grasp at any and all opportunities. The following are some common activities that are uncommonly ripe with romance potential.

Party People in the House

Weekend soirees are veritable couple breeding grounds. When you meet someone at a friend's party, you can be sure that you already know some of the same people. You can play the name game ("Do you know Susan?" "Of course, she's only my best friend." "You're kidding—what about Bob?"...) into the small hours, blow the joint for a late-night stroll, or join forces and party-hop until the sun comes up.

The best thing about hooking up at a party is that while you're having this spontaneous good time, you're simultaneously taking care of the often awkward first date. There is also less pressure to meet again. If you decide to have nothing further to do with this person, you can write the whole thing off to experience. Just don't do anything stupid in the heat of the moment—like declaring your eternal love and giving out your phone number.

The Date Doctor Is In

Q: I (male) like to go out to dance clubs. What's the best thing to wear?

A: *The next time you're out clubbing, scope out the scene looking for the guys at the club who are with the most attractive women. Then copy their style of dress. This strategy should work.*

P.S. Make sure the guy you're looking at is not a pimp; the strategy will surely backfire if that's the case.

I was single for about three years and had pretty much given up on ever finding someone to relate to when I met Darren. It was at a party, and I honestly wasn't there to meet a guy. I figured I'd just have a good time hanging out with my friends. We were dancing, drinking, and having fun when my friend introduced Darren. We started talking and I couldn't believe the strong connection. When my friends told me they were leaving I said "I'll call you tomorrow," and Darren and I just continued to talk. Two hours later he gave me a ride home. He called the next day, and proposed the next year.

—Julie, 31, Makeup Artist

Running in Packs

You can go out on the town with just one or two of your truest and bluest, or you can send out an open invite and wind up going out with a big gang. You do the math, which would offer more promise in the way of dates?

Fraternizing with large numbers can lead to beautiful friendships. Just make sure that you're making the scene with a co-ed group. If you're part of a herd that's strictly same sex, this technique could backfire. Interested parties will be reluctant to approach you if you're surrounded, and you may end the night without so much as one set of digits.

If, on the other hand, you meet a beau/belle in a group setting, the chances of future encounters are high. You can arrange other such outings. With countless opportunities to ply your inimitable charm, you'll be free to take your time enchanting the target of your affections. Once this lovee is hooked on your attentions, you can safely move the relationship onto a more intimate footing.

Social Clubs

Not everyone is blessed with a long list of acquaintances. If you're the reclusive sort or if you have recently moved to a new city, you may not know a soul who meets the soul mate job description. But you don't have to suffer in silence and solitude just because your phone isn't ringing off the hook.

Dinner Parties

Dinner parties, unlike cocktail parties or college-variety keg parties, have a certain charm and intimacy to them. Having a dinner party is a great way to set people up without making them uncomfortable; they're perfect for getting people acquainted, especially if you've just moved to a new city or met a new group of people.

The best kind of dinner party for singles is one in which the host brings together four to six attractive, appealing single friends who don't yet know one another. Preferably, the guests have common interests: two or three love hiking, two are writers, two are WNBA fanatics, all are movie lovers, and so on. This way, everyone will have conversation topics right off the bat that are lively and interesting yet not too personal. Inviting a diverse crowd with common interests helps forge new friendships, which leads to more socializing and more opportunities to mix. This, of course, is what singles want.

You don't have to be a gourmet chef to throw a dinner party. You can fake it, just by trying a tasty-looking recipe in a cookbook, or you can glorify your tried-and-true favorites with a little imagination and care.

Co-hosting a dinner with a more experienced chef and dividing up the work between you is another good tactic. Of course, you can take the easy (if expensive) way out and buy prepared food or hire a caterer. In any event, dinner parties don't have to be formal, but they should feel special.

Dinner party etiquette, though once fairly rigid, is now very simple among friends: guests should bring something to the host (a bottle of wine, a baguette, or a simple dessert); participate politely and affably in conversation; and stay long enough so that everyone can savor the meal and the company, but leave promptly enough so that no one feels awkward.

The real beauty of the dinner party is that inspires guests to respond in kind by hosting dinner parties of their own. This way, a lively ritual among old and new friends will begin, and you'll be meeting friendly faces galore.

For sample recipes for dinner parties (and romantic dates), see Chapter 12.

Most cities now have social clubs that create settings for people to meet. These clubs usually aren't restricted to the unmarried, so they're not the singles groups your mom may have been telling you about. Still, most of the members do happen to be unattached. For a small fee, you can fill your itinerary to the brim with fun-filled activities sure to be jam-packed with hundreds of eligible bachelors and bachelorettes.

Going All The Way

As the song says, sometimes you want to go where everybody knows your name. But what that tune neglects to mention are those times when you can't get far enough away. We all like to make a break for it on occasion. To forget about our daily lives and surround ourselves by the unknown and the unpredictable is what vacation is all about. Housebound vacations are nice, but you have to admit that nothing beats skipping town.

R and R is just about the only thing you'll get out of using your precious time off to sleep in and stay up late with Conan O'Brien. But if you save those pennies, you can wind up seeing sights that few have seen. And if you plan your trips wisely, you'll be up to your neck in romance ops come no time.

Group Tours

If you're looking to spend some quality time with available strangers, there's nothing like a group tour vacation to get you off on the right foot. Wherever you want to go and whatever you want to do, the moon is the limit when it comes to globetrotting en masse.

Can you think of a bonding experience better than spending long hours on the same bus trip? Score a seat next to a friendly companion, and you'll have hours to get acquainted. Lend him your earphones or borrow her magazines—then initiate a discussion about music or some article you're reading. If the chemistry is right, arrange a dinner for two at your next stop. If not, move on, there's more where this one came from.

Singles Resorts

Don't get confused when planning your resort vacation. Certain hot spots cater mostly to couples. Sure, with names like "Hedonism" they may sound like a single girl's or guy's fantasy island, but if you fall for that pitch, you're the one who will be dreaming—of home, that is. Trust us, there's nothing more depressing than sharing a dinner with your platonic pal when the room is full of fawning love birds.

If you don't want to end up as the boy/girlfriendless wonder in a sea of honeymoon suite occupants, you'll have to do some digging. When March Madness rolls around, prick up your ears to find out where the Spring Breakers are flocking. These places are usually bursting at the seams with single sunbathers, ski bunnies, and plenty of nightclubs where you can mingle. You'll have no trouble finding a hot date in such an atmosphere.

If you're of age, youth hostels are another fantastic way to meet wayfarers in search of romantic adventure. Most hostels will provide you and five other travelers with a single room. This is the perfect opportunity to make new friends, hit the town, and then gossip and giggle the night away.

Two of my buddies and I decided to go to Puerto Vallarta, Mexico. I saw Missy our second night out at a local bar. We talked a little, and ended up dancing all night. It turned out that her hotel was just next door, so we saw each other often. Once we even went out to dinner together. When it was time for her to leave, I got her e-mail address and phone number. She lived about a thousand miles away so she didn't think I'd ever call her, but I was serious. First I e-mailed her, then I called her. When I saw that she was open to a relationship, I arranged to visit. Now, I'm looking for jobs in her area, because we decided to move in together.

—CHRIS, 37, MECHANICAL ENGINEER

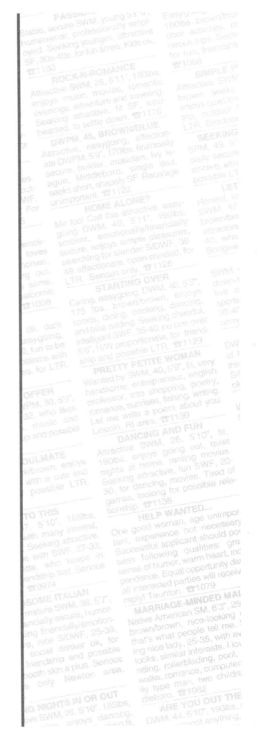

The Love Boats

If you've never seen a single episode of *Love Boat*, you may not know what cruising is all about. Aside from the many couples and families who hit the decks, you'll find scores of singles in their carefully coordinated cruise wear.

The great thing about cruises is that you can quickly find people with whom to spend your time. Since you're around the same group of people day in and day out, you can assess someone's marital status in a matter of minutes. Check for a wedding ring and a lovesick companion. If neither makes an appearance, you're in like Flynn.

Even if you're not the outgoing sort, you can still have fun in international waters. All ships come complete with social directors who make it their business to show you a good time and keep you coming back again and again. These people coordinate fun activities to occupy cruisegoers between ports. Many of the people who partake of the merriment are setting a course for romance, just like you. So you can let the social director's roster of events break the ice and take it from there.

Help For The Lovelorn

Say you've tried just about everything to meet your match and failed miserably in the process. What now? Are you destined to a lifetime of loneliness, pet collecting, and dinners for one? Do you see the task of convincing your married friends to spend boys'/girls' nights out getting harder and harder, until finally you lose the desire for society all together, board up your windows, and get your kicks by scaring unsuspecting little children come Halloween?

Hang in there, all is not lost. Before you resign yourself to dancing with your broomstick for all eternity, see what the experts have in store.

Amateur Night

Whoever said that the best things in life are free knew exactly what they were talking about. Before you bring in the hired guns, why not let those with your best interests at heart give your romantic future their best shot? After all, these are the people who know you best. They understand your "type" and wouldn't set you up with someone they deem less than worthy.

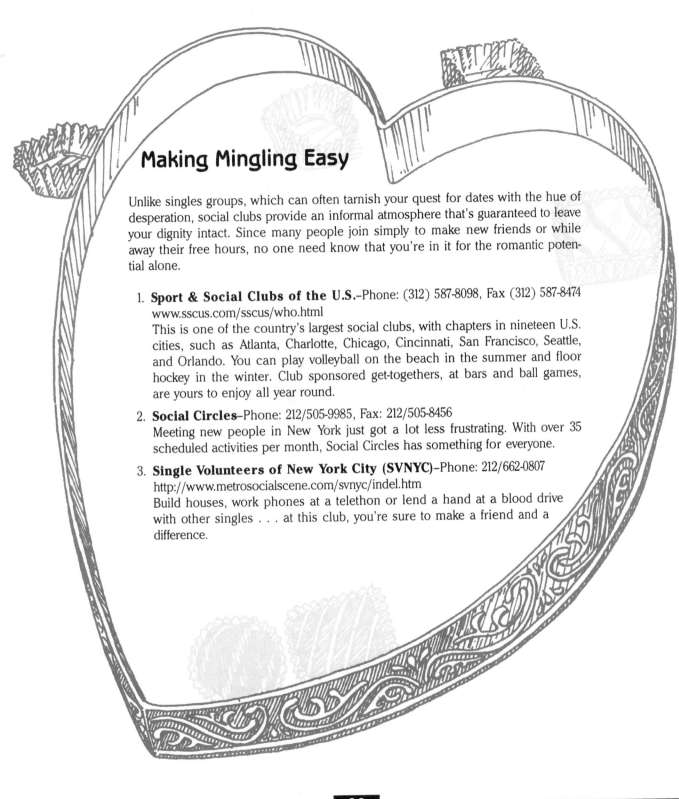

Making Mingling Easy

Unlike singles groups, which can often tarnish your quest for dates with the hue of desperation, social clubs provide an informal atmosphere that's guaranteed to leave your dignity intact. Since many people join simply to make new friends or while away their free hours, no one need know that you're in it for the romantic potential alone.

1. **Sport & Social Clubs of the U.S.**–Phone: (312) 587-8098, Fax (312) 587-8474
   www.sscus.com/sscus/who.html
   This is one of the country's largest social clubs, with chapters in nineteen U.S. cities, such as Atlanta, Charlotte, Chicago, Cincinnati, San Francisco, Seattle, and Orlando. You can play volleyball on the beach in the summer and floor hockey in the winter. Club sponsored get-togethers, at bars and ball games, are yours to enjoy all year round.

2. **Social Circles**–Phone: 212/505-9985, Fax: 212/505-8456
   Meeting new people in New York just got a lot less frustrating. With over 35 scheduled activities per month, Social Circles has something for everyone.

3. **Single Volunteers of New York City (SVNYC)**–Phone: 212/662-0807
   http://www.metrosocialscene.com/svnyc/indel.htm
   Build houses, work phones at a telethon or lend a hand at a blood drive with other singles . . . at this club, you're sure to make a friend and a difference.

Mother Knows Best

You may be your own worst critic, but there's at least one person who is your best publicist—your mother. Here is a woman who makes it her business to sing your praises far and wide. She'll build you up to anyone who will listen. You may groan at the thought of your mom telling perfect strangers about your fifth grade dance trophy, but as they say in Hollywood, no publicity is bad publicity.

While good old Ma may have played an instrumental role in some of your worst date fiascoes, there's no telling when her sixth sense may kick in. If you're constantly snubbing her well-meaning attempts at matchmaking, you may be missing out on some truly great experiences. Since you have nothing to lose and a love life to gain, why not start taking her up on her offers?

Family Matters

If Mom alone isn't enough to keep you in dates, you can call on the reinforcements. Extended families are a great source of dates for those who want to try multiple partners on for size. Those of you with kinfolk to go around are in luck. You may have as many as thirty people working hard on your side.

At the next reunion, let your entire family know that you're in the market. Almost everyone knows one unmarried person who is open to blind dates. Don't be surprised if you end up with a bevy of callers vying for your attentions.

Your Friends and Neighbors

There's no reason to keep your quest for affection all in the family. If you've entrusted your friends with your romantic woes—mercilessly bending their ears and crying on their shoulders—you can trust them to help you succeed in the game of love. After what you've put them through, they have a stake in your romantic rehabilitation.

Coworkers also make for zealous Cupids. Once they get wind of your temporarily unattached status, they'll send so many sons, cousins, and nieces your way you'll hardly know where to begin. Just be careful not to step on any toes as you make your way down the line of available relations. Follow closely the accepted dating protocol laid out in Chapter 6 lest you be branded a weirdo or a pervert. The last thing you want is your cubicle cellmate (you know, the one whose nephew you handcuffed to the bedpost) giving you the old evil eye first thing every morning.

At one of my past jobs, my supervisor and I got along very well. She knew that I was dating, and suggested I meet her niece, Katherine. I said okay. Next thing I know, Katherine is calling me at home. We talked about ourselves for about an hour, and then arranged to go out to dinner. As soon as I saw her, I knew this wasn't going to work. Still, I made the best of it, being my usual charming self. I didn't say I'd call her and didn't kiss her good-night. The next day my supervisor was already asking me what I had thought. It was hard telling her that there was no love connection, but I was glad that I hadn't compromised myself or misled her niece in any way. As a result, our workplace relationship was not affected.

—BRANDON, 25, LAWYER

What's Your Sign? Romance According to the Zodiac

Taurus
In romance with a Taurus, a lot goes on under the surface, out of sight. They're subtle and quiet about what they feel. Once they fall, they fall hard and their fixed natures simply won't allow them to give up. As a Venus-ruled sign, Taureans are true sensualists and romantic lovers. Their romantic attachments ground and stabilize them.

Paid Professionals

Your love search may lead you to a professional's doorstep—and we don't mean the kind that charges by the hour. Plenty of legitimate businesses provide matchmaking services for individuals too busy or too shy to put forth the right amount of effort themselves.

Sure, life would be a dream if we could all spare the hours to take a class, volunteer with a philanthropy, or even scope out the action at a health club. Unfortunately, many workaholics are entirely consumed by burning the midnight oil at the office and can't give dating the attention it deserves.

But it isn't just the monumentally busy who need an extra hand pulling the opposite sex. The shy, introverted single is also entitled to a piece of the happy couple pie. But every time they make the scene, many end up going home unaccompanied and without so much as a phone number.

If you're ready to bid the fruitless searches adieu, the following service providers will help you make a clean break.

Dating Services

With modern technology such as it is, dating services are now capable of shedding light on the blind date. Remember *Love Connection*, that great show of the 80s? Well, that program was basically a televised video dating service. The only difference is that in

real life you have to pay the service for your dates, and not the other way around. But hey, at least you don't have to endure public humiliation in front of millions of people. All things considered, it's a fair trade-off.

Most dating services are also computerized. Which means that you have to spend about an hour filling out what appears to be an inane questionnaire. But don't worry. These people know what they're doing. Your answers will be fed into a computer, and out will come a list of compatible prospects. Some balk at the notion of computer-aided love, but since this method has been known to work, we suggest you not knock it till you try it. After all, the computer isn't charged with making all the decisions for you. You're the one who has to sit down to view the videotapes of your potential partners. You can put the kibosh on the computer's picks any time you like.

As dating becomes more and more arduous with each passing year, dating services are proliferating. Today there's a wide variety to choose from. You can join a service that arranges a set amount of standard dates for a set fee, one that only arranges lunch dates, or even the type that follows a the-more-the-merrier motto to its logical conclusion by only orchestrating group dates. You can even go to date doctors who will send civilians on dates with you to find out what you've been doing wrong. With all the services at your disposal, you are certain to find one that fits your needs.

I would have never considered going to a dating service five years ago. But I have a lot of smart-ass friends who thought it would be fun to pool their money and buy me a membership for my birthday. At first I didn't even consider following through, but then I got curious. I finally showed up, made a video, and checked out some candidates. Two of the women were cute, but one was absolutely gorgeous. We arranged to meet, and I haven't had to use the dating service since.

—Tray, 39, Restaurant Manager

Private Matchmakers

It used to be that parents made all the wedding arrangements for their kids. They even went so far as to choose the proper partner. These were called arranged marriages. As opposed to love

What Are You Looking For?

Take this quiz to find if you're ready for the real world of dating. Warning: You may discover that your zest for rock climbing is simply an attempt to avoid facing another more difficult challenge—OTHER PEOPLE.

1. You went on a great date and had the time of your life, yet you're not quite sure if your partner felt the same. What should you do?
   a) Consider calling in a week's time.
   b) Wait for him/her to call; it is his/her turn after all.
   c) Decide to ask him/her out again. What do you have to lose?

2. You and a very attractive person are alone in an elevator—the clock is ticking. What should you do?
   a) "Accidentally" push emergency stop.
   b) Cast side-long glances, while watching the floors light up.
   c) Strike up a conversation—about the weather.

3. You've asked someone out, only to be turned down. Later in the week, you spot the culprit at a club. What should you do?
   a) Hide in the bathroom; then make a mad dash for the back door.
   b) Ignore him/her.
   c) Act friendly; (s)he was probably just having a bad day.

4. Your date loved the new Jim Carrey flick, but you'd rather die than see it again. What should you do?
   a) Change the subject.
   b) Rip the movie to shreds, and then make fun of your date's taste in film to anyone who'll listen for the rest of the night.
   c) Agree vehemently; you want to make a good impression.

5. It's your first date and you want to look your best. What should you do?
   a) Go with an old standby.
   b) Add a new accessory to a comfortable but attractive ensemble.
   c) Run to the nearest department store for the latest look.

Scoring
Give yourself the following number of points for each answer:

1.	a)2	b)1	c)3
2.	a)3	b)1	c)2
3.	a)1	b)2	c)3
4.	a)2	b)3	c)1
5.	a)1	b)2	c)3

What the Numbers Say About You

If you scored more than 12 points, consider yourself risk-taker extraordinaire—you know what you want and can't be bothered with what others think. Get out the giant Yellow Pages and start dialing for dates.

If you scored 8 to 12 points, you've got the winning combination—you're able to express yourself without alienating others, and you're a born leader with the diplomacy skills necessary to actualize your goals. Start your dating network by calling friends of friends.

If you scored 7 or under, there is really no excuse—after searching for your long-lost spine, practice acting assertive, even if you feel anything but. If others believe you, you must start to believe yourself. Ask yourself out in the mirror, and take it from there.

matches, which were considered crass, arranged marriages were based more on reason than emotion. Prevailing wisdom had it that love would come with time.

If your dating travails have got you waxing nostalgic for this bygone era, have we got something for you. Believe it or not, many countries still make extensive use of the arranged marriage custom today. While we're not suggesting you pack your bags for Pakistan, we do recommend that you check out what our country's private matchmakers have to offer.

A matchmaker's help doesn't come cheap. Nor should it, considering the time and personal attention that each client receives. Introductions are arranged with care by the matchmakers themselves. Customers are frequently attractive, usually successful, and always ready for a permanent relationship. People who are serious about making a commitment are encouraged to apply; those who just want to play the field can do so via...

A Personals Ad to Call Your Own

Personal ads are usually found in the very last pages of most of your local newspapers and magazines. If you have access to the Internet, you can also find plenty of personal ads on-line. Placing an ad that enumerates your many attributes will enable you to reach a broad stratum of society. While newspapers may charge as much as forty dollars per line (Internet personals are often free of charge), it's much easier to sing your own praises to the world than to one particular person. There's no risk of rejection and since it's anonymous, no one can laugh at you to your face. Sounds ideal? Read on.

It's a good idea to write your ad before calling your local rag. The type of respondents who come clamoring at your voice-mail box will depend largely on what you have to say about yourself. All kinds of people read these self-serving little blurbs. Some of these folks have never responded to an ad before, but if you can attract their attention, they just may drop you a line and photo.

So ask yourself, who do you want to draw into your circle of love? Here are a few guidelines to help you:

1. State your gender, the age range you find acceptable, and whether you're limiting your search to non-smokers.
2. People won't part with their pets, so if you're allergic to anything named "Fluffy," say so.

3. If you aren't looking to bill yourself as someone's future gold mine, leave out words such as "doctor/surgeon" (even if you happen to be one), "wealthy," "millionaire," and "generous." These are red letter words for people on the lookout for a meal ticket.

4. Humor is a potent aphrodisiac, and if you can make your readers laugh, you'll have them eating out of the palm of your hand.

5. Describe yourself in terms of the person you would like to see answer the ad. Start by describing the kind of man or woman you're looking for in writing. Is s/he a patron of the arts, attractive, of sound mind and body? Stop writing when anything begins to sound familiar. Now be honest, you just described yourself, didn't you? You probably did it in glowing terms too. This is exactly how you want to present yourself in your ad.

6. Place your ad in a publication that you like to read. People who read the same papers or magazines have more in common than you think.

Once the deed is done, go ahead and call the paper. Extra! Extra! Read all about me! Talk about getting the word out—depending upon which publication you decide to place your ad in, anywhere between 50,000 and one million people may get your message loud and clear.

The best part about placing your own ad is that you get to choose who you want to go out with. Just by taking this step, you've already played your hand. Now all that's left is to kick back and wait for the overwhelming responses to come pouring in.

I wanted to get married soon after my divorce. Unfortunately, everybody I knew was already married. So I decided to put out an ad in the paper. I started dating non-stop. Of course, few of the men were husband material, but instead of depressing me, this gave me more confidence in myself. I met Hank after a few months of this. He was attractive, successful, and had a great sense of humor. To make a long story short, we're now happily married.

—LAURA, 41, RECEPTIONIST

A Personals Response

Of course, you may not want to go to all the trouble and expense of crafting your own ad. This doesn't mean that the personals route isn't for you. Responding to a stranger's ad comes complete with its own set of advantages.

First of all, if you are a newcomer to the newspaper romance game, responding to an ad allows you to get a real feel for personals dating. Should you decide that this schtik isn't for you, you'll have saved yourself a good deal of money.

What's more, reading the ads is a fun business. You can laugh at them all you want without ever hurting anybody's feelings. Just wait, you'll come upon an ad that prompts your response soon enough.

Once you're ready to make contact, simply follow the instructions printed at the beginning of the Personals section. These will explain where to mail or phone in your reply. If you're taking the route of least effort, you may decide to opt for responding by phone instead of toiling over a "Dear SWF/M" missive.

While a voice-mail introduction may appear easy, leaving a message for someone you've never met tends to bring out the babbler in all of us. The following tips should keep your tongue in check when making the all-important call.

1. Less is more. You've never met this person before, so don't overdo it on the hard sell. The more salient points of your personality and appearance should suffice.
2. State what it was that interested you about the ad.
3. Don't talk too fast. If you're prone to talking fast, make a conscious effort to slow down the rush of words. You don't want your listener replaying your message countless times just to get your name straight.
4. Let a friend call for you to make it seem more like a set-up than a personals date. They can go on and on about how wonderful you are, and it will never look like you're bragging.
5. Don't forget to leave your phone number.

Chat Room Savvy

Less than 30 percent of Americans are wise in the ways of the World Wide Web. But with thousands of new recruits hooking up each and every day, the charlatans of the Internet have plenty of opportunity to take unfair home-court advantage. Still, there is a good time to be had in chat rooms, and as long as you approach the medium with a healthy dose of skepticism and caution, you should come out with an enviable cyberbuddy list. Here are some tips to get you started:

1. **Don't believe the hype.** Since the Web's most popular sites usually involve naked celebrities, it's safe to say that the information superhighway is practically teeming with sexual deviants. Remember this when potential paramours describe themselves as the embodiments of physical perfection and worldly success. Don't let your search for a soul mate cloud your better judgment, and take all claims to 36-24-36-type greatness with a grain of salt.

2. **Check out member profiles.** Most serious chat fanatics have profiles in which they divulge their interests to like-minded cyber aficionados. Watch out for people without a profile—they're either hiding something or not serious about using the Web as a meeting ground.

3. **Stick to interest-specific chat rooms.** As cheap-thrill-seekers usually content themselves with scoping out the Teen Chats or the singles sites, Web crawlers on the prowl for a meaningful conversation can usually be found in interest-specific chat rooms. Whether your interest is gardening or the state of the social security system, you're sure to find people who share your passions on the Net.

4. **Picture perfect.** Trading gifs, or photographs, on-line can be a great way to get to know your conversation partners better. However, even this tool of communication has been known to be subverted. People send pictures of their friends, magazine models, or themselves as they looked twenty years earlier—before the hairline disappeared and the morbid obesity had set in. If you're getting pictures that look dated, or simply too good to be true, ask for other photos to either confirm or dispell your suspicions.

5. **Don't give out personal information** Guard your phone number, address, and legal name as heavily as you would your Social Security and credit card numbers.

Instant Connections

While entering a general chat area is a lot like braving a room full of random strangers, interest-specific zones provide an instant connection. The following are just a few examples of rooms that bring people together to talk about a common cause.

1. Stern Chat–Howard Stern fans, look no further.
   http://www.4-lane.com/radiochat/pages/sternchat.html

2. E! Online Chat–If *People* is one of your favorite magazines, you've come to the right place.
   http://www.eonline.com/Chat/

3. PetMania!–Any proud pet owner shouldn't have any problem making friends in here.
   http://talkcity.com/calendar/category/pets.htmpl

4. Food Talk–Foodies looking to trade gourmet experiences and recipes should feel right at home in here.
   http://talkcity.com/calendar/category/cuisine.htmpl

5. PhotoWorld Chat–Shutterbugs unite!
   http://members.xoom.com/photoworld/chat.html

6. Yahoo! Chat: Books and Literature–A book discussion group at your fingertips.
   http://edit.my.yahoo.com/?.src=chat&.done=http://chat.yahoo.com/

7. Gardening Chat–Enter for the tips, stay for the fun.
   http://homegarden.chat.asp

8. Travel Channel–If you're passionate about travel, you're likely to meet your match in here.
   http://www.travelchannel.com/talk/talk.htm

9. Sports WebBoard–Pick a team, any team. Chat rooms for NFL, NHL, MLB, NBA, Soccer, and other sports teams.
   http://www.sportswebboard.com/

10. CNN NewsChat–Current events are the order of the day in this chamber, so read a newspaper, take a position and rant away.
    http://cnn.com/chat/

"Wanna Cyber?"

Anyone who has spent time in an Internet chat room has been confronted by the "Wanna Cyber?" instant message at one point or another. Those of you who unwittingly responded in the affirmative learned a valid lesson about the value of Just say no! This question, of course, refers to cybersex and leads one to wonder just who is it that's actually enticed by such a come-on. But the wannacybers aren't the only types who are looking for love on the Net. Millions of intelligent life forms are also chatting it up, albeit in a manner more becoming to the medium.

To meet the right people on your very own PC you need only log onto the Internet and enter a chat room. There are thousands of rooms from which to choose. You can hobnob with singles of all ages and persuasions in large groups or in private areas. You can search the chat areas for residents of your city or for those who share your interests. You can even exchange photos should the relationship reach a romantic level.

> *Chat rooms are areas where you don't have to worry about making the right impression, and you can be yourself. They offer complete freedom—nobody sees you and nobody knows you, yet everyone wants to talk to you. It's a single person's paradise. At first I would just chat to pass the time. When I got to know some people, and we became cyber-buddies, I got their pictures. Sure, a lot of them send phony pictures, but you can always tell who is lying by asking the right questions. I met Lorraine on-line, and we dated long-distance for a while. It didn't work out for us, but I can certainly understand how so many people find their spouses in chat rooms.*

—BRYCE, 35, TECHNICAL WRITER

Cyber-Jive

If you don't speak chat-roomese, you may have a hard time communicating. Here are some words and symbols that have been known to stump more than a few beginners.

- lol = laugh out loud
- pmp = pissing my pants
- :) = smile
- brb = be right back
- omg = oh my god
- ALL CAPS = shouting!!!
- gifs = photographs
- IM = instant message
- Age/Sex = your cue to type your age and gender, as in 30/f (thirty-year-old female), or 50/m (fifty-year-old male)
- wanna cyber? = cybersex proposition

Chapter 3
A Flawless Presentation

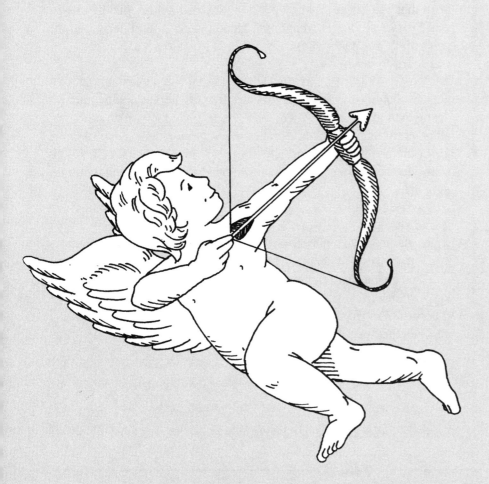

Dating and attraction go together like Batman and Robin, milk and cookies, and Mom and apple pie. Everyone has to bait the hook if they are to be noticed, admired and, consequently, wined and dined. The contrarians can go on and on about looks being deceiving, but nothing will net you a surplus of dates like putting your best pedicured foot forward.

Don't worry, you don't have to be a perfect 10 to lure your object of affection. No, all it takes to be considered the bee's knees is a dab of confidence, a pinch of charisma, and a heaping helping of sex appeal.

Easier said than done, right? It's all well and good to extol the virtues of sex appeal and confidence, but how do the many of us who weren't blessed with this winning formula for dating success navigate the singles scene? It's enough to make people want to wash their hands of the entire sordid business.

Remain calm—there is light at the end of every tunnel. We propose that you begin looking at sex appeal and confidence in a new way. First of all, forget what Frank Sinatra said. "You either got it, or you don't" is a myth whose dispelling is long overdue. You can, and will, learn to get it.

We are all born charmers. Think about it—all babies and little kids are cute. Why? Because they don't worry about looking and acting cute all the time. Their self-esteem is sky high. With time, we all begin to internalize the negative messages we hear every day. We forget the positives and end up becoming our own worst critics. This self-conscious state of mind is hardly conducive to creating a confident aura.

Self-esteem is key to appearing in your best light at all times. But if your self-concept is woefully neglected, you'll have to fake it for a while. By acting like people who think they're all that, you'll soon come to believe it yourself. The trick lies in being consistent.

This chapter will outline the myriad ways in which you can convince yourself that you're worth it. After all, those haughty L'Oréal ("because I'm worth it") models don't have the self-esteem market cornered just yet.

Makeover Madness

Who can resist the oohs and aahs that accompany a good makeover? Some of our male readers may be balking at the notion of getting their hair done and losing a few pounds, but trust us, man or woman, nothing turbo-boosts an ego faster than a flurry of compliments.

Makeovers aren't simply about glopping on a pound of makeup and hair gel. The act of changing from daywear to evening dress doesn't a makeover make. It's about coming out of your shell. It's the ugly duckling turning into a swan, the caterpillar metamorphosing into a bright butterfly before our very eyes. Makeovers are about letting everyone see the real you finally come out to shine and take a bow. David Copperfield has nothing on this brand of magic.

The before-and-after fascination has been used to sell everything from Deal a Meal to toothpaste. In most cases the "before" image reflects a poor posture and a negative facial expression. The person usually looks unsatisfied, frumpy, and, understandably, depressed—three qualities that don't work wonders for the romantically inclined. In contrast, the new and improved version looks vital, confident, and happy. We're not so much attracted by the makeup, hair, and clothes of these revamped images as by the manner in which the people are presenting themselves. So if you're ready to look good, feel great about yourself, and impress everyone you meet, then you're ready for makeover madness.

Image Counts

When you see a woman in a tailored suit holding a briefcase and hailing a cab, one idea comes to mind—professional. When you spot a bike messenger weaving his way through a crowded city street, you'd most likely think—daring. When you notice a mother playing with her child in the park, you assume—family. Everyone you see, from the corner grocer to the president of the United States, has an immediate effect on you, whether you realize or not.

Now, what do you think your image conveys to people around you? Take a moment and close your eyes: Pretend you're watching yourself cross the street on an average day. What images or ideas come to mind?

The Date Doctor Is In

Q: I'm twenty-five and still live with my parents. Will girls get turned off by that?

A: *The reasons for your present living situation make all the difference. If your particular reason stems from an increased dependency both emotionally and economically on your parents combined with a general lack of motivation to get out on your own, the answer to your question is probably yes. Most women, I'm afraid to say, are not turned on by a grown man living with his parents for the reasons mentioned. So shape up and assert your freedom.*

Whatever you take away from this exercise, remember this: the best thing about an image is that it can change at any time. Think about the professional woman playing tennis or running on the beach during the weekend, or the bike messenger coming home to greet his wife and family, or the mother running a meeting in a large boardroom. Changing your image is as easy as changing your clothes. But don't stop there. If you're serious about getting a brand new bag, here's how it's done.

Checking into Image Rehab

Unlike tigers, people often change their stripes to suit the occasion or the people they're with. Most of these changes occur unconsciously. Whether you attribute this to an adaptive social mechanism or to our perpetual need to just get along, we all have a little of the chameleon within us somewhere.

You can also change your image to attract the kind of person you're most interested in meeting. And don't worry about not being true to yourself. After all, it's not as if we're suggesting you do anything drastic like take up rock climbing despite a rabid fear of heights, or become a boxing fanatic when the thought of pugilism makes you sick to your stomach. No, we're simply asking you to consider exploring a neglected side of your personality. Now, is that so very wrong?

Before you dive headlong into the transformation process, you should decide what type of person you'd most like to meet. The following is a breakdown of some of the more common personality types.

Warning: For your convenience, we've managed to classify the entire human race into neat compartments. But as we all know, people will not be defined so easily. We earthlings are a very complicated lot, and you'll often find that no one fits one description to a T. That's why you'll have to do a little generalization of your own. When you meet someone new, try to determine which group they belong to. They could be a combination of several groups, so don't be too quick to judge their personalities.

The Preppy. This person is accustomed to the finer things in life. Often misinterpreted as materialistic, Preppies are simply proud of their immaculate taste and sensibility. They have a tendency to seek out

Beauty, Luxury, Makeovers, and Spas

Searching for a more spectacular look? Yearning to treat yourself to a day of beauty? You're in luck. The world is all too eager to provide you with pure, unrestrained self-indulgence. Go ahead—you deserve it!

In cities, some of the best-kept secrets for massages, facials, and general pampering are hotels. Few people even think of entering hotels in their own cities, but many of them make their facilities available to the public, such as gym and spa memberships and the luxurious treatment that comes along with them. Beyond that, there are sure to be ample choices among locally run spas and beauty centers, many with their own special charm. And then there are those institutions of beauty: Elizabeth Arden and Elizabeth Grady.

Elizabeth Arden Red Door Salon & Spa

http://www.elizabetharden.com/

Elizabeth Arden has Red Door Salons in several major cities, and they're long-renowned for their professionalism and expertise. The spas offer customized skincare, massage and body treatments, healthy lunches, hair care, pedicures, and even special packages for men.

Elizabeth Grady

http://www.elizabethgrady.com
1-800-FACIALS

Billing itself the largest skin care salon company in the country, Elizabeth Grady has over 300 locations and an ample array of services, such as facials, waxing, and eyelash tinting.

Cosmopolitan Virtual Makeover

http://www.virtualmakeover.com

If Cosmo is more your style, their rather sophisticated virtual makeover is a relatively inexpensive product that you can order and run on your computer to manipulate a photograph of yourself in any configuration you desire. Available are hundreds of hair styles and colors, lipsticks, blushes, and features, such as sculpted eyebrows and different eye colors.

those with good educational and family backgrounds, and their viewpoints sometimes run towards the conventional. WASPY, old-money communities boast wall-to-wall Preppies. Other areas have smaller prep concentrations, but if you look hard enough, you can find a preppy mentality anywhere.

The look they're after. Elegant and understated. Pastel designer suits and summer dresses work well for women, while polos and khaki pants are the best choice for men. Hair should be simple but well groomed. A bandana a la Jackie O will work wonders for women looking for a Preppy after their own heart. Makeup should also be kept to a minimum during the day. True prepster males never leave home without a sports coat, as many of their stomping grounds still subscribe to the "Jacket Required" policy.

Slackers. These offspring of the grunge movement value independence and flaunting convention above all else. Often creative and spontaneous, slackers have little regard for hard work and have been known to thumb their noses at "real" jobs. They are fun, interesting people, but don't come knocking on their door if security is at all a concern.

The look they're after. Casual and bold. Jeans, cargo pants, halter tops, and T-shirts will keep you seeing eye to eye. When it comes to these twenty- to thirtysomething bohemians, retro chic is just what the doctor ordered. Think thrift shop, because any outfit or hairstyle that even slightly hints at effort is strictly declassé and should be avoided like the Black Plague. But don't be fooled—achieving this carelessly fashionable attitude takes hard work and dedication.

Hip to be Square. While they may have been on the lower rungs on the high school social ladder, this group is a solid bet for anyone interested in ambition and financial security. While these onetime mouth-breathing, pocket protector enthusiasts may have been shy in the past, they have learned a great deal about social graces and can hold their own in most situations.

The look they're after. Ultra femme and masculine with a mind to match. Since these folks weren't seeing much action in school, they're now looking for the cream of the crop. Form-fitting (note: not obscenely tight and ill-fitting) clothes are a must for anyone who wants to be noticed by this bunch. But top-rate ladies and gents

aren't just about looking good—erudition is important if you want to keep these bookworms interested.

Yuppies. Yuppies value careers, money, and family above all else. They build solid nests for the future and have a strong sense of responsibility. While some are as conservative as sleepless nights are long, others are card-carrying members of the Jerry Brown Fan Club. Of course, most Yuppies are sufficiently enlightened to agree to disagree, so you'll find quite a few Mary Matalin-James Carville-type couples among this constituency.

The look they're after. Polished. Since this group works hard for the money, they don't scoff at showing off their loot once in a while. Jewelry and designer labels are valued by this crowd. But if you can't afford it, try to find inexpensive knockoffs. No one will be the wiser.

Granola Junkies. These outdoorsy types love everything au naturel. Outdoor sports are also a priority, and keeping in shape is not as important as staying healthy. Some G.J.s also rate spirituality very highly. You can often find them perusing the aisles of alternative bookstores in search of total well-being in the homeopathic medicine sections. This group offers much stimulation for anyone seeking a lifestyle well outside the bounds of the mainstream.

The look they're after. Everything including clothes, makeup, and hair should be kept very natural. Sporty gear is very important, as is an ability to ride a mountain bike. You'll never go wrong with a well-worn pair of Birkenstocks or Tevas. Rule number one: Your water bottle is your best friend. For evening, dresses made with organic fibers (preferably hemp) will work wonders, makeup should be present but not seen, and hair should be kept loose and flowing. Men can pull off jeans and a sweater wherever they go, but skip the cowboy boots. For all their nature-loving ways, these folks still like to put a little city in their country ways. Gal or guy, throw in a crystal as jewelry and you'll be the toast of granola junkies everywhere (just make sure you know the kind of crystal you're sporting, along with its extra special purpose, once the time to field questions from inquiring tree-huggers is upon you).

The Trendsetters. While the proper attire and look is key to getting in with these stylers, attitude still reigns supreme. The "I know I

What's Your Sign? Romance According to the Zodiac

Gemini

Geminis love first with their minds. Even a relationship that begins primarily because of a sexual attraction won't last if there's no mental camaraderie. Quite often, Geminis seek friendship first with the opposite sex and once a mental rapport is established, the friendship deepens to love. They can be quite fickle in their affections, sometimes carrying on simultaneous relationships. But once their hearts are won, they love deeply.

The Date Doctor Is In

Q: I seem to attract guys who love to talk about how much money they make—as if I really care. How do I handle this the next times the topic comes up?

A: *First, ask yourself why you're attracting these types of men. If you're wearing tons of jewelry and only wear outfits made by high-priced designers, even on trips to the market, you may have your answer. If not, just tell them that you're recently divorced and instead of getting even, you got everything.*

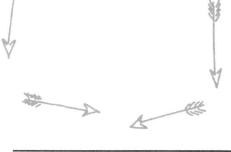

look good" attitude is a constant staple in their presentation. While designer brands are important, these hep cats want to see your own individual style. Pretty boys/girls make fast times and showing off their number one priority. They want to be noticed and may sometimes be a little narcissistic as a result.

The look they're after. Confident, stylish, and totally mod. If you're not sure which approach to take, think all black. Adding some offbeat jewelry and smoky makeup should keep you on an even par with this glam group. Guys should avoid ties at all costs. Tight-fitting sweaters and T-shirts are still the rage. Now pair that with a nice pair of slacks or even jeans and you're in. Leave the tie and sport jacket at home, and never, ever tuck a loose shirt into your pants. Take our advice, and you're bound to be accepted as one of their own.

> *I work in the creative department of a large corporation. Since I love to design and still go out to clubs, I tend to dress with a little more flair than others at the company. There was this hot guy in accounting, but I never noticed him until I saw him out one night. He was dressed so differently, you could tell he had great abs and perfect legs. I didn't even realize who he was until he approached me. You could have knocked me down with a feather duster, I was so shocked. We actually exchanged numbers. I don't usually date with coworkers, but he deserved an exception. Eventually, we went out on a date, and my ex was at the restaurant. The accountant turned out to be a royal snooze, but my ex-boyfriend's dirty look was still worth it.*
>
> —LYNN, 25, COPYWRITER

You should also avoid changing yourself to fit every criteria. The main point of this exercise is to help you determine the type of person you're interested in or have the most in common with. Then, once you've established your compatibility and are confident of working towards a greater good, you can alter your image slightly. Just keep in mind that you are an interesting and valuable person no matter how you present yourself (and if you don't believe that, nothing you wear will ever convince you).

The Grooming Expert

What is good grooming? Is it well-washed hair, flawless makeup, flattering clothes, sparkling teeth, clean cuticles, frequent showers, and manicured nails? Actually, the answer is all of the above. Good grooming is a look that simply says, "I care about my appearance."

So many of us value good grooming in others, but neglect to take care of our own appearance. "Who has the time?" and "It's only a quick trip to the grocery store, why even bother?" figure prominently on our list of excuses. Well, there's a very good reason to bother, and that is because you never know who you'll run into. Why run out of the house wearing sweats and gym shoes, when it takes no more time to put on a nice dress, pants, or shirt? The key to becoming a successful dater is to constantly be on the lookout for dating opportunities, and that means looking your most presentable 24-7. Consider it a small price to pay for love.

> *I was making my weekly visit to the laundromat, and spotted a really attractive woman drying her clothes next to mine. I was shocked since I hardly ever see anyone so attractive in my town, let alone in that laundromat. It was like something out of those Cindy Crawford Pepsi commercials. So I pretended to pass the time, and struck up a conversation with her. When she got up to leave, I asked for her number. She looked me up and down real quick and politely declined. I almost followed her outside to try again, until I caught a glimpse of my reflection in the revolving doors. My hair was sticking up, my shirt was stained, and I looked like something the cat dragged in. Since I hadn't showered, I probably smelled too. It was really pathetic.*

—DAN, 24, STUDENT

Grooming on the Run

In today's hectic world, constantly keeping up appearances is no mean feat. But it can be much easier than you've ever imagined, provided you equip yourself with some tools that will make grooming a fast, easy, and even fun activity.

Beauty Supplies

Avon
http://www.avon.com

The Avon home page, besides being a vast storehouse of products and tips, has a "Virtual Beauty Advisor" which tells you, free of charge, which makeup colors are right for you. And then, of course, there are the famous Avon "ladies," who will gladly offer anything you need in the way of product advice and beauty care guidance.

The Body Shop
http://www.bodyshop.com

If you've been to a mall in the last ten years, you know that The Body Shop, possibly the only international beauty company equally devoted to saving the world and beautifying its residents, has a wide array of sweet-smelling, bright-colored, nature-inspired beauty products. What you may not know is that they too have an increasingly popular "virtual makeover" area on their website.

Clothes Basics

They key to dressing well is to first limit the amount of comfy, cozy home clothes you have at your disposal. We're talking items such as sweats, oversized T-shirts, and hole-infested jeans. Sure, everyone loves lounging around in their favorite set of comfy sweatpants, but home clothes do not make for good street clothes. How many times have you seen someone who looks like they've just rolled out of bed? That's because maybe they have. Our advice: pare down your supply of comfies to the bare essentials, that way you'll be forced to dress in real human clothes come time to go public.

Next, you should find clothes that are both comfortable and attractive. That way you know you'll wear them often. The following items are very low-maintenance and will help both men and women dress better whether on the go or on the prowl.

Women's Essentials

1. Black, white, brown, and gray turtlenecks
2. Simple summer dresses
3. Stretch-denim jeans or comfortable, faded Levis
4. An arsenal of tailored T-shirts in all colors
5. Long skirts you can throw on any time
6. Comfortable but attractive shoes for walking
7. Loose or form-fitting black pants
8. An attractive coat you can throw over anything

Men's Essentials

1. Black, brown, and gray sweaters or turtlenecks
2. Black pants or jeans
3. Well-fitted khaki pants
4. A week's supply of well-fitting T-shirts
5. Loose-fitting blue jeans
6. Navy or black sports coat
7. Rugged boots
8. A black, brown, or navy pea coat you can throw over anything

Fresh Face to the World

The face is the first thing people notice. Get yours in tip-top shape before venturing past the threshold. Your visage is very easy to maintain and doesn't have to cost a bundle to keep looking good. The following bits of advice won't have you bowing your head in shame should any manner of cutie look your way.

Women

1. Moisturize every day
2. Pluck eyebrows; bleach or wax other facial hair as needed
3. Apply homemade facial masks twice a week
4. Don't frown unnecessarily
5. Stay out of the sun
6. Apply self-tanning lotion for added glow

Men

1. Keep clean and moisturized
2. Shave every day or trim facial hair (no visible nose hairs!)
3. Brush eyebrows (mind you that's eyebrows, not eyebrow—if you've got the latter, pull out the tweezers) before going out
4. A fine quality self-tanning lotion never hurt anyone

Hairy Situations

For years, people have been fascinated with hair. Take Samson (of Delilah fame). Snip, snip and poor Samson was bereft of all his preternatural strength. With its ability to cast a spell over entire armies, hair is indeed a very seductive element. The proper maintenance of your crowning glory is critical for both men and women.

Everyone should begin by getting regular trims every three months. If your locks tend towards the oily, you should wash your hair every day. Take a few minutes to create an attractive style before leaving the house. To keep hair glossy and always in control, both men and women should look for styling products that will maximize their hair's natural beauty.

And a word of advice for men: If you're experiencing hair loss, don't try to cover up. The classic comb-over will just make you look more insecure. Instead, try playing up your favorite features. Wearing a bold tie and a top-drawer suit will have you on your way to getting the kind of attention you deserve.

Clothes Busters

You may be sporting the latest in designer wear, but if your outfit includes just one of the following items, all bets are off.

1. T-shirt bearing your name
2. Acid washed jeans
3. Sweaters with reindeer or other cuddly animal prints
4. Leg warmers worn for anything other than dance purposes
5. Fringed, tie-dyed shirts
6. Moccasins
7. Multi-colored suspenders
8. Spandex anything outside the gym

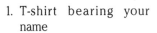

Homemade Beauty

Most of us have bought into the myth that beauty comes at a price. Unless you're comparison shopping for a plastic surgeon or have recently entered into a payment plan with your dermatologist, this old-fashioned edict couldn't be further from the truth. In your kitchen right now lies a virtual silo of undiscovered beauty formulas. And since natural products are safest for your skin, you can rest assured that none of these masks are less safe than those found in your corner drugstore (Warning: Ye of many allergies beware).

Egg Yolk and Honey Toner

This is a great toner that will make your skin look tight and firm. Begin by separating the egg yolk, and, in another jar, mix yolk with 1/2 teaspoon of honey. Apply ingredients and wash off when skin feels tightened.

Strawberry Freshener

Don't try this if you're allergic to strawberries, but anyone else will benefit from this refreshing eye opener. Just mash the strawberries in a plate and apply to face, taking care not to get any on your clothes. Leave on for ten minutes, then rinse clean.

Avocado and Lemon Peel

This natural peel will definitely keep you from spending lots of money at the spa. You'll feel and look great. Just mix half an avocado with a teaspoon of lemon and apply to face. Leave on for five minutes and you'll feel like a new person.

Oatmeal and Honey Exfoliant

This natural exfoliant will remove dead skin cells in moments, leaving you with a fresh and vibrant complexion. Mix half a cup of oatmeal and one tablespoon of honey. Apply to skin, brushing gently. Wash off in two minutes. This skin miracle can be used on face, neck, and body.

Tea Bag/Cucumber Eye Firmers

You stayed out late on a Wednesday, and come Thursday morning your vision is obscured by the bags around your eyes. What do you do? Crying is out of the question—it will only exacerbate the problem. Say what the hey and call it "going for the Clinton look"? Out of luck again, that day is done. Why not place two cold cucumber slices or hot tea bags over your lids, lie back, and enjoy a five-minute snooze? You'll wake up with your eyes wide open.

Hair Silk

To treat overdried, processed hair without spending the extra money on hot-oil treatments, try applying two tablespoons of mayonnaise to wet hair. Comb evenly throughout and wrap with towel. Leave overnight and wash thoroughly with shampoo and conditioner the next morning.

Never Let Them See You Sweat

You probably already know this, but we think it bears repeating: good hygiene can mean the difference between a polite pat on the back and a night of complete debauchery. The choice is yours. The basic rule of thumb is simple: don't stink up the joint. Not to be insensitive to the glandularly challenged, but no one is exempt from taking minor precautions if they want to ensure that a good time is had by all.

By all means, take a shower before any outing. Make extensive use of the soap and sponge. And don't forget the deodorant, a vital component of the grooming process. When things get tense, and when matters of the heart are concerned they inevitably do, you'll be grateful for that added bit of protection.

You should also carry a pack of gum or breath mints wherever you go. The chicks and chucks will go buck wild for that peppermint scent. Finally, ladies and gents can all benefit from a spritz of fragrance. But be careful, less is infinitely more in this department. Unless you're using scented lotion or aftershave, never apply a cologne or perfume directly to your skin. We prefer the "Spray Shower" technique, when you spray the scent into the air and walk through briskly. This method will have your entire being emanating those pheromone-rousing vibes.

To Feel Good About Yourself

- Work out. You've heard it before, and that's because it's true: regular exercise makes you happier, healthier, more fit, and more confident. So lace up those sneakers and go!

- Look as good as you possibly can, in your own unique way.

- Spend time by yourself. Discover what is unique about you, apart from your friends, your job, your ex, and your family.

Keeping Your Cool: Confidence Rules

Any way you look at it, confidence is a tricky matter. Too much of it and you're in danger of being branded a "pompous ass" or an outright "bitch." Too little and you're on your way to monikers such as "pushover," "doormat," "spineless jellyfish," or, worst yet, "mousy." So how does one find a middle ground without wasting years on those painfully frustrating trial-and-error procedures? Well, confidence is a matter of trusting yourself. It's not about putting others down to make yourself feel better, and it's surely not about sacrificing your feelings to make others feel better about themselves. Simply put, confidence is all about respecting yourself, no matter what you do or what other people say.

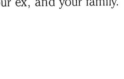

I was in a four-year relationship with a man who constantly put me down, making fun of me in front of my friends and coworkers. Being my high-school sweetheart, I was deeply committed to this man and thought he would change. But he didn't. Finally, with the help of my best friend, I left him. But ever since that time, I've felt unsure of myself and have a hard time meeting new people. One day, after another unsuccessful date, I realized that I was hurting myself more than my ex ever had by constantly putting myself down. So I stopped. It was that easy. It's really amazing how that one day changed my life forever. Now, whatever happens, I actually like myself, and I'm sure it shows.

—JESSICA, 35, MARKET RESEARCH ANALYST

The Confidence Charlatans

Since you can't buy confidence, it suffices to say that money is not a genuine confidence booster. Anyone sufficiently well-off will tell you that flashing a Benjamin-stuffed money clip is the easiest way to get attention in a hurry. But when all is said and done, you've probably attracted someone who is only out for one thing.

But money isn't the only way to abuse the status game. For instance, you can use your good looks, glamorous career, or upper-crust education to create an assertive identity. But in the end, you're sure to find all such efforts futile. While others may be impressed with your accomplishments, they will never get to know the real you. So if you're one of the lucky people upon whom fortune has smiled, make sure you don't confuse this confidence with the real home-grown variety.

A word of caution: If you happen to meet a confidence charlatan, make sure to read the fine print of their personality. This entails paying particular attention to their beliefs, opinions, and actions, as opposed to the self-serving pitch they're trying to feed you.

Another word of caution: Most importantly, never let your confidence levels decline because of someone else's achievements. You never know, they could be exaggerating. Many people who go on and on about their fun and exciting lives are actually insecure.

Someone's desperate efforts to impress you should flatter you, not make you feel worse.

Instant Ego Boosters

Confidence is a learned skill, just like riding a bike or even walking and talking. You can easily make confidence a habit just like any other. Don't be fooled: People who seem to have their act together didn't get there overnight. It takes a certain amount of determination and risk-taking to get yourself to the point where you can bravely navigate the social waters. But once you're successful, and yes, you will be successful, you'll begin to discover that gaining confidence is not as hard as it looks. We've come up with some instant confidence boosters that will get you mingling in no time.

Straight as an Arrow

You probably don't enjoy being told to watch your back, especially if you've long since given up on your posture. But appearing confident is sometimes as simple as straightening your spine. Our mothers knew what they were doing when they told us to stand straight. A slumped posture creates low self-esteem, or at least the appearance thereof. There's a reason why the Hunchback of Notre Dame struck out with Esmerelda.

Exercise: Find a mirror and exaggerate a poor posture. Not very attractive, is it? Now straighten your back and walk around the room. Feel the energy and sense of control coursing through your veins? Every time you meet someone new, pay attention to your posture. Not only will you feel more in charge of the situation, but you'll also make a better impression.

Say Cheese!

The power of a smile should never be underestimated. If you think you're insecure, take a good, hard look at the rest of the world. Most people also fear rejection and walk around feeling anxious and unsure of themselves. Smiling is a safe way to rev your confidence and announce your approachability to the world. Now, don't get carried away and start smiling at everyone you meet. This is such a powerful tool of attraction that you have to exercise extreme caution. You don't want to spread your smiles too thin.

The Date Doctor Is In

Q: I get tongue-tied around attractive women. Is there a remedy for this?

A: *Other than delving into psychoanalysis to uncover any repressed unconscious conflicts arising between your mother and yourself due to early separation anxiety, there is one less complicated solution. Just create an image in your mind of the attractive woman you're talking to doing something really dorky, like breakdancing to country music. This will make her seem a lot less intimidating and thus easier to talk to.*

Once you've chosen a person you're interested in getting to know better, give them a casual smile to let them know you're happy to see them. You don't have to approach them right there and then. But provided they smile back, you'll find they'll soon be inexplicably drawn to you.

Since smiling is a key confidence booster, try to maintain the look and health of your pearly whites. With proper care and daily brushing, you can create an aura of friendliness that will put a bevy of admirers at your command.

Speak Out

Voices have the power to soothe, intimidate, and attract. If you're looking to boost your confidence, you will have to pay special attention to your voice. For instance, do you ever catch yourself whining or complaining? Well, when you do, your voice probably sounds more nasal than usual and not unlike the Nanny's Brooklyn twang. And while Fran Drescher may have her share of admirers, real life nannies should try to keep the whine out of their voice.

A quieter voice also reveals a high intimidation factor. If you're constantly muttering under your breath, people will naturally assume that you're afraid to speak up. And don't forget about pacing yourself. If you speak too quickly, you will come off as lacking the very confidence you want to portray.

So when in doubt about your speaking voice, remember this rule: Speak slowly, speak up, and don't forget to breathe.

Eye Contact

It's not easy looking someone straight in the eye, especially if you're madly attracted to them. But the best way to convey confidence and sexual attraction is to hold long lingering looks for more than five seconds. Heavy eye contact lets others know that you are attracted to them and are not afraid to connect on a deeper level. Just don't turn this beautiful moment into a staring contest. No one wants to be visually harassed or made to feel self-conscious. Make sure you take breaks in between glancing at the object of your affection.

Quiz—Rate Your Shy Q

1. When I see an attractive person on the street, I usually:
   a. Look 'em straight in the eye and smile broadly
   b. Check them out discreetly
   c. Avert my gaze and blush profusely

2. When it's time to put an end to a great date, I usually:
   a. Tell them I had a great time and ask to see them again
   b. Thank them and hope they'll call
   c. Beat a hasty retreat into my house

3. When I do not know anyone at a party, I usually:
   a. Approach someone and introduce myself
   b. Hang out by the food table, waiting for someone to talk to me
   c. Bond with the wall all night

4. I have gone out to a movie alone:
   a. Whenever the opportunity arises
   b. Very seldom
   c. Never

5. When meeting a stranger for the first time, I usually:
   a. Shake their hand confidently
   b. Nod politely
   c. Feel flustered and anxious

6. In school, most people thought you were:
   a. A Socialite
   b. A Drifter
   c. A Loner

7. When talking to your friends about a great date, you reveal:
   a. Everything, including my feelings
   b. All the facts
   c. Almost nothing

Add up the number of a's, b's, and c's you circled, and check your Shy Q rating below.

Rating

- If you chose more than 3 a's, you have a healthy dose of confidence and aren't afraid of what others think of you. Keep up that spirit; it will serve you well in the dating game.
- If b's were your letter of choice, you'll need to become even more outgoing. Ask yourself what's holding you back from enjoying the kindness of strangers. With a little work, you too can make a dramatic impact on everyone you meet.
- For all of you who chose more than three c's, we recommend taking some time off to discover why you have a hard time trusting others. Getting to the root of the shyness matter may be all it takes to make an extrovert out of you.

The Comic Approach

Did you know that a good sense of humor ranks high on the sex appeal scale? Well, if you've ever been on a date that was just ho-hum until someone made a good joke, you probably are aware of laughter's healing power. A good sense of humor is not only entertaining for others, but it also shows that you're not afraid to take chances in life.

If you really want to make a good impression or break the ice, you'll have to do some research. Choose a joke that is neither too lewd nor offensive, and find the right time to deliver it. But as any comedian will tell you: Don't sweat it. The funniest people know how to take a lighthearted attitude towards life. Above all, relax and enjoy yourself, and the humor will take of itself.

Staying in the Know

Have you ever noticed that all intelligent people have an air of superiority about them? Whether their attitude is well-deserved or not, people who keep themselves informed are just naturally more confident and talkative. After all, if they didn't talk, who would know how smart they were?

Replenishing your store of knowledge takes time and should be practiced daily. But if you're in a hurry to make a good impression, it can be as easy as reading the newspaper each day. This activity will provide you with hours of conversation. Just pick out the most interesting topics of the day and talk away. People will take an interest in your conversation, and you will come off as an informed and confident person. It's just that easy.

I met Rod through some friends, and I didn't see what was so great about him at first. Then we started talking, and I couldn't believe how much I was laughing. I couldn't even drink my beer . . . I would have done a spit shot right there and then. Suddenly, he was the most attractive guy I had ever met. We went out for months afterward.

—AMANDA, 23, REAL ESTATE AGENT

Confidence-Boosters

So this isn't a book of affirmations. But we've collected a little set of important goals to remind you of why you should feel entitled to walk into any cocktail party, book signing, high tea, or sports bar feeling like the king (or queen) of the hill.

People with real self-confidence share the following characteristics. Even if you haven't achieved all of these admirable qualities, remember what the objectives are, strive toward achieving them, and chances are it'll become habit-forming. In the meantime, the more you act confident, the more fun you'll be to be around—which leads to increased popularity and the good things that come with it.

Self-confidence is:
- Genuinely liking yourself. This goes without saying.
- Being interested in meeting new people, and acting friendly but at ease when you do.
- Feeling good about your personal achievements, regardless of your social status, amount of money in the bank, fame or lack thereof, looks, educational pedigree, or background.
- Having good will and open-mindedness toward others, regardless of their social status, amount of money in the bank, fame or lack thereof, looks, educational pedigree, or background.
- Being outgoing but not overeager for attention.
- Not needing affection to feel good about yourself.
- Not needing to boast or to prove yourself to be better than other people.
- Being generous toward others and happy about their accomplishments.
- Being able to accept compliments without feeling undeserving or superior.
- Being content and cheerful.
- Remember those strengths you had in college that you don't get to use much at your job? Your figure drawing, your expansive knowledge of '60s film directors, your decent jump shot, your undying love of musical theater? Well, you can still use those abilities—either as you used to or by finding new ways to indulge your creativity. By taking adult education classes, doing volunteer work, getting involved with local organizations, or even enjoying your unique interests by yourself, you expand your horizons, make yourself happier and more interesting, and spend less time comparing yourself to the people on t.v. and in entertainment.

What's Wrong with This Picture?

This next ego booster works on the following premise: If you're too busy worrying about yourself, you'll never truly get to know anyone else. Focusing on your own flaws and inadequacies is unacceptable for many reasons, but one of them is because you will begin to see other people as perfect and will by comparison become even less confident. Another reason to use the "Make Them Squirm" approach is to remind yourself that the dating process is a two-way street. For example, when a job applicant is nervous at an interview, it is usually because they feel scrutinized and put on the spot. But what they have to remember is that every applicant is being selected and selecting at the same time. It's the same with dating. Most people forget that they are in the driver's seat and don't have to impress everyone they meet. Putting your dates to your own test will keep you from having to try and pass anyone else's.

In order to draw attention away from your own flaws, you'll have to turn the tables and focus on the other person's inadequacies. This approach may seem mean and ill-spirited, but when you think about its purpose—sparing your own feelings—you'll become more comfortable performing this fool proof technique. After all, it's not as if we're advocating mental insults; we're just urging you to make the other person feel self-conscious. Once you've completed this exercise you will have learned many things, including that no one is without flaws, everyone struggles with bouts of low self-esteem, and you don't have to be perfect to attract a member of the opposite sex. So what's holding you back? Get out there, and make others work to impress *you*.

A Star Is Born

Picture yourself as a famous celebrity, loved and adored by millions and hounded by a ton of paparazzi wherever you go. Visualize yourself in designer garb, looking absolutely fabulous, as you step up to receive an award for your brilliant performance in the one-(wo)man show, *The Sexiest, Most Desirable Human Alive.* Really get into this fantasy, and hear the crowd chant your name, watch the flash of the cameras, and revel in the scrutiny of your most ardent admirers. Besides being terribly fun and amusing, this exercise, performed before a big date or even during a chance encounter, will instantly raise your ego to new heights.

Just Breathe!

The first thing most of us do whenever we get overly anxious or excited is hold our breath. Considering how easy it is to simply exhale, it seems absurd. But most people just shut off their breathing mechanism at the first sign of tension. That could momentarily cut off the flow of oxygen to your brain and result in an inability to think on your feet. And believe us, when you've just met the person of your dreams, you'll need to have your wits about you. So whenever you find yourself short of breath, take a moment to regroup. Ask the other person a question and take that pause to breathe deeply several times. It can really make a big difference in your comfort level.

So there you have it, a quick and easy reference guide for boosting your ego anytime, anyplace, and with anyone. But take caution: these tactics and strategies are by no means a substitute for real confidence and assurance. That may take more time to develop. But once you commit yourself to forgiving and accepting both the good and bad parts of your identity, you'll never have to resort to faking it again. In the meantime, do whatever it takes to get yourself feeling cool, calm, and collected.

Keep an Eye on Yourself

How are you going to keep an eye on someone else if you can't even look at your reflection in the mirror? The best way to practice the art of proper eye contact is to take a gimlet-eyed look at yourself. Here's how:

1. Look in the mirror
2. Keep looking as you pretend to agree with some opinion or discuss the weather
3. Now add a smile to your chit-chat
4. Try frowning
5. Look away

While exercising, try not to get distracted, and don't break eye contact with yourself. It may all feel a little weird at first, but keep repeating this exercise until you are completely comfortable with maintaining your own eye contact. After several practice rounds, you'll be surprised at how much easier it will be to lock eyes with others.

Chapter 4

Making a Splash

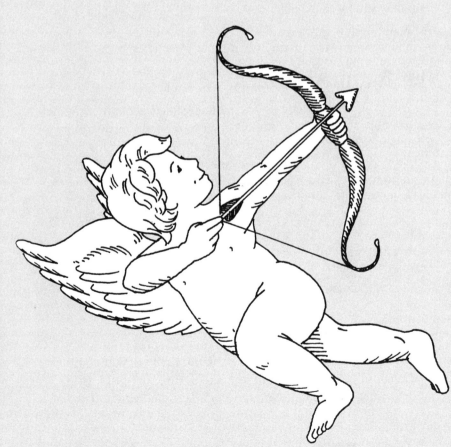

Now that you've bolstered your confidence, honed your image to a razor's edge, and polished your personal style to perfection, you're ready to take your show on the road. True dating gurus understand that great opportunities are either seized or squandered. That's why you're going to have to learn to proactively approach people in a friendly and becoming manner. Don't even think about putting it off, because this is the big moment you've been prepping for. No matter how attractive you fancy yourself, standing around looking cute won't net you the many dates you're expecting.

On the street, in a store, or even in your car, the single people of the world are waiting to be discovered. So unless you're already beating your admirers off with a stick, the time to start rounding up swains and sweethearts is now. While many of us scoff at the arcane notion of a "little black book," you'll need numbers galore to really set your dating life in motion. If a hot Saturday night is what you're after, don't be afraid to gather business cards come Friday. While it may seem passé to collect numbers en masse, a variety of options is still the most cutting-edge way to keep your dating status alive and kicking.

The Right Approach

Doubtless you've all wondered about finding that right approach, the perfect opener to melt that special someone's heart and send him or her scurrying in search of a cocktail napkin and a writing utensil. Well, how do we break this to you gently? It doesn't exist. There's no one way to approach someone because there are just so many factors involved in every meeting. Creating one approach and sticking with it is a tremendous waste of energy. As any village idiot can tell you, you can't please all the people all the time. Setting, mood, and timing have a lot to do with how people respond to one another. So if you're worried about finding a point of entry, focus on the following elements prior to making your move.

Setting the Scene

Romance is a quirky thing. But bring the right setting into the equation, and you may have the formula for true success. It goes without saying, some places are just perfect for finding the date of

your dreams, and others couldn't be more inopportune. For example, if you spot someone having a business lunch meeting, it's safe to say that it's not a good time to have the waiter send over a bottle of their best Merlot. You have to be selective about where you look for dates.

Perfect Timing

When people say timing is everything, they're exaggerating. In fact, it is only half of the right-place-right-time equation. Still, it can mean the difference between getting a phone number and getting a dirty look. You can be in the most romantic place in the world, the absolutely ideal place for finding your true love, but if the timing is off, it's all over. But it's not as if you'll have to pick up on every subtle cue before asking someone out; it only takes a second to assess a given situation before moving in—or bowing out.

For example, while the grocery store may be an ideal place to meet your soul mate, approaching someone engaged in a heated debate over the last bag of fat-free Ruffles is not a good idea. Wait on the sidelines before sauntering over and doing your thing. Once they calm down, they'll be much more receptive to your advances. Whether you're at a party, in a restaurant, or at work, you'll need to pick a time when the other person is not busy talking on the cell phone, calculating the bill, or picking his or her nose.

Moody Moments

If the object of your lustful glances is wearing a surly or depressed expression, keep your distance. Don't try to interfere using the misguided Bozo Technique. What?! You've never heard of it? Maybe this will jog your memory. Picture yourself walking down the street, minding your own business, when some bozo looks you straight in the eye and tells you to "smile!" Warning: Never try this. Unless your aim is to practice random acts of viciousness, and annoy as many people as possible, no good can come of this technique.

Watch for facial cues to gauge moods. Ask yourself, "Would I make that face if I was feeling happy, calm, and satisfied?" If the answer is no, try to catch them when they're in a better mood. After all, you, too, would be grateful for this extra bit of consideration.

The Scene of the Crime

Crimes of the heart are committed every day, but none are more heinous than approaching someone in any of the following places:

1. A funeral
2. The XXX aisle at a video store
3. A crowded elevator
4. The lingerie department
5. A dark alley
6. A bridal shop

The Date Doctor Is In

Q. My best friend, Bob, and I often hit the town together and go out to parties. We're both pretty attractive, but for some reason he gets all the girls. He tells me it's because I talk too much about myself. Is there any truth to that?

A. *While you shouldn't be embarrassed to shine in the spotlight and talk about yourself, there is a limit. If, after talking to a woman, you find that you know no more about her than you did when you first said your hellos, you are indeed monopolizing the conversation. Droning on and on about your job, childhood, love life, opinions, and interests is a great big turnoff. So start listening to your conversation partners, or prepare to spend every Saturday night hitting the town with Bob.*

Group Dynamics

If three is a crowd, then you may want to avoid approaching large groups for fear of being trampled. While more may be merrier, a tight-knit pack of singles can definitely put a damper on your plans. Unless you're looking for a challenge, where all eyes are literally on you, the best way to navigate crowded waters is to divide and conquer. You can either try to catch that person's attention from a distance and motion to another part of the room, wait until they set off for the bathroom, or ask them to dance. Either way, it's best if you separate that person from their clique. Certain things, such as accepting a date, should not be a group decision.

Charm School

Any way you look at it, charm is a tough racket. You just never know when an attitude or gesture will charm someone and when it will repel. Take the musty old standby, the kissing of the hand. One woman may swoon at the idea of a man pressing his lips to the back of her hand. The same move may be all it takes to send another woman in search of the nearest lavatory. Once again, studying the object of your affection in advance is key. Some women believe that charm is all about batting their lashes and flashing some skin. But the truth of the matter is that charm has very little to do with physical persuasion and a lot to do with your ability to mentally challenge the other person. This involves a certain element of playful manipulation. A wink of the eye, a private smile, and even a brush of the hand can propel your charm quotient into the stratosphere.

On a final note, don't forget about the fine line between forced and natural charm. If your actions stick too close to convention, your charm is in danger of appearing unnatural. Guys who believe that their charisma rests solely upon opening plenty of doors and pulling out their share of chairs are bound to come off as unimaginative. Gals who work the "little old me" act into the ground will also turn off their share of gentleman callers. Above all else, try to live in the moment. Instead of relying on the wisdom you've gleaned from romantic comedies, stay true to the situation and to your companion. Not only will you make your love interest feel attractive and unique, but you're bound to make a great impression.

Pay Attention

Instead of coming right out and saying that we live in a world of self-centered people, let's just say that most people's favorite topic of conversation is themselves. This universal trait can operate in your favor if you work with it, not against it.

If you meet someone attractive, put on your crack investigative journalist's cap and get to work. Ask potential paramours questions about their lives—the what, where, when, why, and how of their banal existence. Look them straight in the eye while they answer your questions. If your mind begins to wander, pretend you're listening. A few nods and grunts of agreement should be all it takes to keep the illusion alive. Slowly but surely, this strategy will make them feel like they're the most important person in the room, and you will be the recipient of their gratitude.

The interview technique is also a good way to get the goods on someone before you decide to ask him or her out. That's why we recommend that you actually listen to the answers you're given. You can learn vital bits of information that may make or break your decision to get to know that person better.

The Eye of the Tiger

Using your eyes is never inappropriate. After all, everyone is allowed to look. In a store you're free to say that you're just looking, at a museum you're warned to look but don't touch, and everyone is always telling you to look before you leap. So using eye contact to charm is a relatively safe bet.

Begin by occasionally letting your eyes drift off in the desired direction. Once you've established contact, look away. Repeat this exercise, and finally look the person straight in the eye and smile at them. This eye game is very alluring and can be powerful. So use it at your own discretion. But remember not to stare. Not only is this extremely annoying, you scare off your target audience.

When it comes to winking, we believe less is more. Some people's attempts make them look like they're struggling to extract a bug from their eye. If you must wink, keep it to a minimum or risk making a spastic impression. If the other person is at all interested, they will notice.

One night my friend and I were at a local bar checking out the scene. That's when I noticed this really cute guy standing by the bar. Imagine my glee when he looked straight at me and winked. I was right about to make my move when my friend told me, "Hey, check out that guy, he must have winked at every girl in the bar." I was really embarrassed and relieved. I would never go out with someone like that.

—SUSAN, 24, COMPUTER TECHNICIAN

A Touchy Subject

Touching someone can be charming, but do it the wrong way and you're likely to end up with a red handprint along the side of your face or a beer stain down the front of your shirt. Women are far more likely to bristle at a stranger's touch than men, so guys must take extra care. But any guy being fondled by a woman is liable to get a certain idea, so unless the woman has only one thing on her mind, she'd best keep her hands in check.

If you're engaged in conversation, you can use touch to heighten the already romantic mood. The key is to make it look as natural or accidental as possible. For instance, if you lean over to get something from the table, let your arm lightly touch your partner's. Or you can touch his shoulder when something witty is said.

Touch is one of our most precious and sensitive senses, so make an added effort to be careful. Never touch someone forcefully or grab them in any way. Not only is this tactic an instant turnoff, but it borders on harassment. So if in doubt, skip the groping until you're better acquainted.

The Body's Secret Language

How you sit, stand, and hold yourself speaks volumes about your state of mind. In order to develop a charming body language, you should practice the mirroring technique. This strategy is based on the idea that people are attracted to like-minded individuals. So if you literally copy their body language, you can quickly convey that you have a lot in common and would like to explore even more common ground in the near future.

For example, if someone is sitting with their legs crossed towards you, it means that they are open to getting to know you. Mirror that pose and you're on your way to making an instant love connection.

Speak Easy

Our voices have unlimited power to soothe and seduce. Take 1-900-G-A-L-P-A-L-S or B-O-Y-T-O-Y-S, where the voice is their one and only tool of seduction—and business is booming. Once you learn to make the most of what nature gave you, it's only a matter of time before you can put someone under your spell by simply opening your mouth to speak.

Here's a tip: Don't follow their lead. If someone is speaking very quickly, try to slow down the exchange by monitoring your pace. On the other hand, if someone is talking too slow and you want to energize the exchange, practice the art of fast-talking. But never raise your voice; by speaking in a muted tone, you'll force the other person to lean in and pay closer attention to what you have to say.

Witty Ways to Win a Lover

You've probably heard some people say that there's nothing quite as sexy as intellect and humor. You yourself have probably been won over by someone who's not your physical type but can tell a joke like nobody's business. Recall how many times you were ready to dismiss someone only to discover that they have a wit that puts Woody Allen to shame. Intellect is very appealing because it challenges others to be better and smarter people. When we encounter people with serious brain power, it just makes it that much harder to dislike them. Plus, if you sharpen your wits, you will be able to enjoy verbal sparring, which is the standard rite of passage for any great relationship.

Be Playful

Let's see if we're all on the same page: flirting is *not* a serious pastime. Right? It is a fun activity that everyone should engage in from time to time and thoroughly enjoy. When you take the fun out

Not All Questions are Created Equal

Much like during a job interview, there are good and bad questions to ask when first meeting someone new. The following list should give you a head start on becoming a top-notch interviewer.

Appropriate Questions

1. What do you do?
2. Where do you live?
3. How do you like your job?
4. Are you married?
5. What do you do in your spare time?
6. How do you feel about recycling?

Inappropriate Questions

1. How much money do you make?
2. Do you prefer the top or the bottom?
3. What kind of car do you drive?
4. How do you feel about children?
5. Are you gay? (note: assuming that you yourself are not)
6. How old are you?

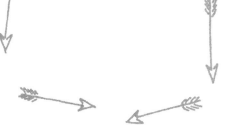

of flirting it can create a high-stress situation that has very little to do with enjoying yourself. Flirting is about exploring the kid in yourself. If you think about it, it's really the last form of noncompetitive play allowed to adults. So remember not to put any undue pressure on yourself, because much like dating, flirting is all fun and games.

The Charmer's Worksheet

If you think you've mastered the art of being charming, you're probably right! Now use this worksheet to reinforce all the knowledge you've gained. Once you're ready to get out there, review your answers before the big date because you never know when you'll need to pour on the charm.

- How will I use body language to entice that special someone?
- Should I stare at my date?
- Will talking about myself turn them off?
- When and how is it okay to touch someone on the first date?

Power Flirting Strategies

There's a shameless flirt in everyone that's just waiting to cut loose. But people often forget where they left the on-switch to their charm, flirting ability, or sex appeal. Long work days, endless errands, and a million little urgencies often conspire to keep you from committing to the flirt's credo: flirt brazenly and perpetually. These suggestions will keep you in high flirting gear around the clock.

- Make eye contact and smile
- Listen closely to what the other person is saying
- Touch someone playfully
- Make a silly face
- Throw your head back in laughter
- Wear flowers in your hair (guys may want to think twice)
- Blow a kiss

The Great Wits of World Literature

If your comebacks and one-liners can use some work, brush up by reading the following books. Now you can finally learn the art of the quick-word draw. Note for the literarily impaired: The following books all come in convenient, easy-to-read movie versions.

The Taming of the Shrew by William Shakespeare

Much Ado About Nothing by William Shakespeare

The Importance of Being Earnest by Oscar Wilde

Come-Ons, Kiss-Offs, And Everything In Between

Natural charm is all well and good, but getting to the point where you can actually work it will take some doing. For instance, you can smile, pout, and make eyes at the fine-looking coffee shop barrista all you want, but when it comes down to bagging a date you'll need to pull out some fancy footwork to make the approach. No need to throw your best autumn coat over an oncoming puddle; getting someone's undivided attention is easier than it sounds. All you have to do is choose a style that fits your mood and personality. Once you're set on your game plan, nothing can stop you.

The Personalized Pickup

Most people go gaga at the first sign of original thought. Maybe it's because we're living in terribly derivative times, or maybe it's because few people have the energy, desire, or wherewithal to come up with a new angle. Regardless, the minute someone approaches us with a line we've never heard before, we definitely take notice.

If you're someone who has a knack for thinking on your feet and can come up with a unique approach, never miss the opportunity to use your amazing gift. Treating each potential date as an independent person will net you major bonus points in the creativity department. As for all of you who haven't been blessed with this particular brand of talent, you'll have to push your observational skills to the limit in order to learn something unique about the person you're eyeing. For example, are they wearing an unusual hat, do they look like they're waiting for a friend, or is there something special about the setting you're in? If you customize your approach to match that particular moment in time, you'll be living your own love story before you know it.

I think I've heard every line in the book, so I'm usu-ally very wary of strangers coming up to me. So one day, I'm getting my hair done at this posh salon my friend had recommended. I end up getting into an argument with this snooty colorist about getting chunky highlights. All of a sudden, this guy comes up to us and says, 'I don't know what the problem is, but if I was lucky enough to go out

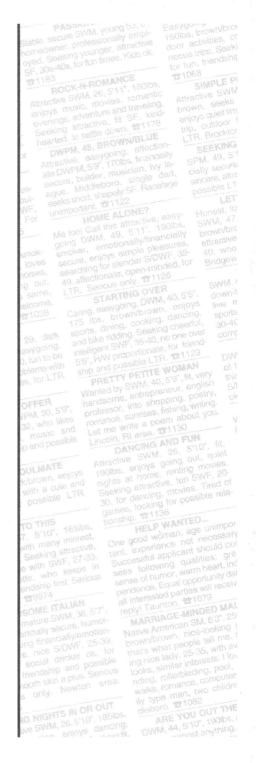

with you, I wouldn't waste time arguing.' And you know what happened? I left the salon to have a drink with him. I was that flattered and grateful for his assistance. Soon after, we were married, I got my highlights, and I still get goosebumps every time I tell the story of how we met.

—LISA, 29, ADVERTISING EXECUTIVE

The Wild and Wacky World of Pickups

If trolling for dates tends to bring out your wild side, you're in luck. Most people will love your attitude towards life and dating. Just consider the banality of the everyday: waking up, shaving, showering, riding or driving to and fro, and finally, falling asleep on the couch while watching reruns of *Sanford and Son*. We're not trying to depress you, we're just demonstrating the obvious—nobody minds being amused, amazed, or bewildered from time to time. So if you get the urge to do something outrageous, go for it. You never know when someone is looking to add a little spice to their lackluster existence.

Practical jokes can break the barrier between you and that special someone you're dying to meet. For example, you can come up to two lads/ladies at a bar, saying to one of them, "Hey, someone in the back wants to talk to you." Once the undesirable element is gone and you're left alone with the hottie of your choice, you simply say, "There's really no one looking for her/him, I just wanted to get a quiet moment with you." It's funny and flattering. Of course, you are always free to improvise your own approach. Just remember that when it comes to matters of the heart, you can be as spontaneous and wild as you like. We only pray you don't come up with anything quite as corny as dressing up in a policeman's uniform to arrest your heartthrob for stealing hearts all over the city.

The Aggressive Pickup

Some people believe in taking matters into their own hands. So if you want to get to the point quickly, you can appropriate the aggressive routine as your own. Telling someone you won't take no for answer may be old hat, but you'll be surprised at how many times this ploy works. Decisions, decisions, who needs them. By

being aggressive you're actually preventing someone from having to make yet another decision in their lives.

Yet there is a group of people that love to take control of a situation. When you use the aggressive approach on such a stalwart independent, you may easily end up at loggerheads. So a word to the wise: Persistence and harassment are two totally different brands of bagel. For best results, use the aggressive approach only if you know when to call it a day.

The Flattering Pickup

Flattery is also a very effective way for worming your way into someone's good graces. If you can deliver a compliment without appearing downright obsequious, then you may just find yourself using this traditional come-on over and over. The key to giving good compliments is to first discover what that person values most. For example, a woman wearing brand spanking new designer shoes may welcome your appreciation of her taste in footwear. On the flip side, a man going out of his way to make you laugh would most likely appreciate your giggles and vociferous belief in his ability to grace the stage of Caroline's Comedy Club.

Most importantly, be discreet. Do not make a great big fuss over the person lest you embarrass them unnecessarily. People like to be noticed, but nobody likes to get soaking wet as you drool all over them.

The Seductive Pickup

Few things in life can compare to meeting someone well-versed in the art of seduction. But if your seduction methods border on the obscene and perverse, your skills are in need of some serious work and you'll be safer using the many other approaches provided. If, on the other hand, you've yet to get a drink thrown in your face and have never so much as been escorted out of a bar for unbefitting conduct, the seductive approach may be just the thing.

All you need to do is think of a very provocative image to get yourself in the mood. Are you thinking? Good. Now when you approach someone, use a very slow gait and stare at them as if they're not wearing any clothes. Yes, this is legal and can work for both men and women. Actually, it's the surest way to get someone

Flattery Safe Zones

Sincere compliments may get you everywhere, but obnoxious passes will do you no good. The following list should clue you in to what's safe and not so safe to flatter.

Women Flattery Do's

- Hair style
- Eyes
- Manicure
- Necklace or watch
- Shoes
- Handbag

Women Flattery Don'ts

- Anatomy
- Hair color
- Blouse
- Pants
- Makeup
- Engagement/wedding ring

in the mood. When you finally open your mouth to speak, remember that less is more for the seductive pickup. You can also choose a dignified compliment, such as, "I find you very alluring." This method is simple, understated, and totally irresistible—guaranteed to arouse curiosity every time.

The Poor-Little-Old-Me Pickup

There are different varieties of this approach. Some of these include making a big, fat display out of pretending you're lost, dropping something (preferably something other than a hankie), and searching for a misplaced item. There are many benefits to this approach. You never have to put yourself out on the line or reveal your true intentions. When it comes to approaching someone new, this one's definitely the safest way to go.

Almost everyone you'll meet has a pressing need to help someone even more clueless than themselves. Call it the desire to feel superior or the Mother Teresa complex, the end result is the same: most people will lend a helping hand to a person in need. While this damsel-in-distress approach has worked for millions of women throughout history, gentlemen need not be too proud to make extensive use of this technique. Translation: If you've never so much as stopped to ask for directions, now may be the time.

One day, I was driving along when I spotted someone I wanted to meet. She was walking with some friends, and I was stopped at a red light. I racked my brain for something to say. But anytime a guy screams out of a moving vehicle, women assume he's a lewd jerk. I was almost about to lose my chance, when I decided to ask her for directions. She walked over to my car and we started talking. I got her number and called the next day to "thank her for her assistance." Suffice it to say, my instincts paid off.

—Rob, 28, Sales Representative

Flattery Safe Zones

Male Flattery Do's

- Necktie
- Eyes
- Watch
- Briefcase
- Shoes
- Hair style

Male Flattery Don'ts

- Pants
- Hairpiece
- Anatomy
- Wallet size
- Engagement/wedding ring

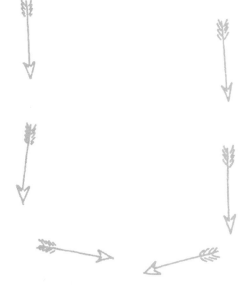

Smooth Operator:
More Sample Pickups

Situation: In line at the bank
Strategy: Toss your coins

This strategy is equivalent to dropping a hanky, but much more revealing in this day and age. You have nothing to lose—as long as you don't drop any quarters. As (s)he joins in the scramble to retrieve your loot, open with this gem: "A penny for your thoughts." (S)he's bound to crack a smile.

Situation: Bar
Strategy: "Survey Says!"

When you walk into a bar, it never fails that the one person you're interested in is busy chatting with a large group of friends. When this happens, it's time for the trusty notepad. Assume your most dignified air and walk right up to the group, under the guise of taking a survey for an article you're writing. Come up with a creative title and ask away. Single out your target for a more informative one on one.

Situation: Restaurant
Strategy: Slip 'em a note

You're both having lunch with friends; unfortunately, it's at different tables. How can you cross paths without involving a waiter and a glass of wine? Scribble a message, making sure to include all the vital stats (e.g., phone number), and deliver it yourself. Keep the conversation brief: "I thought you may want this" says it all.

Situation: Grocery store
Strategy: Make a little mess

Get in the same aisle and reach for the sky, or at least the highest shelf. You'll probably topple some merchandise in the process, but that's the point. If that special someone doesn't try to excavate you from the rubble, (s)he's not worth it. If (s)he does, laughter will be the only opener you'll need.

Situation: On the street
Strategy: "Where am I?"

This strategy instantly makes him a knight in shining armor to your damsel in distress, or allows her to finally find that one special guy secure enough to admit he's lost. (S)he need not know that you're asking to be pointed in the direction (s)he's already going. Strike up a conversation as you stroll.

The Honest Pickup

There are times when honesty is truly the best policy. You may be skeptical, but you'll never know until you try it. While you can't call honesty a tactic, many a dating aficionado has sworn that it's the best approach possible. It involves simply walking up to the stranger of your choice and politely asking their name. You can even tell them that you'd be interested in getting to know them better. While this approach is not for the faint of heart, we heartily applaud anyone who can take that kind of risk.

The Last Word on Lines

The majority of singles have probably heard every bad line in the book. So why is it that so many new ones keep cropping up? Some people will argue that the worse the line the funnier it is. And we've all been briefed on the connection between humor and love. Yet there are the detractors of that position, people who insist that bad lines are really an indication of insecurity, vulgarity, and lack of originality. Whatever school of thought you happen to subscribe to, there's no such thing as a truly bad line, just a bad delivery.

For example, take the line "Come here often, baby?" Now, imagine a drunk and drooling guy delivering that line while scratching his overgrown potbelly. Pretty bad, wouldn't you say? No doubt, a tum-tum-tum-tum-TUMS moment. But, don't reach for the antacid just yet. Here's the flip side: imagine a well-groomed man delivering this tagline while smiling and obviously enjoying the joke. See? We told you, it's all in the delivery.

I'm embarrassed to say this, and most of my closest friends don't even know. But I met my current boyfriend right after he pitched me one of the worst lines I've ever heard. Being that he was a construction worker, I assumed he did that all the time. But when I was walking home past the construction site the next day, he ran after me and apologized for his behavior. He told me someone dared him to scream that. I still don't know whether that's true or not, but bad line and all, I was hooked.

—KATERINA, 34, ARTIST

Comedy Central

People who can laugh at themselves and the whole dating business will definitely rack up extra credit in the delivery department. If you can show someone you're having fun while casting your lines like a pro, you may just get a warm-hearted greeting for your trouble. So whatever your line, good or bad, serve it up with a heaping dose of smiles and laughter.

Dead Serious

Now let's explore the darker side of human nature. While some people may go in for the comic stylings of Robin Williams, others would prefer the Steven Wright approach. There's no need to stifle a dry and caustic wit. You too can deliver any line you wish—just do what comes naturally. If your brand of humor finds a receptive audience, great. If not, it's best to call the whole thing off. If you have to change your personality, the jig is up. There are plenty of people who will appreciate you for who you are and what you have to offer. The trick is to find them.

A Line for Every Occasion

Provided you take the right approach, almost any line can land you that much-sought-after date. But in certain places, circumstances, or settings, personalizing your dialogue may work even greater love wonders. We've brainstormed some common scenarios and site-specific dialogue. So get ready to learn your lines, because you're about to become a major star in the dating business.

Grocery Store

> *You:* Can you tell me where I can find the Portobello mushrooms?
> *Love Interest:* Right over there, in the fresh produce aisle.
> *You:* I don't know if you agree, but it's tough cooking for one, isn't it?

(Follow with an observation such as, "By the time I get around to the lettuce, it's already wilted. A Somali family can eat for a year on what I have to throw away each week.")

Honesty, Shmonesty: The Liar's Approach to Finding a Date

Radical honesty may be all well and good for some people, but not everyone can stand the heat of the boy/girl scout lifestyle. If you are able to tell a lie and have a tendency to let even the slightest pangs of guilt slide off you, then these strategies may just be what the doctor ordered:

- Borrow your friend's Porsche for the day and claim ownership
- Ask someone for directions while standing outside your house
- Scream the name of your imaginary dog "Freddy" and wait for help to arrive
- Run through the street yelling "Help" to get attention
- Faint before their very eyes
- Lose a contact

Party

You:	Do you know if (name of partygoer) is here tonight?
Love Interest:	I don't know (name of partygoer).
You:	So who did you come here with?
Love Interest:	Just some friends...

Book Store

You:	Have you read this book? I'm looking for a present for my mom.
Love Interest:	No, I haven't. But I bought my mom this other great book last year. She loved it.
You:	Great. Maybe you can help me find it...

Health Club

You:	Who invented this machine, the Marquis de Sade?
Love Interest:	It's actually easier than it looks. Here, let me show you.
You:	So I've been torturing myself for hours unnecessarily. Maybe you could show me what this next machine is all about...

The Park

You:	It's really a beautiful day, isn't it?
Love Interest:	Yes, it is.
You:	So what kind of bike is that? It looks really fast.
Love Interest:	It is. Do you ride?

In Line

You:	Did you know Americans spend 500 hours of their lives waiting in line?
Love Interest:	It sure seems like that now.
You:	You really should try (name of store). The lines there go much faster.
Love Interest:	Thanks, I'll keep that in mind.

Museum

        You: I've been here for ten minutes, and I still can't figure it out. What about you?

  Love Interest: I think it's (their opinion).

        You: I hadn't thought of that. Are you an art student?

  Love Interest: Not really, it's just something I enjoy from time to time.

        You: Me too...

While most conversations are not as predictable or even as smooth as the above, all you need to do is jump-start the discussion. If you seem interested in someone's opinion, it's most likely that you'll get an earful. Once you've opened the lines of communication, you'll be ready to seal the deal.

Hook, Line, and Sinker

Most salespeople will tell you that even the most carefully crafted presentations can fall apart once it comes time to close the deal. Second thoughts and apprehensions can set in at any time, so don't go counting your chickens even if everything seems to be going according to plan. Even if you've done an amazing job of breaking the ice, a million little factors can interfere with your ability to confirm the date.

While it's true that sometimes people get nervous or tense while asking for a date, there are proven and effective strategies that will help you get the job done. After all, you've done the hard part; approaching a perfect stranger isn't easy. So pat yourself on the back; you're ready for the big time.

Get an alibi

People are always looking to liven things up a bit. And what better way to do it than at a concert, comedy club, or a benefit? Never mind that you don't have the tickets yet. Just pretend you do.

Once you decide on the event you'd like to attend, explain to the other person that your friend canceled out on you at the last minute and you have an extra ticket. This will not only make you seem popular and social, it will help your date feel safer accepting a

The Date Doctor Is In

Q: I have a hard time talking to my date's answering machine. Are there any secrets to mastering this particular dating torture device?

A: *I'm sorry to say that the only secret is not to get involved at all—with the answering machine, that is. When first dating someone, nothing is worse than leaving an embarrassing message, for the obvious reason that you can't take it back! Your disastrous message is left there and all you can do is just spend your time thinking about how much of a loser you are. Not to sound pessimistic, but it's only natural for people to be nervous about leaving messages when they're just getting to know someone, so they are bound to say things they did not mean. Trying to make up for it only worsens the problem, digging the hole deeper. My only advice is that you dial* *67 *(an effective caller ID blocking method) before dialing the number, and then hang up unless someone answers. Once you've gone out a few times you'll feel comfortable enough leaving as many messages as you like.*

date with you. After all, if someone else has already consented to hang with you, you can't be all that bad.

Be spontaneous: Hey, I've got a great idea!

When asking for a date, it's best not to put too much pressure on someone. By making your plans sound spontaneous, you allow that person the freedom to choose. You'll also be able to catch them off guard. Hopefully, you can come up with a fun idea at short notice, like renting rollerblades or sharing a hot dog. This strategy will keep you from seeming too anxious and will make you look like a fun and outgoing person. Any way you look at it, you win!

There's safety in numbers

This one works especially well for guys. Nowadays, a girl can't be too careful. If you think about it, she really doesn't know you from Jack the Ripper. Oftentimes, women prefer going out with large groups to allay their anxieties and fears. So why not spare her the extra work of calling on her friends?

One way to win over someone fast is to recommend an outing that involves a group of your friends. A concert, sports event, or bar are perfect ways to get your closest set of pals and your new beau together. And this approach doesn't come without its own set of advantages: Not only will you make your date feel safe, you can collect your friends' feedback before things get too hot and heavy.

Keep it quick

In these frantic, fast-paced times, most people loathe the idea of committing their time to something that is doomed to fail. Not that your date will be a disaster, but since neither of you knows the other too well, try to limit the level of commitment as much as possible.

Think back to some of your unfortunately long dates when you realized that your companion was not Mr./Ms. Right, or Mr./Ms. Maybe for that matter. It's tough hanging in there when all seems lost. So spare yourself and your date any loss of precious time by suggesting a brief outing. You can invite the person for a drink after work or even a stroll in the park. And if a love connection happens to strike, you can always extend the date past the allotted time limit.

Lend your idea

The art of suggestion has gone neglected for too long. But if used correctly, suggestions can be a powerful way to incite someone to ask you out. All you have to do is plant the idea in their minds. We knew a guy who would always end each conversation by telling the girl that he accepts her invitation to dinner. He would then proceed to get her number. Usually, the other person was so dumbfounded that she just agreed to go along. It was her idea after all.

Spare your time

If you're looking for a cool and nonchalant way to ask for a date, you've hit pay dirt. This strategy is as old as time itself, as it is based on the idea that most people want what they cannot have or what is in scarce supply.

When getting ready to ask someone out, just inform him or her that you have some extra time in your schedule this coming weekend and would like to take him or her out. This way you appear casual yet in-demand. And if the theory of supply and demand holds true, you're bound to succeed.

Heart-studded sleeve

Let's get down to brass tacks: There's absolutely nothing wrong with a little straight talk. Just because most people have a hard time exposing their true colors to the scrutiny of strangers does not mean that you're bound to be penalized for taking the plunge. If you feel more comfortable telling someone that you are interested and would like to get to know him or her better, go for it! There are millions of well-adjusted singles who aren't particularly fond of perpetual mind games and who would respect you for your bravery and candor.

Whatever approach or combination of methods you choose to close the deal, you're bound to succeed eventually. So don't make the mistake of using these power selling strategies on just anyone. Choose your targets wisely. Anyone who overuses these potent tools of seduction may just end up with more than they bargained for.

Getting The Digits

Some people make a sport out of it, others just view the number-scoring process as a necessary evil. But whatever way you look at it, your dating life would not exist without those seven magic numbers. If asking someone for their phone number sends you into a full-blown panic attack, try giving the following techniques a try. See if they don't have you breathing a whole lot easier.

Smooth Operator

It's as easy as dropping a piece of paper on the floor and saying, "Hey, you can write your number here." When performing this trick, make sure you don't make it look too obvious. Practice looking surprised before trying this with someone new. But even if the person sees straight through this routine, it can get a chuckle out of them and land you the date you're after.

It's Nothing Personal

There are people out there who are just loath to give out their home numbers. Maybe they've had it with late-night booty calls or maybe it's a safety precaution, but some people will go to any lengths to avoid giving you their home number. Work numbers, provided they're employed, are another matter altogether. Unless they're a VIP, most people love taking personal calls during work—it helps them while away the monotony of their daily work routine.

Besides being a safe way to get to know someone new, giving a work number can help you land a lunch date. When you call during work hours, you can bond over how mundane your work is and then suggest a meal at a nearby restaurant to break up the routine. There's even a new dating service that sets up busy professionals on lunch dates—it's obviously a trend that's here to stay.

E-mail Savvy

Of all the modes of communication available today, e-mail is by far the least intrusive. Virtual strangers give up their e-mail addresses without a second's hesitation. Everyone loves to get e-mail—the novelty just never seems to wear off.

Exchanging e-mail is also a great way to get to know someone before going out on a date. Writing an e-mail letter requires only a modicum of commitment and you can take your time responding. There are many singles who have launched great friendships and even better romances using this approach.

Not only can you e-mail your thoughts and ideas, you can begin exchanging funny jokes and notes. Pretty soon you will have won your paramour's trust. A more direct interface is sure to follow.

> *When I first met my wife Rose, she was on the brink of breaking up with her boyfriend and didn't want to get involved with anyone new. Since I was so interested, I was uncharacteristically persistent. I convinced her that giving me her e-mail address wouldn't interfere with her relationship. Soon, we were having great conversations over the e-mail on a daily basis. I would rush home just to see if she had sent an e-mail. Through writing to Rose, I realized that she wasn't only attractive, she was smart and funny as well. When we finally went out on our first date, we didn't have any of those first-date jitters. It felt like we were old friends.*
>
> —BRAD, 26, ACCOUNTANT

I Could Have Talked All Night

Showing your appreciation for someone's speaking ability will not only flatter the other party, but will help you talk them into continuing the conversation via phone. Just tell them that you enjoyed talking so much that you would love to continue the discussion at a later time. Stroking people's ego is a great way to get their number permanently tattooed on your phone book.

Follow-Up

If you want to take your conversation to the next level, you should think seriously about talking about a specific subject matter like careers, new technological gizmos, or cars—any subject that will require you to do extra research. Keep them talking until you hit upon a subject that is near and dear to their hearts. Then

Private Phone Matters

There are times when you simply cannot bear to part with your phone number. Whether you're not interested, simply repulsed, or just playing a high-stakes game of hard-to-get, you do not have to give your phone number to every Tom, Jane, or Sally that comes along. Exercise the following options and save yourself from a lot of unnecessary mad dashes for the caller ID monitor.

1. Tell them that you just moved and are between numbers
2. Explain that you forgot to pay your phone bill
3. Write down a fake number
4. Explain that your baby wakes up every time the phone rings
5. Ask for their number, and never call back
6. Tell them the FBI is wiretapping your lines
7. Run like the wind

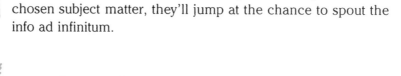
Five Fabulous Failures

At one time or another, all of us will meet with failure and rejection. But that should in no way stop us from trying. Rergardless of whether you fall flat on your face, going out on a limb is an accomplishment in its own right. Think of the following former rejects whenever the temptation to retreat into the safety of your inner sanctum and never take a chance again strikes.

1. **Michael Jordan**
   Who hasn't heard this tale? Jordan didn't make his junior high school basketball team.

2. **Stevie Nicks**
   First album's sales were so minimal that she and partner Lindsey Buckingham were dropped by their record label.

3. **Jerry Seinfeld**
   Bombed the first time he performed stand-up.

4. **Drew Barrymore**
   Laughed out of auditions upon her return to Hollywood from drug rehab.

5. **Gary Shandling**
   See Number 3

once it's time to get the phone number, you can ask to contact them for more information. Since they're such experts in the chosen subject matter, they'll jump at the chance to spout the info ad infinitum.

Dealing With Rejection

Getting rejected is tough. Even the most confident people have a hard time dealing with a firm "No." You may have done everything just right, you may look absolutely breathtaking, but (and perish the thought!) there will be those monstrously insane moments when you are faced with the realization that someone out there, beneath that pale moonlight, is neither thinking of you nor loving you tonight. Some of you may fight the notion with all the violence of a seven-year-old raging against a tablespoon of castor oil. But if you learn to take rejection in stride, it will serve you well both in the long and short run.

As one of today's all-time favorite (and most overused) quotes puts it, "What does not kill us, makes us stronger." And when it comes to rejection, this statement couldn't be any more apropos. Being refused or rebuffed can actually serve as an invaluable learning experience. If you accept the fact that you will have to overcome obstacles in life in order to achieve your goals, you will soon become a more together and successful person. It is rejection and failure that reveal our limitations and motivate us to overcome them. Perpetual success may feel like a dream come true, but it is only through failure that we learn about who we are and who we want to become.

And while we're on the subject of rejection, remember one golden rule: There's no such thing as rejection, just a lack of good sense on the part of the rejecter. Take Brad Pitt, for example. Would any ladies in their right mind refuse a date with this man? And what about Michelle Pfeiffer—how many of you guys out there would kick her to the curb? Probably not many. But surprise, surprise, both of these gorgeous stars experienced their fair share of heartbreak. So if you're confronted by someone who turns out not to have a firm grasp on reality (a.k.a. your obvious charm), you're in good company.

One night I was reading a magazine at the local coffee shop, and this really attractive guy walked in. He bought himself a drink and looked around for a place to sit. He came over to my table and asked to sit down. I was really excited and flattered at this point, because he was very attractive and had the confidence to sit at my table. He began talking to me and I was sure he was going to ask me out. But after finishing his drink, he started to walk away. That's when I told him to wait. He looked kind of confused when I asked for his number. He basically said that he wasn't interested because he was involved with someone else. I then stupidly asked him why he had sat at my table if he didn't want to get to know me better. That's when he told me that the chair at my table was the only empty seat available. I was really embarrassed at first. But when I told my friends, they helped me see the humor in that situation.

—Brenda, 39, Computer Programmer

Saving Face

The problem with rejection is that it's often not the refusal that hurts so much but having to get out of a sticky situation. Many of us have a tendency to pout, spew invective, or storm away in a huff when confronted by a flat-out, unapologetic "No." And who could blame us? It's hard to walk away with your head held high when you've just had your hopes dashed.

But rejection doesn't have to be so painful. There are many graceful ways to extricate yourself from this sticky situation and maintain your dignity in the process. Once you learn some key techniques for handling rejection, you'll not only feel okay about yourself but actually feel even better than before you asked for a date. Sound too good to be true? We'll let you be the judge.

Be Polite

If you've ever subscribed to the theory of "killing with kindness," now is the time to make ample use of it. If you are rejected, you can save face by simply putting on your polite hat. You can say how

nice it was to talk to him or her, or even mention something about staying friends in the future.

Politeness will give you a sense of superiority that no act of rudeness can. This way you'll also come off looking like the bigger person for having the grace and character not to harbor a grudge.

Recommend a Set-up

This technique can really kick your sense of dignity into high gear. What we are about to reveal is an age-old secret known and used by a select few for generations. This rejection-coping strategy works wonders, no matter what situation you're in.

Next time you innocently ask for a lad's or lady's number, only to get blown the big kiss-off, you should immediately explain that you were hoping to set them up with one of your single friends. By using this approach you will be saying that you never really cared about going out with the offensive individual, and would even go so far as to pass them around the table like a stuffed turkey. In one fell swoop, you'll have won back the upper hand. And let's face it, isn't that what it's all about?

Appreciate Their Honesty

If you thank someone for being honest, you just may be able to turn a negative situation into a positive. People love to think of themselves as down-to-earth and straightforward individuals. Give them that and you'll be giving yourself an exit line the likes of which even Bogart would envy.

Keep Smiling

Okay, getting rejected hurts. It can make your vision blur, bring a lump to your throat, and may even cause you to stifle a gasp. But whatever you do, never let someone see your pain. No matter how sensitive a nineties person you consider yourself to be, come the next morning and you'll most likely feel like a giant ball of goof. And say you run into that person again? You hardly want them and their friends to break into tears at the sight of your pathetically fragile ego.

Take it from us: Keep your cool by plastering a permanent grin on your face. Even if you feel like you've just had the wind knocked

right out of you, you will begin feeling happy. That's the beauty of a smile; if you can fake it for a little while, it will lift your spirits as well as those of everyone in your vicinity.

> *I've always had a hard time dealing with rejection. But I never thought I was capable of doing what I did. One night, me and my friends were out and I met a girl who I instantly felt attracted to. She really seemed to be interested in me, until another guy came along. She began talking to him, and when I asked her to dance, she completely ignored me. So, in my completely inebriated state, I took my revenge the only way I knew how. As I was leaving, I told my competitor that the girl had contracted a sexually transmitted disease. I thought I was being really funny and clever, until I discovered that the guy she was talking to was her husband. The next thing I knew I was lying on the floor. He had hit me. I guess I couldn't really blame him.*

—ROB, 28, PIANO TEACHER

Recovering From Rejection

People lie to themselves on an hourly basis. And in the name of keeping your confidence, we're all for it. You see, rationalizations aren't really lies anyway. They're a vital component of our psyche's self-defense infrastructure. Rationalizing in the face of rejection will help you go on with your life as if nothing ever happened. A well-chosen and timely rationalization can have you walking on air despite a most cutting insult to your pride. There's no need to let others affect how you feel about yourself. You will emerge exempted from the negative opinion of others. Much like any popularly maligned superstar (Pamela Anderson, Jean-Claude Van Damme, and the like), you will choose to believe the cheers and ignore the jeers. Here are some ways you can begin on your journey toward recovery.

Steep Competition

The best way to alleviate any unnecessary heartache is to convince yourself that, contrary to what you were told, your rejecter is involved with someone else. Just because you didn't spot a wedding

Rejection Blunders

When it comes to rejection, there is definitely a wrong and right way to handle it. Some people would beg to differ, claiming that any behavior is justifiable in the face of such an all-out slight. But never forget that two wrongs don't make a right. The more obnoxious you act, the more injured and desperate you will appear—thereby proving to the object of your spurned affections that they were right about you all along. Avoid this dastardly fate by adhering to the following list of what not to do after being rejected:

1. Bawl like a baby
2. Slap the rejecter's face
3. Place your hands over your ears, screaming "I can't hear you!"
4. Deny having asked them out in the first place
5. Call them every name in the dirty word handbook
6. Indignantly scream, "How dare you?"
7. Spill a drink in their lap

band on their finger doesn't mean that they're not attached. Many people simply don't want to proclaim their coupled status to the world. And who knows, if they're not married, they're most likely living with someone. Or if that's not the case, they've probably been dating someone for several years—no doubt, their high school sweetheart. When it comes to healing the wounds of rejection, blaming it on the system of first-come-first-served can send your self-esteem into the stratosphere where it belongs.

A Troubled Soul

There comes a time in all our lives when dating ceases to seem so important. Remember to apply this rationale to the next person who rejects you. There are many events that can put a damper on someone's dating spirit; they may have just been fired from a job, suffered the loss of a pet, or watched their house burn to the ground. Any number of disasters could have descended upon your romantic interest mere minutes before you came along to ask them out. Now, ask yourself: How can you, a mere mortal, compete with such calamity? Even Don Juan wouldn't be able to seduce someone in such dire straits. Chalk it up to bad timing, and you'll walk away with a spring in your step.

Plenty of Fish in the Sea

Getting rejected is a walk in the park once you convince yourself that there are millions of available fish in the sea who would give their right gill to go out with you. Just because you happened to stumble upon an unsuitable fish doesn't mean that there aren't others out there who would be your perfect match. Tell yourself this and you will rebound from rejection almost instantly, leaving yourself free to ask new people out and find someone who truly cares for you.

Not the Sharpest Ginsu in the Set

It's all too true: not everyone was blessed with the natural intelligence necessary to understand and appreciate your indisputable greatness. The world is indeed an imperfect place, so don't be too hard on those who are dwarfed by your considerable intellectual prowess. Instead, take a lesson from the experience and stop asking

random half-wits to spend time with you. Tell yourself that next time you will only select those people who are your mental equals.

This line of thought can make the difference between "I'm a loser" and "You're a loser." Blaming others for your lack of success may be a petty and childish way to handle rejection, but as long as you keep this dialogue silent, there's no reason why you shouldn't indulge yourself.

You Were Doing Them a Favor

The difficulty rating for this rationalization is quite high, so bully for those of you who can pull it off without a hitch. Start by telling your recently rejected self that you never really liked the other person to begin with. In fact, the only reason you even felt obligated to ask them out was because, ever the good Samaritan, you felt sorry for them. Using this rationalization will require that you actually begin feeling sorry for the other person. You can start picking out their weak points almost immediately. A lack of style, insipid conversation, weak chin, or facial tic are all fair game. Then, start congratulating yourself on your selflessness and generosity. If you can convince yourself, you're home free—and you've done your good deed for the day to boot.

Friends in Need

Good friends can be instrumental in lifting you out of the rejection blues. As your so-called support network, they should zealously represent your best interests at this low point of your dating career. Of course, it's up to you to initiate the group healing process. You can choose from either of the following two options, or combine them when combating the more serious cases of depression. First, you can proclaim an open season bash fest on the rejecter. Feel free to begin the festivities with, "Could you believe I was rejected by her/him? Who does she/he think they are?" Or, if you prefer, you can try to get your friends talking about what a great thing the evil naysayer lost out on. "She/he doesn't know what they're missing. Right?" is a great launching pad for such a discussion. If your friends are worth the paper your birthday cards have been printed on, they'll chime in with many things about you that are not to be missed. After all, that's what friends are for.

What's Your Sign? Romance According to the Zodiac

Cancer

Cancers can be evasive when it comes to romance. They flirt, they're coy, and all the while they're feeling their way through the maze of their own emotions. They enjoy entertaining at home because it's where they feel most comfortable, surrounded by all that's familiar to them. Some Cancers dislike the courtship of romance altogether and prefer to get right down to the important questions: Are we compatible? Do we love each other?

To live with and love a Cancer, you have to accept the intensity of their emotions and their imaginations.

Chapter 5

The Date Planner

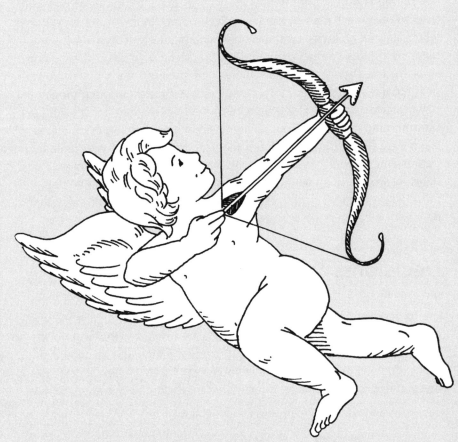

Many people believe that a good date is an act of divine intervention. They argue that spontaneous and exciting dates cannot be planned; they can only "happen." But what many of these people don't realize is that creating a date that looks effortless and impulsive takes time, foresight, and preparation.

The to-plan-or-not-to-plan question is easily resolved if you think about someone who excels in his/her profession. A ballerina, for instance, is able to make her every move seem effortless and easy. Is that because ballet is truly effortless? No, it's because a ballerina has to study for many years before she can attain a level of expertise that makes even the most difficult dance moves look easy. Emergency room doctors are another example. Those who watch the show *ER* often see emergency room doctors making quick and seemingly spontaneous decisions in order to save people's lives. These MDs rarely have the time to think about what procedures to use, and, therefore, have to rely on their eight years of medical school and work experience. But while the doctors seem to have an easy way with their patients, it actually took them years to perfect their ability to think spontaneously.

Dating is no different in that in order to make it look easy, you will have to study and plan in advance. Even if you think you were endowed with a natural ability to woo the opposite sex, it never hurts to have a plan. First dates can be very grueling. You're nervous, your date is nervous, and neither of you needs the added stress of worrying where your next meal is coming from, or whether you've brought enough money to pay the cover charge. These unnecessary concerns can actually hamper the romantic mood and your ability to enjoy the date. So once you've taken care of the details, you can feel free to be yourself and make a great impression on your date. In order to take the guesswork out of your first dates, we've come up with a date planner that should eliminate any and all of your questions and worries. So if you want to start off every first date with a bang, using this planner will ensure that you do just that.

Decisions, Decisions

If you've been brave enough to ask someone to go out with you, it is up to you to decide upon the circumstances of your date. After all, the person who asks (a.k.a. you) usually ends up paying, so it's only fair that you decide how your hard-earned cash will be spent. Plotting the time and location is a luxury that you've earned. So make the most of it by picking a destination that you enjoy and feel most comfortable in. Right now, it's all about you.

In order to decide where you want to go, try to come up with a list of places you and your friends like to visit. Then choose your favorite place from this list. You can also choose by trying this exercise: Imagine that you just won a million dollars and you could do anything you wanted. What would you pick? And while you may have chosen a plan that exceeds your present means, you can choose a more budget-friendly activity that resembles the one in your dreams.

Plans B and C

In a perfect world, your date would agree with every idea you come up with. Unfortunately, some people like to have a say in what they do. Go figure! So it's not at all unlikely that after planning the perfect night your date will decide that your plans are somehow flawed. Instead of getting upset, you'll benefit from having a backup plan.

The importance of leaving your options open cannot be stressed enough. Besides your date's preferences, there are a number of little things that may go wrong. For instance, traffic may be bad and you may miss the movie you planned on seeing. Or the cash machine you planned on using may be out of order. You never know. So when planning the date, make sure you have an alternate date route to fall back on. After all, who's not better off safe than sorry?

During college I was madly in love with a girl in one of my classes. Our relationship slowly evolved from study partners to friends. One day I told her how I felt and asked her to my fraternity formal. I was all ready for the big night: a limo, a tux, and a corsage. When I came to pick her up she was wearing jeans and a plaid flannel shirt. I was shocked. Apparently she thought we were going to a barn dance. I asked her if she could change, but apparently all her formal dresses were back in her hometown. She was so embarrassed. But unwilling to blow the date, I quickly changed into the pants and sweater I brought along just in case we got tired of the formal thing. She was really relieved. I then suggested we spend the night cruising around town in our own new limo. We had a great time. We went to a local diner and then to a bar. It was a riot. I think she enjoyed the date as much as I did.

—DEREK, 23, GRAD STUDENT

What's Your Sign? Romance According to the Zodiac

Leo

Leos are passionate. They can also be impulsive, particularly when their egos are stroked. For the most part, Leos need to feel needed and need to know they are loved before they commit entirely. Once they're committed, everything is bigger than life and brighter than the sun. Courtship is often a series of dramatic gestures: five dozen roses that arrive at your office, an erotic call at three a.m., or a chopper ride over Manhattan.

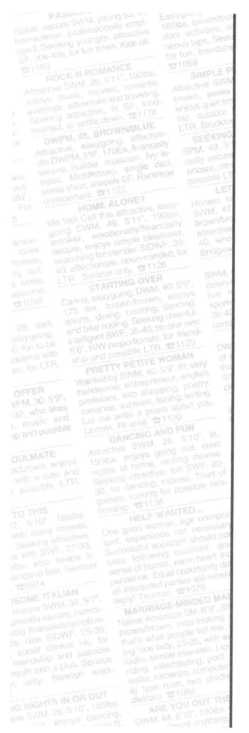

Day and Night

Deciding whether you want to plan your date during the day or evening hours is an important step. Daytime dates have a tendency to be more casual. If, say, you met your date in a dark nightclub and you're not sure whether you're truly interested, a day date can be a great way to fend off expectations and pressure. There's something about the daylight that helps people get to know each other, without feeling the need to be romantic.

Days are also ideal for people who love the outdoors and who want to plan a date involving sports, hiking, or relaxing on the beach. If any of these ideas appeal to you, try to reserve some daylight hours for getting to know someone new.

Nighttime is great for cutting loose and letting it all hang out. If you're a night owl and wouldn't dream of dining before nine o'clock, then you'll have to wait till sundown to frolic with your dates. For those serious first dates, when you need to set a very romantic mood, you can't beat an evening of dinner and dancing. So if you're really attracted to the other person and want to put them in the mood, choose the late evening hours to carry out your wildest date fantasies.

Penny Wise

Let's get something straight: a great date is not something money can buy. That settled, we can move on to the very important topic of how much cash you're willing to pony up. Some people prefer to skimp on the questionable dates and go the extra dollar for those whom they want to impress. We suggest that you use your best judgment in any situation. But no matter how much you like the person, spending too much money on a first date is never a good idea. If you set an inordinately high precedent, living up to it is liable to land you in the poorhouse.

Spending too little on a date is also not recommended, since you may actually end up insulting your date. Moderation is the name of the game. Take your date to a reasonably priced full-service restaurant (as opposed to self-service fast food). Unless you're on a very special date a good rule of thumb is to let the dining establishment dictate how much to spend. Don't tack on the extras like a bottle of premium wine and caviar unless you want to spoil the guest of honor. If your date orders the most expensive item on the menu, try not to grip the edge of the table and by all means refrain from any acts of outright physical violence.

If you're really unsure about your evening's companion, stay away from restaurants altogether. This will curb your impulse to insist that they order only salad and save you the embarrassment of being labeled a skinflint of the highest order. A bar is the ideal spot for a "maybe" date. Stick to drinks and claim inebriation after the third round. You'll end up spending less and won't come off looking cheap in the process. So once again, use your best judgment, and remember, money is only as important as you make it.

Dating Brainstorms For Every Budget

What would you do if you had a dating assistant to generate date ideas, plan your evenings, and take care of every last detail? That would come in very handy, wouldn't it? Well, that's exactly what we're about to do for you.

Forget staying up late worrying about the details, forget planning a boring date, forget trying to remember where you're supposed to be at a given time. For the first time in history, we have formulated the most complete date planner ever. In the following planner, you will discover a list of dating ideas. You can choose a single idea if you're low on time, or combine several for a long-lasting good time. Each date comes with its own code, ¢: inexpensive, !: adventure, $: lavish, and @: artistic or cultured. Each date also comes equipped with a complete list of supplies, as well as steps that you need to take to make this date everything it can be.

That's right, all that's left for you to do is find the date, set the time, and enjoy yourself. So go ahead and pick a date, any date. Now that you've got your handy-dandy date planner at your side, you're bound to have a good time!

The Dining Duo

Depending on how much money you're willing to spend, this date may run you an arm and a leg. To insure that you don't over-spend, check out the menu beforehand. When planning a dinner date, make sure to scope out the premises before the big event. If

Dinner Checklist

❏ Preliminary walk-through

❏ Price appraisal

❏ Reservations

❏ Credit card

❏ Coat and tie or cocktail dress

❏ Appetite

you're really looking to impress and get to know your date, you should plan well in advance to reserve the best table in the room. Check out the layout to determine the table that is most secluded. If the date is going well, you may just benefit from some extra privacy.

Since restaurants come in all price ranges, it is wise to get a look at the menu beforehand. If there are no prices listed on the menu and you have to ask, you can't afford it. Another financial point to keep in mind is credit cards. Do they accept them? Since about 99 percent of all restaurants do a little jig at the sight of credit-toting patrons, you should have no problem passing plastic. But on the off chance that your credit is no good, make sure before it's time to shell out the cash or local check only.

When choosing a restaurant you'll also have to establish the type of cuisine you'll be sampling. Some people will avoid Italian joints at all costs, claiming the pasta is too difficult to digest with dignity. Much like the language, French food is a really romantic choice for those intimate dinner dates. While dining with a vegan or a dieter poses a special challenge to the date planner, even these obstacles can be surmounted by investing a few bucks in your city's Zagat survey.

Clientele will also play a big role in your choice of dining establishment. If you're looking to liven up the hours, you should steer clear of places that may be too stuffy and serious. There are plenty of great restaurants that boast a lively atmosphere as well as great food. So just in case your dinner date isn't all you hoped, you can still enjoy yourself by taking in the general merriment.

A final note: some restaurants are notoriously hard to get into. If you've chosen a hip spot that's all the rage, you may have to make reservations weeks ahead. So whatever you do, don't procrastinate. It's never too soon to make a reservation.

Movie Madness

Movies can be problematic when you're talking first date. On the one hand, they can prevent people from getting to know one another. Conversely, what better way to get to know someone than to sit next to him or her in the dark? Whatever your stance on the movie issue, there's plenty of fun to be had while taking in a flick. You can study your date's silhouetted profile to your heart's content and exchange your views on the movie once the film has ended. Pulling the old stretch-and-yawn maneuver is also a quick way to

Mr. and Ms. Cheap

No matter how frugal the person, no one appreciates being called a cheapskate. Even the most notorious tightwads like to think of themselves as extremely generous. We've come up with a quiz that will separate the true cheapskates from those who are merely financially challenged.

1. What coin denomination would you to kneel down to retrieve?
   A. A penny
   B. Anything silver
   C. I only stoop for dollars

2. When you and your friends go Dutch at a restaurant, how often do you end up calculating everyone's share?
   A. Every time; people can't be trusted
   B. Sometimes, when asked
   C. Never; I can't bother myself with such trivialities

3. How often do you look over your receipt?
   A. Always; a penny skimmed is a penny earned
   B. Sometimes, if the cashier doesn't look honest
   C. Never; it's just money

4. How often do you turn off all the lights before leaving your house?
   A. Always
   B. Sometimes, if I can remember
   C. Never; the more lights, the less chance I stand of getting robbed, and that would cost far more than any electrical bill

5. Would you dine with someone you disliked for a free meal?
   A. Always; who said there was no such thing as a free lunch
   B. Yes, if there were other people I liked there
   C. Never; I'd lose my appetite

6. Do you wait for a trip to your doctor's office in order to read your favorite magazines?
   A. Sure, why spend the extra money
   B. Only if it's a frivolous zine
   C. Please! What a silly question

7. How often do you find yourself discussing money?
   A. Every day
   B. Several times a month, around bill time
   C. Almost never

8. How often do you clip and use coupons?
   A. Always
   B. Only for high-priced items, like restaurants and car washes
   C. Almost never

Scoring: Judgment day has arrived. To find out whether or not you've been leading a cheapskate's lifestyle, tally up your score and refer to the letter you selected most.

If you selected six or more Cs, then you don't have a cheap bone in your body. But you're not getting off the hook that easy. Judging by your responses, you may want to rethink your spend-thrift ways. A lighthearted attitude towards money has its time and place, but when you start acting irresponsibly, you may find yourself in debt. While you may be on the right track in not taking the green stuff too seriously, you may want to consider setting up a budget, just in case.

If you selected six or more Bs, then you have absolutely nothing to worry about. Your attitude towards money is as healthy as they come. You understand the value of a dollar but would never let it rule your life. Congratulations!

If you selected six or more A's, take heed; you may be a bigger cheapskate than you anticipated. Before you get too down upon yourself, consider that you probably picked up this behavior while growing up. It may be that your parents were overly concerned about material security or it may be that you had to work too hard for your money throughout your life. Regardless of the reason, penny-pinching is not native to your constitution, so there is hope for change.

The best way to conquer your love of money is to simply part with it. No doubt about it, you can definitely benefit from splurging every once in a while. But don't overdo it at first. Start small by treating yourself to a frivolous present. Next, increase the amount you spend on gifts come holiday season. Before you know it, you'll be able to drop a hundred bucks on a date without cursing inflation for the rest of the week. Your friends will like you better, you'll do more repeat date business, and your standard of living will increase. Hey, you may even start earning more money. Just remember: Money has no value unless it is spent. So take that to the bank.

Movie Checklist

❏ Select a movie

❏ Choose a place

❏ Pick a time

❏ Don't forget the extra cash for popcorn and candy

❏ Buy tickets

establish whether mutual attraction is one of the things you two have in common.

When planning your movie date, the single most important decision you can make is what film to see. This is the hard part. Don't go with anything too violent, sappy, or sexual. After all, it is your first outing, and you don't want your date squirming in his or her seat. Most people believe that romantic films are perfect for first dates. But we must beg to differ. All romance is not created equal. If the movie you've chosen deals too tragically with the question of love, your date may misinterpret your intentions. So unless you're convinced that you really like the person, save the melodramatic sagas for a later date.

Great first-date movie selections are usually labeled as such. *My Best Friend's Wedding, Jerry McGuire, When Harry Met Sally,* and the like were all branded great date movies upon their release. Romantic? Sure. Comedies? Yes again. Romantic comedies are the movies of choice for first dates. Nothing too serious, nothing too adolescent, just good, clean fun.

Of course, these won't work if you're not at all into your date. To save a sparkless date it's best to see a semi-serious movie that you have both had your eye on. This way everyone gets something out of the experience. Steer clear of romantic comedies at all costs. These films have a tendency to invest those not involved in relationships with a feeling of melancholy. You're liable to mistake your film-prompted mood for desperation and make promises you can't keep to your date. Stick to somber films that have received a good critical response. Whether you agree with the reviews or not, you'll be inspired to converse and debate. After the movie you can take a walk and exchange your ideas.

Art Gallery Opening

Taking a date to an art gallery is a favorite among seasoned date-goers. Not only can you impress your date with your arsenal of art terminology, you can also learn about the other person's likes and dislikes. The key to making this date a wild success lies in choosing a popular opening and briefing yourself on the artist's background prior to setting foot on the premises.

Since the last thing you want is to attend a one-person, one-guest show, the more popular the event, the more competent you

will appear to your date. A poor showing can bore your companion and sour the entire date. Not only will a popular show keep your date from dozing off, but it's bound to be filled with all manner of well-heeled art patrons. And if you get right down to it, the best part of attending an opening is playing "let's make fun of the most pretentious guests."

But in order to make sure that you're not the one who's the butt of all jokes, you'll have to research the artist beforehand. Call the gallery and ask to receive information about the featured artists. They're usually only too happy to oblige. Then, study up on the life and times, as well as the influences, shaping the artist's work. But once you're in the know, make sure not to spread the good word too thick. No one likes a know-it-all.

While refreshments may be served at the opening, you should make an effort to eat before you go. Noshing at the hors d'oeuvres all night is considered to be in very bad taste. So if you don't want to look like a faux art lover who is only in it for the free eats, treat an art gallery like a feast for the eyes, not for the stomach.

Gallery Checklist

- ❏ Selection of artist and gallery
- ❏ Background information on artist
- ❏ A working knowledge of art terminology
- ❏ Entry fee
- ❏ Full stomach
- ❏ Wear comfortable shoes

The House of Games

Amusement parks aren't just for kids anymore. Riding wild roller coasters, crashing into each other on bumper cars, and trying to win stuffed animals for your date—now what's more romantic than that? For fun-loving singles, amusement parks can be a great way to spend an adventurous and exciting time.

Should you decide to take your date to an amusement park, you'll have to find one that's not located too far off. Anything over an hour's drive should be shunned at all costs. Because you don't want to commit yourself to a long first date, a conveniently located park should do the trick.

Once you've selected a park, make sure your date is aware of your plans for the evening. Because unless she or he is crazy about the idea of having a thrilling first-date experience, you may be in for a difficult evening.

Several important factors remain to be considered before going to an amusement park. First, you'll have to prepare yourself for any calamity. The worst thing that could happen to you on this date (getting stuck on a malfunctioning ride aside) is that you may become nauseous on a ride and embarrass yourself in the process.

Amusement Park Checklist

❑ Credit cards
❑ Gas
❑ Casual clothes
❑ Empty stomach

We recommend that you don't indulge yourself with any big meals before taking on the rides. You should also warn your date, just in case they're not familiar with this drill.

Next, remember to dress comfortably for this casual occasion. This is a somewhat physical date with a high blooper factor. Favorite shirts get ripped in the heat of the moment and dresses are blown up by lightning speed rides. Comfortable shirts, jeans, and pants should suit guys and gals alike in this venue. And if you're planning on hitting the water rides, wear white at your own risk.

And here's a final note: Do not waste all your money on winning a plush toy to impress your date. Some people, and we're not naming names, can get ultra competitive when playing the shooting games or trying to knock down pins for ponies. Very few people will be impressed with your ability to throw a baseball through a dime-sized slot. So when in doubt, save your time, money, and energy for the actual date.

I had just broken up with my boyfriend and was trying to date more. So one evening this guy took me to a huge amusement park. They had these horrifying roller coasters, and I was really scared. I told him I liked amusement parks, but I was referring to the smaller rides. And instead of going home or riding the smaller rides, this guy insisted that he get all the fun his money could buy. So he proceeded to ride every roller coaster while I waited below. I was really bored, but I didn't have another way to go home. So after like four hours of just standing around, we went home. Needless to say, we never went out again.

—LISA, 23, PUBLIC RELATIONS

Picnic Lovers

Ahhh, the great outdoors. Just you, your date, and thousands of six-legged critters lounging around and enjoying everything that nature has to offer. Picnics are great for first dates. You can talk all you want while enjoying the fruits of your labor in the kitchen.

The first course of business is picking out the picnic spot. Ideally, you'll want to pick an area closely situated to a tree for leaning. And if the natural landscape affords it, a nice lake or

Creative Date Ideas

- **Outdoor summer concerts.** Whether it's handbells, pops, a symphony orchestra, bluegrass, jazz, or big band, outdoor concerts are unparalleled for relaxing and enjoying your date's clever conversation. Picture a warm evening, soft breezes, a picnic, a blanket, you, your date, and the dulcet tones of the local philharmonic wafting over you. Sound perfect? Yes, we know. But bring bug spray, just in case.

- **One-of-a-kind festivals**, such as the Burning of Zozobra in Santa Fe, New Mexico, the Zucchini Festival in Eldorado, Ohio, The Geek Pride Festival in Boston, Massachusetts, or The Johnny Appleseed Festival in Fort Wayne, Indiana. The enthusiasms of these diverse crowds are sure to provoke interesting observations and chat.

- **Film revivals.** Let's face it—as much as we all love the likes of Julia Roberts and Hugh Grant, nothing compares to the classics. The romance and originality of Old Hollywood—whether it's Bogie, Audrey Hepburn, film noir, screwball comedies, Hitchcock, or silent-screen classics such as Buster Keaton and Charlie Chaplin—is hard to beat. When you want to offer your date a night that feels more special than just "going to the movies," try one out of the archives—we guarantee you won't be disappointed.

- **Early morning adventures.** It's 6 a.m. What could be more romantic than skulking around in a marsh with your date, a set of binoculars, and a good command of birdcalls? If birdwatching's not your bag, how about a refreshing two-person morning jog through the city park? You can even try the decidedly unconventional before-work breakfast date. If you manage to get out of bed and do any of these other-side-of-the-clock activities, you'll love the feeling of starting the day with an activity that's just for you—as opposed the usual ones which are focused on your boss.

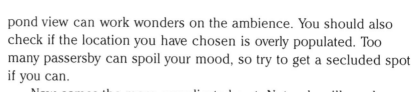

pond view can work wonders on the ambience. You should also check if the location you have chosen is overly populated. Too many passersby can spoil your mood, so try to get a secluded spot if you can.

Now comes the more complicated part. Not only will you have the task of amusing your date, you'll have to feed him or her as well. You can either prepare a gourmet meal yourself or have it catered. But whatever you do you'll have to come equipped with the basic gourmet picnic fare—wine, cheese, fresh bread, pâté, and ripe fruit. The combination of fresh air and good food is bound to give your date that extra advantage.

To complete the festivities you may want to bring along a Frisbee, musical instrument (if you play one) or a CD player to set the mood. There is nothing more romantic than eating a great meal, working it off with a Frisbee, and then sealing the evening with a great melody and who knows what else.

Picnic Checklist

- ❏ The perfect location
- ❏ Picnic basket
- ❏ Blanket
- ❏ Food: wine, cheese, bread, pâté, fruit
- ❏ Insect spray
- ❏ Post-meal activity: Frisbee, CD player

Dancing the Night Away

Let's get one thing straight: If you can't dance to save your life, then choose another game plan. Unfortunately, most people who truly can't dance have no idea that they're so inept. Take Elaine from *Seinfeld*. When she started kicking up her heels and elbows during an office party, she was all thumbs and had a hard time living down the shame. We're not trying to give you a complex. All we're doing is trying to save you any unnecessary embarrassment. The best way to gauge your dancing queen/king quotient is to ask your most trusted friends for their advice. No one is going to tell you that you suck on the dance floor, so forget posing any point blank questions. Instead, tell your friends that you're considering taking your date dancing and ask them what they think of the plan. If they suggest you do something else, by all means, take their advice.

For those of you who *can* hold your own, dancing dates can be a highly stimulating experience for all involved. Provided you don't offend your date with one too many pelvic thrusts, you can dip, twirl, and sway the night away.

Depending on your dance preference, you will have to decide on an appropriate place to take your date. Unless you're both punk fiends, slam dancing is strictly off limits. Swing can also be a bone

Dancing Checklist

- ❏ Money for drinks and entry fee
- ❏ Comfortable clothes and shoes
- ❏ Money for drinks
- ❏ An alternative dance club in case the door policy is too strict

of contention for individuals who can't jump and jive. In fact, there's no one dance that's universally accepted. So your best bet is to discuss your plans in detail with your dance partner before the date.

When dancing with your date for the first time it is wise to avoid any aggressive or sexual moves. In a nutshell, keep your hands where your date can see them. No one wants to be pawed and groped their first night out. Of course, there are exceptions to that rule. Just to be safe, make sure to take your cue from your date. If he or she is keeping their distance, try to respect their personal space. You should also allow your date the freedom to decide when and how long they want to dance. Don't pull your date onto the dance floor just because your favorite song is playing. They may not share your enthusiasm.

Other dancing do's include comfortable shoes and appropriate clothes. When selecting your clothes, make sure to wear something that fits the venue you'll be attending. Being refused entry by the doorman is a humbling experience and probably not something you want to have happen while you're trying to impress your date. For country dance clubs, you can't beat a swanky pair of cowboy boots and a cowboy hat. If you're heading out to a swing bar, make sure your look is hopping by wearing your finest vintage threads. And nothing says salsa like a tight red dress or a sleek black suit. Wherever you're going, dressing the part will make your dancing experience that much more enjoyable.

When my date told me we were going to a new club, I was excited because I love going to new places. I knew the nightclub scene in my hometown pretty well, but I had never heard of the one she suggested. When we arrived, I realized it was an all-access club, meaning anything and everything goes. People were making out on the floor and there were really strange whips and chains all over the walls. I decided to give it some time, until a guy and a girl came up to us and asked if we wanted to play. When my date turned out to be interested in their offer, I politely excused myself to go to the bathroom and hightailed it out of there through the back door.

—STEVE, 26, PERSONAL TRAINER

Beach Checklist

- ❏ Sunglasses
- ❏ Beach towel
- ❏ Sunscreen
- ❏ Attractive bathing suit
- ❏ Cooler for drinks

A Day at the Beach

Who wouldn't love an outing to the beach? Providing that the weather is fine and the water is swimmer-friendly, the beach is a very alluring date zone. You'll be able to rub tanning lotion on each other and even check out one another's physiques without getting too intimate. There is something about the sand, the surf, and the smell of tanning lotion on a hot, sunny day that acts as an instant ice breaker. Such dates make it absolutely impossible for anyone to keep their guard up for long.

The most important consideration for a beach date is looking good and feeling comfortable. If you're feeling bloated or just plain fat, you're bound to be self-conscious. In this case, maybe the beach isn't the place for you. But if it's only a matter of finding that perfect bathing suit, you've got nothing to worry about. The key is not to expose too much. Unless you're in Europe, or even Miami for that matter, men should avoid cavorting in anything smaller than a regulation-sized pair of boxer shorts. Women, too, should save their thong bikinis for another time. Even if you have a killer bod and are just dying to show it off, resist the urge to unveil. A little mystery can go a long way.

Another consideration is your tan. There is nothing more appealing than a great tan. So if you're lacking in that department, remember to apply self-tanning lotion a week in advance. And for the women out there, make sure you don't wear too much makeup to the beach. Even if you're head over heels over your date, too much makeup can spell disaster on the shores. Keep it natural, clean, and subtle. And skip the mascara, no matter how waterproof. But do bring sunscreen.

When it comes to water games, do not take this time to bond with your inner child. Some people just can't resist splashing and spraying people with water. Rule number one: There will be absolutely no dunking. Of course, you may want to engage in some light splashing, but only if the other person initiates it.

Museum

Exploring each other and the cultures of the world simultaneously can make for a memorable and fulfilling date. The great thing about going to a museum is that awkward silences are easily

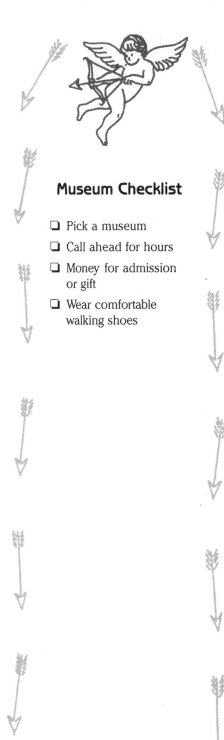

prevented. There will be plenty to talk about once you take in the displays and voice your opinions. You can also save money on admission by calling in advance and finding out on what day the free-admission period falls. You can choose from a variety of museums. Who says art is the only way to go? There are dinosaurs and scientific advances and nostalgic memorabilia...oh my! Any way you go, you're bound to learn something about the world and your date in the process.

When viewing the exhibits, you will benefit from asking your dates what they think. Some people are none too keen about offering their opinion for fear of appearing ignorant and being ridiculed. When dealing with such a companion, playing dumb and feigning utter cluelessness should make short work of opening the lines of communication.

You'll also come off looking the prince/ess if you pace your gait in accordance with your date. If he or she seems content to stroll idly while gazing at the displays, do not try to rush him or her through the museum. You'll only end up appearing pushy and frustrating your date.

Museum Checklist

❏ Pick a museum
❏ Call ahead for hours
❏ Money for admission or gift
❏ Wear comfortable walking shoes

Sports Nuts

For sports fanatics, sharing the experience of a competitive event with a companion can be very gratifying and exciting. You can munch on hot dogs to your little hearts' content, start a riot by rooting for the visiting team, and even yell until your vocal cords collapse from sheer exhaustion. Where but at a sporting event are such things possible?

When asking your date to attend a game, try to choose a sport you both enjoy watching. If you happen to already have the tickets in your possession, then these will have to dictate the time and place. Otherwise, determine your date's favorite sport and team before popping the big question.

On such a date, romance may or may not enter into the picture. But either way, there's no pressure to pile on the charm. Keep your clothes as easy as possible. Stiletto heels and business suits should be saved for another occasion. Show your team spirit by wearing a logo-emblazoned sweatshirt or jacket. The great thing about a sporty date is that you can be as casual as you like. If you table your

Sports Date Checklist

❏ Choose an event
❏ Sporty clothes
❏ Tickets
❏ Money for extras

Theatre Date Checklist

❏ Pick a show
❏ Tickets
❏ Stylish clothes
❏ Opera glasses

predilection for face-painting (it may be part of your personality, but some things are best kept for last), you can really let it all hang out.

In all the freewheeling sports date excitement, you're liable to forget that you're still on a first date. Try not to let this slip your mind. Obnoxious behavior, like picking fights or screaming obscenities, remain off limits. While some conduct may be acceptable among friends, there are limits to what you can do and say on your date.

You should also make all the sports venue amenities available to your date. That means beer, hot dogs, peanuts, pretzels—all the cornucopia plied by the vendors. If you asked for the date, be so kind as to treat your companion to the full experience.

A Night at the Theatre

Ballet, musicals, opera—whatever your poison, a night at the theater should quench the thirst for an enchanting experience. While you may not be able to bond by talking through the show, you will be able to measure your compatibility by comparing notes after the performance.

When selecting an event, try to keep your tastes in mind. Do they run towards the dramatic, the instrumental, or the operatic? You decide. Once you've bought the tickets, you can offer an invitation. This way you'll know right away if your date shares your taste for the arts.

Try to take in a show you've never seen before. If you know what's going to happen and your date is in the dark, it may cause an unnecessary rift between the two of you. It's much more rewarding to share a new experience together.

Deciding the sartorial issue can be tough going. Unless you're sitting front and center at the opera or have managed to score tickets for opening night, you may want to rethink the formal wear. Elegant, well-tailored clothes are a must, but getting overly gussied is never advised. Chic suits and dresses for women are a must, while gentlemen would do best to don suits and ties.

Finally, if you've attempted to save money by purchasing tickets in what's called the "nose bleed" section, you can still save face in front of your date. Secure two pairs of opera glasses to improve visibility. After setting sights on your seats, your date will appreciate the considerate and gallant gesture.

Trailblazers

Anyone wishing to get out in the great outdoors and travel via bicycle, foot, or rollerblade would appreciate the benefits of a trailblazer date. Just pick your mode of transport and off you go.

When choosing a mode of travel, try to ascertain how compatible your date's skills are. If they have a hard time biking or inline skating, then hiking may be your best bet. Make sure to clear up the issue of transportation before the date. Discovering that your date doesn't blade is *tres* awkward when you're standing outside his or her door brandishing two pairs of rented skates.

You would also do well to choose a scenic route. Any path along the lake/sea/oceanfront is a good idea. But even if you're landlocked, there are plenty of routes to choose from. So consult and do a trial run before heading out into the great wide open.

Clothes should be comfortable and sporty. If the Spandex fits, wear it. Shorts, pants, T-shirts, and gym shoes will also suit the occasion for both men and women. And don't forget to bring a light lunch and cold drinks, just in case you begin to feel the weight of your journey.

Shopping

If you've been meaning to do some shopping but just haven't been able to get around to it, this is a great way to kill two birds with one stone. You can shop for various items on your "to-buy" list while enjoying the pleasant conversation and company of your date.

When planning a shopping date make sure you choose a shopping locale rife with possibilities. Picking an open mall or an area abounding in small stores and boutiques can provide you with plenty of opportunities to while away the hours of your date. You can stroll hand in hand while enjoying America's greatest pastime and making a valuable contribution to the gross national product. Now, ask yourself, what could be better than that?

Once you've chosen your shopping location, you should ask your date where he or she would be interested in going. Instead of just charging full speed ahead to the stores of your choice, you would make a better impression by alternating between your date's choices and your own.

Trailblazers Checklist

❑ Scenic trail
❑ Comfortable clothes
❑ Insect repellent
❑ Binoculars
❑ Drinks and snack
❑ Emergency first-aid kit
❑ Compass or map

Shopping Checklist

❑ Shopping location
❑ Credit cards
❑ Comfortable Shoes
❑ Empty your trunk

Extreme Measures Date Checklist

❏ An extreme activity
❏ Comfortable clothes and safety gear
❏ Credit cards
❏ Emergency first-aid kit

Patience remains a virtue on the shopping circuit. While you may hate the idea of waiting around at the makeup counter or spending more than fifteen minutes picking out tennis shoes, exhibit no signs of restlessness to your eager companion. An inability to play the waiting game has soured many a great love affair in the making. Don't worry: after a few more shopping dates, you can whine and complain until you get your way.

You should also avoid making anything other than food purchases for your date. This field trip isn't about buying your date's affections; it's about enjoying a date at your favorite mall. If your date seems to have his or her eye on something, make a mental note just in case your relationship progresses to the next level. Should your date look to you to fund their wardrobe, refuse to play the Sugar Daddy/Mommy by ignoring their hints.

Extreme Measures

Adrenaline junkies take note. If the traditional wine and dine date leaves you high and dry, you can parlay your love of extreme sports into a date extraordinaire. Skydiving, bungee jumping, whitewater rafting, and cliff diving are activities that are sure to make a lasting impression.

Of course, to many people the sky is literally the limit. They would sooner call Dr. Kevorkian than throw themselves from a moving aircraft. Yet there are others who, while wary of initiating the ultimate thrill ride themselves, would jump at the chance if someone they knew presented them with the idea.

If you're a risk-taker and would love to meet someone who shares your love of danger, then asking your date to join you on a wild expedition will tell you everything you want to know about his or her lust for the hazardous life. You may have to do a little cajoling, but they'll thank you in the end. However, if your date seems dead set against your plan, do not force the issue. You will then have the option of choosing another activity or finding someone more adventurous.

Selecting an extreme activity will depend on you. If you've always wanted to try skydiving, now is the time. Or, you may want to choose an activity that is the least expensive or most accessible. Call around your area or ask friends to find a viable and affordable alternative.

Eclectic Date Ideas

The novelty date: Showing that you're both fun-loving and slightly campy, the novelty date is a good way to have a good time and indulge your creativity, all without having to fork over $50 for a fancy dinner.

- **Local carnivals.** Ferris wheels, carnies, candied apples: they all spell "good time." The nostalgia factor is high, and you may find yourself overcome with childlike enthusiasm; you might find yourselves entering a three-legged race or a pie-eating contest.

- **Agricultural fairs.** Watch a herd of oxen pull enormous cement blocks, then root for your favorite kid in the tractor-driving contest. Pet a llama at the petting farm, then make your own honeycomb candles and exchange them with your date. If you and your date are both city slickers, all the better!

- **Go-cart tracks.** Driving a go-cart is a lot more fun than driving a car. You can turn faster, you don't have to worry much about safety, and you're practically sitting on the motor. Nothing will break the first-date ice faster than a few invigorating spins around the go-cart track—just remember, if you get stuck with a slow car, it's bad manners to block your date like a NASCAR driver.

- **Family fun centers.** Mini-golf, bumper boats, skee ball—all in the name of good clean fun. You can win anything from button candy to clock radios with your skee ball tickets. And don't forget to stop at Dairy Queen on the way home. Remember—it's not just childish, it's fun!

- **Karaoke.** If you can pull off a good karaoke performance, chances are you'll win your date's heart right then and there. There's something intoxicating about karaoke's magical blend of camp, charisma, and improvisation, and if you can look and sound good while doing it, more power to you. A few tips: choose a good song, have fun with it, and don't try break dancing during the instrumental sections if you don't know how.

Animal Kingdom Date Checklist

- ❏ Your favorite zoo
- ❏ Sunny, warm day
- ❏ Camera
- ❏ Credit cards and cash for tickets and lunch
- ❏ A coin for making tough "where to go next?" decisions

Finally, when you're all set to take the plunge, make sure your date is feeling okay about the activity. Remember never to pressure anyone into doing something they're not comfortable with. And it's all right to turn back if your date is apprehensive, no matter how much you've planned or waited for the big event. Should your date back out at the very last minute (as in right on the ledge of the bungee platform), you can still go solo. Your date should have no problem with this strategy considering how much you put into setting up this date. In fact, he or she may decide to join in the merry-making after watching your successful performance.

Wild Animal Kingdom

As children we had plenty of opportunities to explore the zoo's wild animal kingdom. But as adults, we just can't seem to make the time to join the animal-loving throngs. If you don't break into hysterical sobbing at the site of animals in captivity, the zoo is just as much fun today as it was when you were still back in day-camp.

Taking your date to the zoo is certain to prove a jolly good time. You can check out the fierce lions and tigers, take in the monkey madness, or play with the small and friendly creatures at the petting zoo. Any way you look at it, this date is custom made for the animal lover in all of us.

To really enjoy your zoo experience, you'll benefit from reading the educational descriptions of each animal. You can learn about the mating, sleeping, and hunting habits of your favorite animals, or discover new animals you didn't even know existed.

When setting up this date, keep in mind that bright sunny conditions and warm weather are ideally suited for making your day at the zoo unforgettable. Check the weather forecast before phoning your love interest.

Once you've entered the zoo, make every effort at compromise with your date. If you're wild about the zebras and your date goes ape for the monkeys, then you may want to forfeit your turn or toss a coin. Quarreling over animals is a no-no in the dating game. You should also make sure to rest your weary feet and get some refreshment during your exploration.

It's plain to see that your dating options are truly unlimited. All of these dates, or any combination thereof, are a great way to get to know someone on a more personal level. But regardless of where you go and what you do, the key to having a great time has been, is, and always will be your ability to connect and be considerate of your date. So get out there and have a great time. But remember, wherever you go, whatever you do, it's who you are that makes a world of difference.

It's All In The Packaging

Getting ready for your first date is not something to take lightly. Your first impression will have a lasting effect on the outing, so do not be nonchalant or careless when preparing your outside package. While you may feel that looks and appearance are of no importance, your date may see things a little differently. So don't be difficult; a little primping and fussing never hurt anyone.

Why Clothes Make the Wo/Man

Your clothes are an extension of who you are and how you would like to be treated. Risqué attire may send the message that you're interested in something more than friendship, while business suits may leave your date wondering why you're so serious.

In the clothes department, striking a nice balance is crucial. And then there's the not-so-small consideration of dressing for the time and place. Whatever you do, avoid buying a new outfit for a first date. Wearing your favorite outfit will give you the peace of mind that a new and untested ensemble can never hope to equal.

Evening Wear for Her

This is your first date, correct? If so, you're probably not sure of your interest level. This is precisely why we strongly caution against showing up in revealing clothes. From now on, you should take low-cut shirts, midriff-baring sweaters, tight pants and short minis out of your

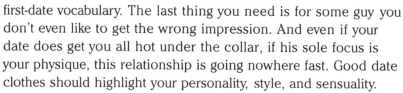

Evening Outfit Options for Her

- Strappy dresses, small cardigans, high heels, elegant choker
- Palazzo pants, bodice skimming shirt, cardigan, long beads, flattering flats
- Tight-fitting pants, long tailored jacket, high heels, funky evening bag
- Tight knee-length skirt, short jacket or cardigan, high heels or boots
- Long flowing skirt, silk blouse, pretty camisole, flats, silver earrings

Evening Outfit Options for Him

- Ribbed turtleneck, black sports coat, jeans, black shoes
- Form-fitting black pants, bright man-made fiber shirt (untucked)
- Black, gray, or brown V-neck sweater, white T-shirt, black corduroys, motorcycle boots

first-date vocabulary. The last thing you need is for some guy you don't even like to get the wrong impression. And even if your date does get you all hot under the collar, if his sole focus is your physique, this relationship is going nowhere fast. Good date clothes should highlight your personality, style, and sensuality.

Comfort is a top priority. If you don't feel good, you won't look good. No two ways about it. Buying new shoes, a new dress, or a new pair of pants can lead to a dating disaster. Something may look great in the dressing room, but sit down and watch that seam run. New shoes are notorious date spoilers. Imagine the two of you strolling down a boulevard. No, scratch that. He's strolling, you're hobbling. Unless he picks you up and carries you to his white horse, this isn't exactly the romantic scene you pictured earlier, now is it?

Unmentionable Matters

When selecting lingerie for your first date, remember that comfort is your main consideration. Garter belts, tight corsets, or leather bodysuits should remain hidden in your drawer for a later time. It's hard enough making conversation without having to fidget with your bra straps all night long.

Evening Wear for Him

When dressing for a night out, most men think that their options are limited and don't put as much time as they could into picking out their clothes. While men's style may not be as multifaceted as women's (sorry guys), a great look is all in the details. The cut of the shirt, the color and pattern of the tie, the socks and shoes, all contribute to creating a strong impression.

The most common mistakes made by men are dressing too casually and not taking enough style gambles. Women love a man who dares to be bold and expresses his individuality through his clothes. Really, it's true. We can't tell you how many times we've met someone attractive only to be turned off by their lack of style. It would be unfortunate if every woman who met you thought, "What a great guy. I'd love to do a makeover on him."

And no one is saying that you have to dress à la David Bowie circa 1970s glam rock to score big. Not at all. Just pay careful attention to the details and try to look through men's fashion magazines on a monthly basis. Then incorporate your favorite looks with more traditional attire to become the ultimate sharp-dressed man.

Day Wear for Her

We didn't recommend dressing too provocatively for evening dates, and we are even more adamantly against it for a daytime date. If you can believe it, bustiers, stiletto heels, and short skirts look even cheaper and more tawdry in the daylight. What's more, dressing this way during the day may not only make you feel self-conscious, it can make your date feel uncomfortable.

Choose clothes that flatter your physique but that are comfortable as well. If you're embarking upon an active date, you can wear athletic gear that is somewhat revealing, but never overdo it. For example, you can wear leggings, but with a loose-fitting T-shirt. Or you can wear a tank top, but cover up with an unzipped, hooded sweatshirt. It's all about striking a pleasant visual balance.

And don't take this casual green light as an excuse to go out wearing your pajamas. Looking casual should take just as much time and preparation as dressing up, so make every effort to look your best no matter what's on your agenda.

Day Wear for Him

All you guys out there, heed this important warning: Do not, and we repeat, do not make the mistake of underdressing. Just because you will be spending your time walking around during the sunlit hours doesn't mean you can throw on any dirty old thing. Remember, stains are more visible in the daylight. Day garb must be as impressive as your evening wear, so don't waste this opportunity to show off your impeccable sense of style.

Grooming and Hygiene

Now that you're dressed to impress, you can go on to other important matters like makeup, grooming, and good hygiene lessons. Even if your clothes scream style god/goddess, no wardrobe choices can save you if your hair is a mess and your breath is a vampire repellent. It's all part of making a great impression. While most of our male readers should skip over our little makeup lesson, anyone who neglects the grooming and hygiene instructions does so at their own peril.

Day Outfit Options for Her

- Shorts, T-shirt, sneakers
- Jeans, tank top, sneakers
- Knee-length skirt, walking sandals, button-down shirt
- Long or short summer dress, pretty choker, strappy sandals

Day Outfit Options for Him

- Slightly baggy jeans, well-fitted, solid color T-shirt
- Khaki pants, crisp white shirt, running shoes
- Long-sleeved shirt, baseball hat, running pants

Cover Girl

If you're worried about the art of makeup application, you can rest assured that we have the answers to your most pressing questions. Makeup can be a difficult business. Apply too much and you end up looking like Bozo's ugly step daughter, too little and you're in danger of blending into the beige background. The key to applying makeup is to study your face and emphasize your positive characteristics. If you have a great mouth, then play it up. If your eyes have a star quality, then help illuminate them.

Most importantly, do not change your makeup routine too much. You may hate the results and feel uncomfortable all evening. It's best to work off of your old routine and improve your technique gradually over time.

Skin

To make skin look soft, radiant, and smooth you should first apply a moisturizer. Next, to even out your complexion, choose a foundation that closely matches your skin tone and apply with a makeup sponge (remember the Buff Puff?) for easy coverage. A dusting of pressed or bronzing powder should come next, and you can seal the deal by applying a rosy blush, working from the apple of your cheeks upward.

Eyes

Depending on how strong a lipstick color you've chosen, eyes should balance the face. If your lipstick is dark and bright, you may want to play down your eyes with little or no makeup. But should you choose a nude or light lipstick, you can create a dramatic, eye-opening look. First, apply concealer around your eyes and lids to prime eyes. Then, completely outline the eye with brown liner and add mascara. When applying mascara make sure to wipe off any extra buildup on the brush with a tissue to prevent eyelashes from clumping and appearing Tammy Faye-ish.

Lips

Lipstick should never be applied until you've brushed your lips with a toothbrush to get rid of flakes, dabbed a little concealer on your lips to dry and neutralize the surface, outlined your lips with a liner (be careful not to stray from the edges), and then filled in your lips with a matching lipstick. The result will be a perfectly kissable pout.

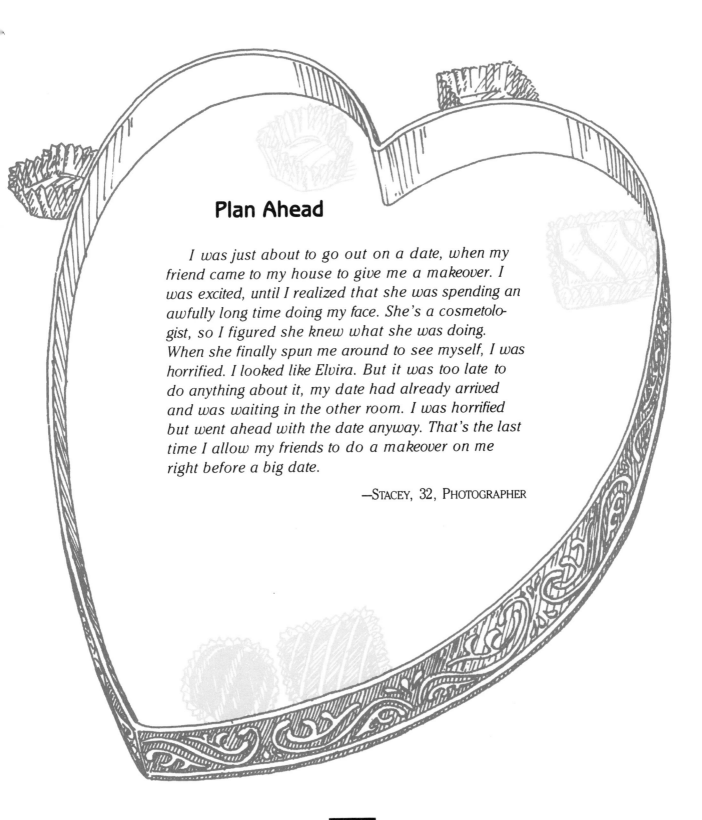

Plan Ahead

I was just about to go out on a date, when my friend came to my house to give me a makeover. I was excited, until I realized that she was spending an awfully long time doing my face. She's a cosmetologist, so I figured she knew what she was doing. When she finally spun me around to see myself, I was horrified. I looked like Elvira. But it was too late to do anything about it, my date had already arrived and was waiting in the other room. I was horrified but went ahead with the date anyway. That's the last time I allow my friends to do a makeover on me right before a big date.

—STACEY, 32, PHOTOGRAPHER

A Hairy Business

Both men and women should make every effort to keep their hair neat and simple for a first date. It is better to keep your coif as similar to your everyday look as possible. A dramatic new cut right before a big date can end in tears. Men should consider going to the barbershop for a trim, while women may want to enlist the aid of a seasoned stylist to save time and make a great first impression. Even if you're against going out of your way, the least you can do is wash your hair. Dandruff flakes and cigarette smoke residue are the fastest ways to ruin what could have been a beautiful friendship.

Shower and Breath Check

You should always take a shower one hour before your big date for ultimate freshness. Don't scoff at the deodorant stick sitting in your medicine cabinet. You may be cool, calm, and collected now, but who knows what you'll be feeling two hours into your date?

When it comes to fragrance or cologne, a dab will do you. Too much may provoke an allergic reaction. And while we're on the subject of toiletries, let's not forget the toothpaste. Brush your teeth like they've never been brushed before. And don't forget the emergency Binaca or mints for those romantic post-garlic-bread moments.

Money Check

Asking your date to spot you a fifty, ditching your date in search of a cash machine, or opting to spend the night washing dishes as your date looks on are eventualities that can be avoided with a little pre-planning. While credit cards may serve a vital function in your cashless lifestyle, you should fill up your money clip with the real deal just in case the credit card machine breaks or the ATM is out of order.

Gas Check

If your tank isn't at least halfway full, and you're not planning on running out of gas in a pathetic attempt to seduce your date, you'll have to fill it up before venturing out for any escapade. Try to take care of this matter early in the day, as leaving it for the last minute can cause tardiness. There's nothing less fashionable than being late to a date.

Map Check

Even if you know where you are going, it would be wise to take along a map just in case your plans change. In fact, if your car isn't packing maps at all times, you may want to make a pit-stop at your local Rand McNally retailer. Whether on a date or on your way to a date, if you're a person who hates to ask for directions for fear of having your navigational/urban wilderness survival skills called into question, a map is the only hope you have of steering a smooth course to your destination.

Pre-Date Pep Talk

With all the material trappings in place, you're set for your date. Or are you? Let's see: money-check; gas-check; clean hair-check; hmmm...what could be missing? How about the right attitude. If you haven't already done so, go ahead and get psyched up. Do whatever necessary to get in the zone. No one is watching, so prance in front of the mirror, flex your muscles, tell yourself you're a rock star. Then get a glass of wine or a cup of tea and sit down for a relaxing moment. Aaaah.

Makeup Mishaps

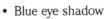

From time to time, even the most well-meaning and knowledgeable female can make a major makeup blunder. The key to avoiding makeup mishaps is to simply avoid the trendy and rely on the classic. So if you've committed any of the following beauty crimes, treat your experience as one to grow on.

- Blue eye shadow
- False eyelashes
- Green mascara
- Pancake makeup
- Warrior blush streaks
- Razor-thin eyebrows

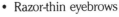

Chapter 6

First Encounters of the Date Kind

The day of reckoning is finally upon you. You have traveled a long and often treacherous road to get to this point. Great gains have been made and many losses suffered. You've mastered the art of asking someone out, dealt with the inevitable rejections, and now here you stand, the comeback kid, triumphant with date in hand. You might as well break out the massage oil and bubble bath; your work is done.

Now, didn't that feel good? We're all entitled to a little self-satisfaction now and again. But let's not get carried away. There's still plenty of work to be done. True, you've passed many important rites of passage, but there are a lot more dating challenges where those came from. If you have diligently applied the lessons of our dating acumen, you're past the point of no return. There's no sense in undoing all the good you've done by reverting back to your old habits now.

When you think about it, the actual date experience is the most exciting and enjoyable time in a single person's life. It's a time when anything can happen, when all the doors are open to you, and you decide what comes next. There's nothing more exhilarating than standing at the precipice of your future. And that is exactly how you should look at each first date, as a journey into the short- or long-term future of your love life.

Every person you date has the potential to become the love of your life. The great part about dating is that you never know who that person will be. You can have a perfect first date, but come date number two you're hard-pressed to suppress a yawn. Or you can have a disastrous first date, when everything that can go wrong does, and still end up forsaking all others so long as you both shall live. So, as guesswork clearly won't pass muster, you'll have to learn to go with the flow and accept whatever surprises come your way. The fact is you can never predict when and why love happens. Ain't it grand?

Since you'll never know what's waiting around the corner, we want you to make the most of each and every date. That means putting all your energy into every encounter, no matter how hopeless the situation may seem.

The Setup

The phone is an invaluable tool for setting up the date. The setup conversation is not the best time to reaffirm how much you want to

see the other person. It is but a brief conversation during which you remind your date at what time and place you will be meeting. Think of it as the courtesy confirmation call your barber or stylist makes prior to an appointment. Many people make the grave error of chatting it up for hours with their soon-to-be date. Not a good idea. The key is to keep from divulging all your best stuff before the date, lest you make the actual meeting anticlimactic. The following are some of the most common mistakes people make when confirming the date arrangements.

The Phone Stalker

Should your future date be unavailable, you will want to leave a message. Take heart; if your date legitimately agreed to go out with you, he or she will return your call. There are some people who just can't stand the idea of talking to an answering machine, fearing they will say something ridiculous in the process. So these people, and you know who you are, proceed to call their dates every hour on the hour. Used to be that this pastime was a safe pursuit. No longer. With the advent of caller ID, your date will be able to detect when and how many times you called during the day. They will be none too pleased to discover that the person they may have thought was The One is, in actuality, none other than your run-of-the-mill phone stalker. So no matter how desperately you want to relay the particulars personally, if you should find your date absent, leave a message on your first try, or suffer the consequences.

The Never-Ending Message

Like most people, you too have probably been plagued by the extra-long message bandit at some point in your life. You stroll innocently to your answering machine and see twelve messages on your display. You immediately grow enthusiastic at the discovery of your newfound popularity. Then, you hear the first message, and your heart sinks. It suddenly dawns upon you that twelve people didn't call you today; one person called you and left you twelve continuous messages. The horror!

While an answering machine does carry a certain degree of pressure, there's no reason to tie up someone's line forever. It may be natural to get off track in your confusion, but avoid leaving

What's Your Sign? Romance According to the Zodiac

Virgo
Virgos are often inscrutable in the affairs of the heart. They seem remote and quiet, then open and talkative. One moment they're glad to see you, then the next they act like they could care less. This is only the Virgo need to perfect what is. Virgos generally don't entertain romantic illusions; they see what's there in finely carved detail, like an X-ray, and then they try to improve on it. Don't take it personally. A Virgo is never harder on the people she loves than she is on herself.

rambling messages. Sticking to your name, number, and the time and place of your rendezvous will prevent you from blubbering and revealing too much information.

Wine Tips for Dating

1. Red wine can temporarily stain your teeth, although it brushes right off.

2. If you have plans to do something after dinner, you should consider drinking lower-alcohol wine. There is a big difference between 11 percent and 14 percent. German white wines are usually low in alcohol.

3. No jug wines or screwcaps, unless you are looking to end a relationship.

4. Don't overspend, as it can intimidate the other person and make you appear to be pompous and/or insecure.

5. Always ask the other person if they would like more wine before pouring it into their glass.

6. When pouring wine, always pour yours last.

7. Don't feel the need to finish the bottle.

The Phone Monopolizer

When calling to arrange your date, make sure you don't end up talking into the wee hours. As mentioned earlier, you'll want to keep your pre-date phone chat short—ten minutes max. Follow the lead of Hollywood, where it's standard practice to let the suspense build before spilling the beans. The less your date knows about you in the beginning, the more of an advantage you'll have.

You should also abstain from monopolizing the conversation with full-length descriptions of what you've planned for the date. While you may have gone to a lot of trouble, you should try to make the experience seem as effortless and spur-of-the-moment as possible. Talking too much will also prevent you from hearing any objections your date may have to your agenda. While you may not want to accept any dissent from the ranks, you would benefit from hearing your date out. Maybe he gets motion sickness on roller coasters, or maybe she's allergic to strawberries; either possibility may impinge upon your Disneyland-going or berry-picking plans. You'll never know until you make an effort to clam up and listen.

Call Waiting

No one, and we stress, *no one* likes to be put on hold for long periods of time. If you should happen to receive a call during your confirmation call, keep it as brief as is humanly possible. Telling the other caller that you're on a long-distance call should do the trick. And don't try to do us one better by trying to ignore the call waiting altogether. Not picking up the call can signal that you are too anxious and, even worse, desperate to seal the deal. So, by all means, take the call, but make it short and sweet.

If, on the other hand, your date should leave you hanging on hold, cut them some slack. While you may hate to be kept waiting, handle the situation with patience. Do not hang up and do not express your resentment. At this early juncture of your relationship, any such act may end the date before it's even begun.

Get Off the Hook

Getting off the phone is, alas, just as difficult as dialing the number. If some of your dates pride themselves on their gift of gab, you must try to make your getaway as seamless as possible. While you don't want to spend all night listening to empty chatter, neither do you want to send the message that you don't want to spend all night listening to empty chatter. The key to making a graceful exit is to allow your phone buddies to think ending the call was all their idea. If, for example, they mention all the work they still have to do, tell them that you'll let them get back to work. Or, if they're prattling away about all the things they did that day, feel free to say, "Oh my, you must be exhausted. I know! What do you say we talk tomorrow?" This way no one gets hurt, and you don't endanger your chances of getting a date in the future.

You can also try staging a stunt, like a pot boiling over or a knock on your door. This way they will let you off the hook and will harbor no ill will come date time.

This girl who lives on my block asked me to go out with her one night. I agreed and gave her my number so she could call me to arrange the plans. I was pretty excited about the date, but when I didn't hear from her that week, I started to wonder what was going on. A couple of days later, I received a formal invitation in the mail. Thinking it was from one of my many engaged friends, I put it aside. That night I looked at it again but discovered that it wasn't a wedding invitation, it was from her. The girl who asked me out sent me an invitation with the date, time, and place of our date written on it. There was even an RSVP card, just in case. I was very impressed that someone would go to such lengths for me.

—TOM, 37, BROKER

The Ten Commandments Of Dating

You've made the plans, confirmed the plans, and now it's time to get down to business. The date portion is one of the most savory dishes on life's expansive menu so prepare to sample your fair share. You probably don't want to hear any lectures about the dating do's and don'ts, so we'll just skip the do's and get straight to the don'ts. Just as Moses handed down a set of laws, or commandments, if you will, for us mortals to follow, so shall we bring forth the laws of dating. Should you break a commandment or fail to follow the formula for perfect dates coming up in the next section, you should prepare to endure all the torments of dating hell. Don't come crying to us when your phone doesn't ring the next day, and don't go calling on the mighty powers that be to reverse the situation. No, you and your love life will do better if you just follow the rules. That said, let's get on with the show.

Commandment #1: Thou Shalt Not Ignore Thy Date

Paying close attention to your date's every move is not up for discussion. There are some people who feel like they have to leer at every attractive person that walks through the door. Most dates would get offended by this sort of behavior, taking it as a personal insult to themselves. So unless you're intent on hurting your companion's feelings, keep your eyes and ears directed at your date at all times. If you made your date feel like they're the only person in the room, you'll have gone a long way towards living up to your role as the perfect date.

If you happen to take your date to a party and feel like mingling with some of your friends, keep in mind that your date's happiness is your first priority. Be extra attentive by doing small things such as bringing drinks, initiating conversation, and making all the right introductions. You can bet that your little acts of kindness will not go unnoticed.

Commandment #2: Thou Shalt Not Drink or Become Intoxicated

Even if you're not driving, excessive consumption of alcohol and other recreational drugs is strictly prohibited. If you've ever been forced to sit through the film *Blind Date*, in which lovely Kim Basinger proceeds to get sloshed during a night on the town with Bruce Willis, you know that there's nothing less attractive than a perfectly nice date who's three sheets to the wind and feeling no pain. As far as first impressions go, this behavior can put you at a disadvantage.

The best way to avoid becoming too drunk is to eat plenty before the date. That way you'll be able to absorb the alcohol faster. And even if you're just looking to chase the butterflies out of your stomach, forgo the booze in favor of some deep breathing exercises.

Commandment #3: Thou Shalt Not Talk about Thy Ex

Whether you've just broken up, happened to run into your ex that day, or just can't help digging up the past, talking about your ex is a first date *faux pas*. The last thing your date wants to hear about is how horrible or great your ex was. As far as your date is concerned, you've never ever gone out with anyone before.

Many people think that dredging up a former love will somehow make them seem more desirable. This couldn't be further from the truth. Your date is more likely to think that you're having a problem letting go and are on the rebound. If they're smart, they will never want to see you again. If they're not, it's you who should be running the other way.

Commandment #4: Thou Shalt Not Lie

First dates are all about getting to know each other and being honest. If you happen to be out of a job, living with your parents, or hard up for cash, by all means don't lie about it. You can omit the information, so long as you fess up when asked point blank. Don't equivocate, don't change the subject, and don't make up some elaborate ruse. If the date proves successful, and more follow, you'll eventually be exposed for the charlatan that you are. And, besides, if your date can't accept you exactly the way you are, then you're better off finding someone who isn't so superficial.

While still in high school, I met this really cute guy at my health club. But I was only a sophomore in high school, and he was a senior in college. So, I lied and told him I was a freshman in college, and he seemed to believe me. He even asked me out. In order to go out with him, I had to sneak out of my house and then pretend I knew what college life was about. I made up a major, lied about the classes I was taking, and pretended

The Date Doctor Is In

Q: How much detail should I reveal about my sex life on the first date?

A: *This depends on how you feel about your date. If you detest him/her to the point that you'd rather spend your life celibate than ever see them again, you can reveal anything you want; tell them you're a vestal virgin. On the other hand, if there is even the slightest chance you will go out again don't bring up the topic; nothing is worse than listening to someone on a date talk about their past boyfriends or girlfriends.*

P.S. Disregard last statement if your ex-boyfriend/ girlfriend or fling was a well-known model or celebrity.

I lived in the dorm. I even mobilized all of my friends to cover for me, just in case my mom called looking for me. After two weeks of this activity, I was too tired to even enjoy going out with him. I realized what a hassle it was to keep lying, and told him the truth. He never wanted to speak to me again, but I really couldn't blame him.

—Maggie, 23, Accountant

The Wine Ritual

You ordered the wine, and you are shown the label. Is it the right year? If you ordered a "reserve," make sure it is not a lesser bottling from the same producer. So far, so good. Tell the server to keep the cork, unless you collect corks; it is of no use to you once you have verified that it hasn't rotted during its years in the bottle. Do taste the wine while the server is there. Any problem should be addressed immediately. Your server should then pour wine for everyone at the table.

Commandment #5: Thou Shalt Not Commit an Act of Road Rage

When transporting your date from one destination to another, thou shalt obey the rules of the road and be courteous to other drivers. If you happen to be cut off by a kamikaze driver or even get thrown the bird, act as if nothing happened. Do not, and we repeat, do not proceed to chase down the offender or slam on your brakes to get revenge. Not only will your date be paralyzed with fear for his or her safety; he or she will remain disgruntled for the duration of this, your first and last date together.

Commandment #6: Thou Shalt Not Show Up Over Twenty Minutes Late

When it comes to dating, timeliness is next to godliness. The worst thing you can do to your date is keep them waiting. Nobody likes to sit around wondering whether they're being stood up, especially if they're already nervous about going out with someone for the first time. Before heading out for the outing, make sure you have scheduled plenty of time to pick up your date. You should also avoid scheduling any other activities for at least one hour before your date. Many dates have been known to be canceled right from the get go because of tardiness. Make sure you're not one of the many casualties in the race against time by allowing plenty of room for error.

Commandment #7: Thou Shalt Not Come on Too Strong

It's considered in very bad taste to make lewd comments about your date's appearance, touch them without permission, or insinuate wanting to get more sexual. Unless you're looking for nothing more than a basic wham-bam-adios-amigo—which, by the way, you're still not likely to score using these tactless methods—keep your sexually charged particles in line.

When getting to know someone for the first time, most people prefer to keep things on a platonic level. That means putting a nix on the sexual advances, or, if you prefer Pig Latin, ixnay on the exualsay advancesay. At least have the decency to wait until your date is more comfortable with you. Most importantly, never try to push your date into a sexual situation. Always err on the side of caution—even if while their lips are saying no, their eyes are saying yes.

Commandment #8: Thou Shalt Not Use Thy Cellular

In the name of insufferable bores everywhere, deactivate your cell phone while on your date. Should your friends be trying to reach you they can leave a message on your voice mail. Using a cellular phone during your date can be a major turnoff. By talking on the phone, you're saying that your date is not significant enough to captivate your attention, implying that your work and friends are much more important. That's not exactly the message you want to convey to someone who has kindly agreed to go out with a cell-phone-flaunting-Sal/ly like yourself. If you cared enough to go on the date, keeping things lively should be your top priority.

Commandment #9: Thou Shalt Not Talk about Building a Family

Few things are more frightening than going on a first date and being confronted with the issues of marriage and family. Such situations make most people stop and look around to make sure they're still in America—as opposed to Pakistan, where one meeting is all you get before striking an arrangement.

Before sizing up your date for mate potential, take a breather and get a little perspective. You've only just met a little while ago. If you happen to be looking for Mr/s. Right, keep your plans to yourself or risk scaring off potential suitors. Remember, whatever will be, will be. Grilling your date about their desire to have kids will only make you seem foolish and desperate. If you want to find out whether someone

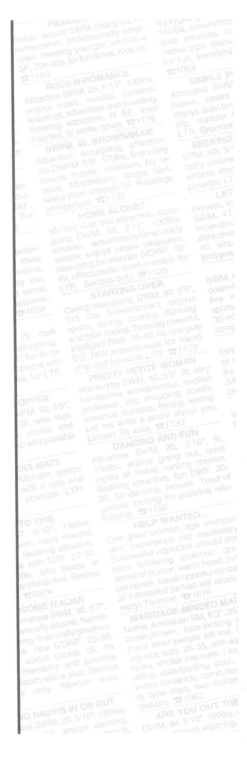

would make a good husband or wife, try studying their behavior instead. Actions will always speak much louder than words.

I remember one date that started off really well. She was gorgeous, a great conversationalist, and seemed very ambitious, at first. But halfway through dinner she launched into this long tirade about how she wanted to meet someone she could marry and then quit her job. She kept looking at me, like she was waiting for a response or something. Frankly, I was having a hard enough time just trying to swallow my food after that confession. To cut the conversation short, I quickly finished my meal and complained of a stomachache. I dropped her off, and never called her again. Talk about putting way too much pressure on a first date.

—MICHAEL, 36, PERSONAL TRAINER

Commandment #10: Thou Shalt Not Whine Too Much

If "I want" figures prominently on your list of most frequently used phrases, then prepare to monitor your behavior during date hours. Bossing your date around or pouring on the old "bitch and moan" routine when you don't get your way are sure-fire ways to spoil a romantic mood. If you have your heart set on doing something particular, take the lead—just make sure your date is fine with your arrangements. If, on the other hand, you've let your date take control, either voice your dissent right away or pretend you're enjoying the 100-degree weather and the two-hour hike. The prima donna attitude will make you seem spoiled, selfish, and definitely not second date material.

Going Out With A Bang

Now that you've got the basics of dating down pat, you are in pretty good shape for the date. If you're wondering about all those little things that can make a big difference, you have a point. While a basic set of guidelines is all well and good, nothing beats good old-fashioned attention to detail for sending your companion into a tailspin of appreciation.

Chivalric Codes

During the Middle Ages, English knights obeyed a strict code of chivalry.

We don't need to point out to you that etiquette's changed over the years, but just for education's sake, here's a quick rundown of traditional social graces so that you know what rules you're bending if you choose to do so.

- A gentleman may hold a door open for a lady to pass through first, although this has ceased to be a hard-and-fast rule. Practically speaking, the first person to arrive at a door should hold it open for the next, and that person should smile or say "Thank you" at the gesture.

- A gentleman allows a lady to enter and exit the elevator first and holds the door to prevent it from closing on her.

- The gentleman walks ahead of a lady coming downstairs.

- A gentleman walks on the curb side of the sidewalk with the lady on the building side to prevent her from being splashed by passing cars.

- Gentlemen rise when a lady enters or leaves the room or when she leaves or returns to the table.

- A gentleman follows the lady to their table in the restaurant (because the maitre d' precedes her) and steadies her chair as she sits (although the maitre d' will likely do so).

- In movie (or other) theaters or sports events, the man allows the woman to walk ahead of him into the row; he sits on the aisle. If two or more couples attend together, the women sit between the men.

- When driving a car, a gentleman unlocks the passenger door from the outside, helps the lady to her seat, then closes the door before opening his own. He also gets out first on arrival to help her from the car. (Note: according to dating lore, if the woman reaches over and unlocks the man's door before he gets to it, she likes him.) If the woman drives the car, the man still helps her in before taking his passenger seat.

Ten Things You Should Never Say to Your Date's Parents

While we all have those awkward foot-in-the-mouth moments, the less you have of them around your date's parents the better. Because parents have such a strong influence on their children, you will want to avoid uttering any of the following statements:

1. "So where do you guys keep the booze?"

2. "You must be very proud of your grandson/daughter."

3. "Now that sleeping around has become so dangerous, I am ready to date a nice boy/girl."

4. "What a coincidence! Can you believe they had the same poster at my detox clinic?"

5. "Being locked away at the state pen all those years really taught me to appreciate the love of a good man/woman."

6. "I'm not ready to settle down. I'm just enjoying playing the field."

7. "Al/Ally is so lucky. I wish I didn't hate my parents."

8. "We'll be back in the morning."

9. "Whooyee, you guys must be loaded!"

10. "All of you look nothing alike, are you sure she/he isn't adopted?"

Because our goal is to ensure that each and every one of your dates turns into a great triumph, we have come up with a point-by-point description of each and every phase of your date. To make sure that not a single moment of doubt creeps into your outing, we will follow you from the exact moment you greet your date at his or her door to the exact minute you drop him or her off. So now that your dating course is all mapped out, what are you waiting for? Your only responsibility from this point forth is to have a good time.

Going Through the Pickup Drive

Many people have a hard time with this preliminary date activity, and with good reason. Meeting your date at the door can be likened to the opening of Pandora's Box. Even though you may have met your date before, you never know what's going to come out—personality traits, dark secrets, maybe even a person you really like. Whatever happens, one thing is certain: you're face to face with the unknown, and that could be scary for anyone.

Three's Company

Before picking up your date for the evening, you should always find out if he or she is living with family members or roommates. That way you will not be surprised when his or her whole *mizpucha* comes to the door to take a look at you. If you're not prepared for this critical moment, you may be caught off balance and be nervous as a result.

If you are expected to meet a roommate, friend, or relative while picking up your date, be polite and honest. Do not try to be overly charming at first, since you're not even sure as to how you feel about your date. Simply talk about your job, your plans for the evening, or ask them a little bit about themselves. Keep the subjects of conversation as innocuous as possible, and try not to reveal anything too personal at first sight.

The Waiting Game

Should you catch your date unawares and still getting ready, try to be patient and avoid the temptation to go off searching through his or her house. Don't encourage your date to take his or her time and then proceed to rifle through whatever personal effects you can find. The best thing to do is read a magazine or watch TV.

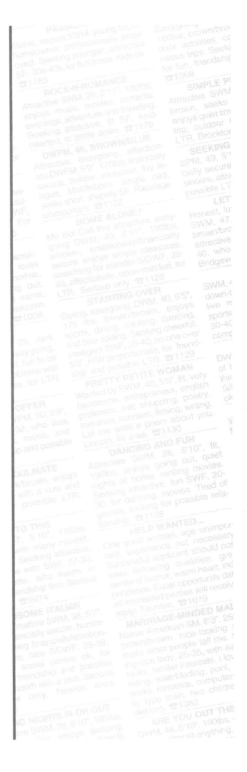

But of all the missteps to take, quite probably the most appalling is the honking of the horn and the turning on of the high-beams in your date's driveway. No matter how casual or unconventional you want to appear, you're now bordering on rude. So get yourself on that stoop before you sabotage the whole date.

Taking the High Road

Transporting your companion to your destination is not an activity to be taken lightly. Any number of road hazards may pop up along the way. If you adhere to the following laws of driving etiquette, and take the precautions to heart, you should come out of the car unscathed.

Greased Lightning

When tooling your date around town, you should first make sure that your vehicle is in tip-top condition. That means no old newspapers crowding the passenger seat and no edible leftovers in the glovebox. A car wash and an air freshener should top off Operation Clean Car nicely.

Smoking Hazard

If you're a smoker and your date isn't, you really should abstain from lighting up until you get outside. Opening windows in the dead of winter or at the height of summer heat will have your date plotting your slow and painful demise. Keeping them closed will make your passenger feel like they're being smoked out. So unless the weather is fine, and you have a convertible, combat your nicotine fits with gum and breath mints while riding in the jalopy.

My Way or the Highway

Watch out for the stereo; it can be a deal-breaker. There will be times when your companion is less than thrilled with your choice of music. If they feel the need to touch that dial, don't get bossy with them. You're already in the driver's seat; it's time to let your date have some control. Who knows, maybe the exercise will broaden your musical horizons. The same thing goes for the thermostat. If your date starts fiddling with the controls, by all means let him.

Wining and Dining, Part I

Wine by the Glass Is Usually a Rip-Off

The markup on bottles of wine is far less than the markup on mixed drinks. Many customers now order a glass of wine in place of that initial cocktail, so smart restaurant operators make sure that they make the same money on that drink and mark up wine by the glass accordingly. A better value is premium wine by the glass, a category in which the markup is more in line with the wine program than with the martini program. These premium wines by the glass are a convenient service for those who can't agree on a bottle or don't want to drink that much.

Enjoying Wine with Your Dinner

Just as at home, in a restaurant you have some control over the enjoyment of your wine. Is this white too cold? Let it warm up on the table and in the glass, and taste the hidden flavors as they emerge. Is the red too warm? Your server should cool it for you in ice water for five minutes or so. Your server should be pouring it for you—in proper glassware, never more than half full—though it's okay to pour it yourself. Don't drink it all before the food arrives (unless you're planning to buy another bottle, of course).

The Magic Rule

In a good restaurant with fairly priced food and wine, wine as good as the food will cost about twice the price of the average entree.

Unsafe vs. Safe Date Food

There are some foods that just don't make the dating cut. If you're brave and uninhibited, go right ahead and sample these items. But if you fall on the cautious end of the spectrum, try choosing from the safe date food list instead.

Unsafe Date Food:

1. Ribs
2. Big salads with extra dressing
3. Spaghetti or angel hair pasta
4. Fried chicken
5. Oversized hamburgers
6. Garlic/onion anything

Safe Date Food:

1. Fish
2. Steak and potatoes
3. Soups
4. Sushi
5. Lamb or duck
6. Ravioli or tortellini

Since everyone thinks they know the best route to take, you and your date may clash in the navigation department. Some people are just not comfortable following the beat of a different drummer. If your date is convinced that you are taking the longest path possible, try to meet his or her demands. If your date's directions turn out to be wrong, you can feel that much better about yourself. But never, ever say "I told you so" during the first date.

Safety First

Finally, make an effort to keep both hands on the steering wheel and eyes on the road at all times. Because it's your first date, you may get distracted by the conversation or the looks of your date. But don't fall prey to this impulse. There will be plenty of time to stare deeply into each other's eyes or debate the state of health care once you get to your destination.

Dinner Time

No matter what you do, or where you go, there will come a time when you have to satisfy your hunger. The reason so many people choose to break bread on their first dates is because eating with someone can tell you volumes about who they are. So if you want to pass the dining test, make sure your table manners are practiced and polished.

Meet and Greet

Since you're the one who made reservations, you'll have to take the lead when approaching your host or hostess for the evening. Inform them that your party has arrived and wait patiently to be seated. Should your table be occupied or in the process of being cleaned, do not take this opportunity to show off by blowing up at the host. They are only doing their job, and you'll end up looking like a first-class bully.

Today's Specials

When deciding what item to order, you should consider that some foods do not make for great date meals. And while they may taste great, the difficulty of eating or digesting them may prove more than you can handle. If your date asks for a suggestion, then you have full freedom to recommend whatever it is you think he or she

would like. But if your date seems to be considering the choices, curb the urge to butt in with your personal faves. Finally, and this hardly bears mentioning, ordering for your date is absolutely out of the question, unless he or she has given you the go-ahead.

Table Talk

During dinner you will be called upon to provide stimulating conversation. There's no getting around this requirement, so come prepared. The best way to improve your table talk is to simply ask questions and discuss current events.

The rules for asking the right questions are twofold. First, you should try to ask open-ended questions rather than those easily satisfied by a one-word answer. For instance, if you're interested in finding out what a person does for a living, your best bet is to ask, "So what do you enjoy about your line of work?" rather than, "What line of work are you in?" The first question necessitates that your date give their opinion, while the second asks for little more than a job title. The difference lies in the awkward silence you'll experience once they've made their response.

You should also avoid asking anything too personal on the first date. Subjects having to do with marriage, sex, or income should be put off for another date. If your dinner companion is interested in revealing something about their private life, they will do so of their own accord. Do not pry, because if your date isn't telling you everything, chances are you're better off in the dark.

Before your date even begins, you should try to collect a reserve of sample topics of conversation. Catching up on MSNBC, CNN, CNBC, and other news programming should fill your coffers with conversation topics galore. You can then freely select topics that are of interest to you on the date. If your companion is interested in the subject of your choice, they will take the conversation in the direction of their choice. To keep the discussion rolling as smoothly as possible, remain flexible and open to new subject matters. Most importantly, forget the PC police and trust your date with your honest opinion. If you play it too safe, you'll sap all the fun right out of your *tête-à-tête*.

During a date with some guy I picked up at a party, he began asking me all about my love life. Like how many people I slept with, whether I was sexually uninhibited, and so on. I was stunned. I tried to play it off, but he just kept persisting. I think he thought he was being funny, but I certainly wasn't getting the joke. After another five minutes of this interrogation, I told him it was none of his business because he would never know what it was like to sleep with me. He was so embarrassed he called the waitress and asked for the check. He even gave me money for a cab. What a relief.

—SARAH, 26, DENTAL HYGIENIST

Mind Your Manners

If you're out at a nice restaurant, dressed to kill, but can't find the right fork to save your life, then you're simply out of luck. No matter how well you hide them, there's no escaping bad table manners. If you can't tell a salad fork from a dessert fork, you'll be dead in the waters of most fine-dining establishments. Unless you plan to compensate by taking all your dates for shakes and fries (no forks, no problems), you'll have to brush up on your dining etiquette.

First off, there will be no talking with your mouth full. Men take note, for you are the most frequent offenders. Even if you have the world's wittiest thing to say and you're dying to let your humor flow, put a muzzle on it lest you repulse your date. Nothing spoils an evening faster than spraying your date with semi-chewed potato chunks.

You should also abstain from making any chewing noises or offensive grunts while munching away. The key to becoming a silent diner is to chew slowly and with your mouth firmly shut. That way you won't embarrass your date or disgust neighboring diners.

Utensils are another hot-button issue. Many people are divided on the utensils question, especially when it comes to eating meat on the bone. We're here to tell you that when it comes to the first date, you're better off playing the conservative card. Even if your entree includes a lamb shank or chicken drumstick, you must tackle it with your knife and fork. If this goes against all your moral principles, refrain from ordering the controversial item altogether. And, while eating with your hands may be acceptable at certain restaurants, licking your hands is never permitted. Contrary to what you may have heard, nothing merits being called "finger-lickin'-good" on the first date.

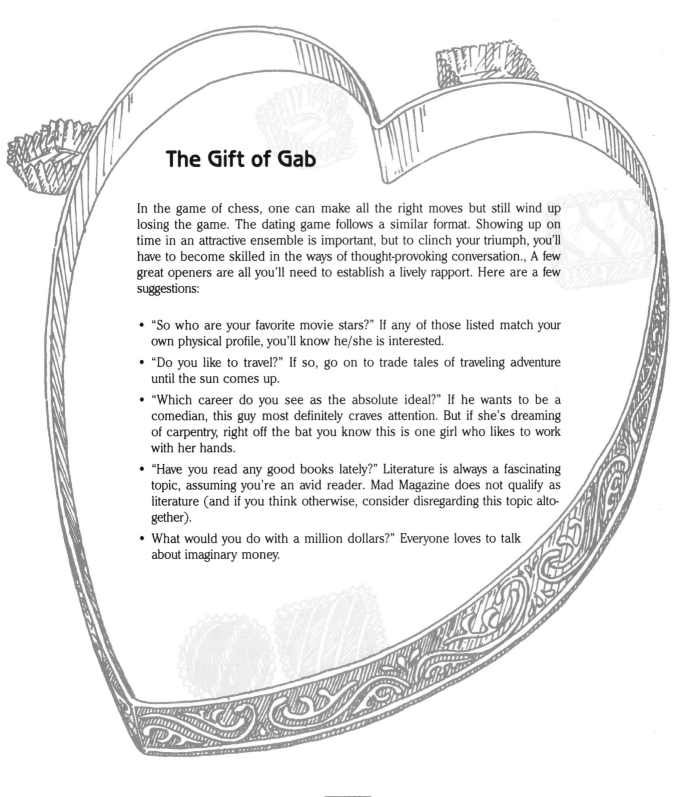

The Gift of Gab

In the game of chess, one can make all the right moves but still wind up losing the game. The dating game follows a similar format. Showing up on time in an attractive ensemble is important, but to clinch your triumph, you'll have to become skilled in the ways of thought-provoking conversation., A few great openers are all you'll need to establish a lively rapport. Here are a few suggestions:

• "So who are your favorite movie stars?" If any of those listed match your own physical profile, you'll know he/she is interested.

• "Do you like to travel?" If so, go on to trade tales of traveling adventure until the sun comes up.

• "Which career do you see as the absolute ideal?" If he wants to be a comedian, this guy most definitely craves attention. But if she's dreaming of carpentry, right off the bat you know this is one girl who likes to work with her hands.

• "Have you read any good books lately?" Literature is always a fascinating topic, assuming you're an avid reader. Mad Magazine does not qualify as literature (and if you think otherwise, consider disregarding this topic altogether).

• What would you do with a million dollars?" Everyone loves to talk about imaginary money.

The Date Doctor Is In

Q: If a woman asks me out, should I still pay if I want to make a good impression?

A: *Many people will tell you that these are the nineties and you don't have to pay if you're asked out. But in my experience, this strategy has a high failure rate. Most women don't appreciate such a fair-minded attitude. On the rare occasions that I have let the woman pay, I found that their interest in me had substantially waned by the second date. So if you want to make a good impression, make sure you can afford it by bringing all your cash and credit, and being free-handed during the date.*

Last but not least, never attempt the long reach on a first date. If you need something on the opposite end of the table, simply ask your date, who will be more than happy to oblige. Leaning over the table is not only awkward, but it is the leading cause of food-related accidents and high dry-cleaning bills.

Pay Your Way

We don't blame you one bit for being a little squeamish about this phase of the dining experience. The question of money never fails to bring out the worst in people, but try as you might, there's no avoiding it on a date. Most people have a hard time gauging when a person truly wants to pay his or her way or if he or she is merely being polite. So here's the drill: If you asked your date out, footing the bill is your responsibility. Should your date decide to chip in, refuse the offer twice. If your date persists, suggest that he or she only pay for the tip or split the bill. If your date continues in his or her attempts to cover all costs, now is the time to acquiesce.

Men's Aside

Guys, you of all people have it the hardest. Many a cheapskate-testing woman will pass through your life. A lot of these women may be perfectly nice, independent-minded people, but they have been taught that a man who doesn't insist on paying is cheap and petty. If you're a staunch defender of the ERA this may be hard for you to accept, but many of the women with whom you go Dutch will never return your calls again. It's a sad fact of life, but then again, no one said that sticking up for your beliefs would be easy.

If you happen to be the one who's protesting your date's expenditure, you must be prepared to pay for the whole dinner. Settling the account is not as easy as it appears. The key to becoming a smooth payer is to simply fork over your credit card without so much as looking at the bill. Checking the bill for mistakes will only disconcert your date and make you look miserly in the process. And what's a few bucks when your reputation is at stake?

Once it's time to calculate the tip, make sure you don't spend more than thirty seconds agonizing over it. Doing so may make you seem unsure of yourself. To speed the calculations along, simply divide the total by ten and multiply by two ($80/10 = $8, $8 x 2 = $16.00). And voila, that there is your tip! Another handy dandy little rule of thumb is to double the tax. Unless your waiter literally spits

in your spaghetti before your very eyes, don't skimp on the gratuity. After all, this is their livelihood we're talking about.

One last bit of advice: should you feel the urge to tell your date how much you've spent on dinner, bite down on your tongue—hard. You should never, ever, ever, reveal the cost of your date. Doing so would be the worst possible mistake you'll ever make.

Saying Good-bye

There are those dates that you wish would never end, and then there are the others. Whichever category your date happens to fall into, a polite exit is a must. That's right, this is not the time to tell your date what you really think of them. Neither is it acceptable to sneak out during the movie or jump into the first available cab as your stunned companion helplessly looks on. And even if you're trying for a happy ending, calling out "Hey! No fair!" when your date gives you the cheek or the pat on the back is also out of bounds. Following our suggestions should make all your good-byes that much sweeter.

To Escort or Not to Escort

There's nothing tougher than deciding whether your date wants to finish the date by saying good-bye in your car or be escorted to her door. When in doubt, the best thing to do is to simply ask.

If you're really anxious to leave, however, you may be able to get away with simply making sure your date gets in her house or apartment safely. Tell her that you'll watch from the car to make sure she gets in all right. Your date will appreciate the effort even if the date didn't go that well.

One thing you should never do is to drop off your date and burn rubber as soon as their feet hit the pavement. Even if you absolutely despised your date, there are better ways of handling the situation.

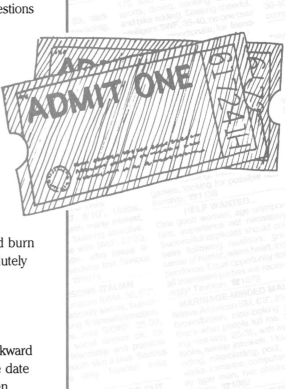

To Kiss or Not to Kiss

The after-date smooch has to be one of the event's most awkward moments. Unless you've already snuck some loving in during the date itself, the romantic ice between you may not yet be broken. When deciding when to kiss someone for the first time, you will have to first decide how you feel about him or her and then try to determine whether or not he or she would be receptive to your advances.

Call You Later?

Even if you had a very unsatisfying date with little or no chemistry, some people will want to end things politely by telling their date that they will call later. This is our advice: Do not tell someone you'll call them unless you really mean it. There's no point in raising someone's hopes when there's absolutely no chance that you'll call. Or, worse yet, if your equally dissatisfied companion takes your words at face value, he or she might be forced to screen all calls for the coming week. So save everyone a lot of trouble—if you're stuck and can't find a nice phrase to tie up the loose ends, just tell your date that you had fun and thank him or her for going out with you. No matter how comfortable it is to end each date with the I'll-Call-You-Later bit, you should abstain from using this phrase unless you absolutely mean it. Try "sweet dreams," or "drive safely." Hey, even "have fun" is better than an ersatz "I'll call you."

On Second Thought

There's nothing more confusing than that hour after your date when you're sitting around wondering what happened. Sometimes mulling the date over in your mind can feel a lot like watching your life pass before your eyes during a train wreck. One minute you're cruising along, sipping a beverage and enjoying the scenery, and the next you're curled up in the fetal position screaming for mommy.

If you end the date feeling more anxious than when you started out, you may be processing some cues and signals that your preoccupied mind did not have time to register while you were on your date. After all, forming all those first-date impressions is hard enough without having to make sense of them all to boot. So if you're feeling a little unsure about your date, don't get down on yourself. You may be just starting to put the pieces together. And what you may have accepted as normal during your date may, upon reflection, begin to appear totally incompatible with your values and lifestyle. Since this is the time during which the fate of most relationships is decided, spend it wisely by using your head.

Kissing Up Quiz

To determine your date's level of attraction to you, take this quiz and you'll find out everything you need to know before putting yourself in humiliation's way by venturing a kiss.

1. Did your date touch you at any point in the date? Yes_____ No_____

2. Did your date compliment your looks? Yes_____ No_____

3. Did you get the feeling your date wanted to see you again?
   Yes_____ No_____

4. Did you get the feeling that your date wanted to prolong the evening?
   Yes_____ No_____

5. Did your date pay a lot of attention to you? Yes_____ No_____

6. Did you and your date have a lot in common? Yes_____ No_____

7. Did your date look happy during the outing? Yes_____ No_____

Scoring:

Five or more yes's is a sure sign that your cohort wants you to plant a big kiss on them. But don't start in with the hands just yet. Anywhere between one and ten nice (by this we mean, not too wet, not too dry, not too hard, and not too soft) kisses should suffice in most instances.

Three or more yes's means that your date may be interested in you. So first test the waters with a small peck on the cheek. If your date looks disappointed, then maybe they were looking for something more. But if your date starts backing up after, or even before, the peck, you may be finished for the evening.

If you scored less than three yes's then your date may not be as receptive to your romantic overtures as you may have hoped. But as nothing is foolproof, you may want to go ahead and ask their permission before trying your luck. Mixed messages have been known to happen, so you may be pleasantly surprised.

Your Date Is Seeing Someone Else

Sometimes we hear something that we just can't register at first. If your date tells you he or she is in a relationship, our natural tendency is to just let it slide. Our desire to not stir up trouble is a natural reflex. So we often end up accepting something negative.

If your date is seeing someone else or several other people, you may have your doubts about that person after the date. After all, if you're looking for a monogamous relationship then you don't need to waste your time on someone who doesn't share your penchant for exclusivity. While you may have let this little bit of information slide during the date, you may want to rethink going out on a second date if what you really want is a committed relationship.

Of course, if a good time is all you're after, this person may just be what the love doctor ordered. The most important thing is that you don't compromise your values for anyone else.

Your Date Is Trying to Hide Something

If your date was uncommunicative, had a hard time looking you in the eye, and avoided answering your question directly, your post-date apprehensions may have merit. Some people hide a fair share of skeletons in the closet, and you'll either feel more interested in the mystery of it all or confused as to what kind of person your date truly is. But don't let curiosity get the best of you. Often, people may be hiding a lot more than you'll ever want to know. When you feel this to be the case, go with your gut and don't pour on the third degree. For all you know, you're scratching at the surface of some recent wounds, and hurting your date in the process. Give them time to trust you, and you'll hear their story.

Now, if you believe that your date is truly hiding some godawful secret, keep away. Who knows, she may be a he in she's clothing or worse. Your intuition is often right, so give that little inner voice a shot at being heard.

Your Date Is Only Interested in One Thing

Actually, depending on whom you talk to, that one thing can be one of three. First, and most popular, is sex. Second is money—always a major bummer. Third, of course, is marriage. If your date is putting on a good show for any one of these three possibilities, you've got some thinking to do. Since we're not here to judge, we'll tell you the truth. Let's start with

money. Many people who fall in love are only too happy to be wanted for their income tax brackets. This way, with the aid of a pre-nup, they can be certain that the object of their affection will never fall out of love. But this is a sad way to start a relationship. Our advice is that you make every attempt not to fall in love with someone who is only into testing your credit limit.

With money and marriage you're in luck. If your date has been sending strong signals in either direction, you need only consider how you feel about these issues to come to a satisfying conclusion. But don't be too quick to thumb your nose at either. After all, what in the world is so wrong with either an hour of fun or a lifetime of happiness? If, upon reflection, thoughts of love (long-term or otherwise) still leave you cold, you're better off calling the whole thing off.

Your Date Is Very Argumentative

Confrontation is not for everybody. Those of us who run like the Road Runner from the conflict coyote may not always see an argumentative person for who they are during the date. But if you're sitting around wondering why when you expressed your fondness for Andrew Lloyd Webber your date, an admitted musicals-devotee, launched into an anti-*Phantom of the Opera* tirade, you're probably suffering from a delayed reaction. This is not uncommon for most peace-loving people. Trying to make the date go as smoothly as possible, most people react to a contrarian by simply working twice as hard to keep everything in sync. If, in hindsight, you realize that what you're up against is a conflict-thriving individual, your next move should be to save yourself the nerve damage and call it quits.

Your Date Expressed Views You Can't Respect

He or she may have made all the right moves and sent your heart into the outer reaches of the pitter-patter zone, but once you get home something crosses your mind that turns your smile upside down. One of your date's offhand remarks is now making you cringe, and you're left to wonder whether they really meant it the way it sounded or if it's a simple miscommunication. If you can't figure it out for the life of you, the best thing to do is to broach the issue again on the second date. If, on the other hand, you're fairly certain that you and your date are at odds on the issue at hand, you're better off moving on—make no mistake about it.

The Date Doctor Is In

Q: How do you politely invite someone into your house after a great date?

A: *The key here is honesty. In any potentially intimate situation, people's B.S. detectors are on super sensitive. So try to keep cheesy lines at bay. What you want to do is tell your date what a pleasant time you're having being with them and that you would like to prolong the evening. Then simply ask them if they'd enjoy hanging out and talking inside. That's all there is to it.*

Chapter 7

Better Safe
Than Sorry

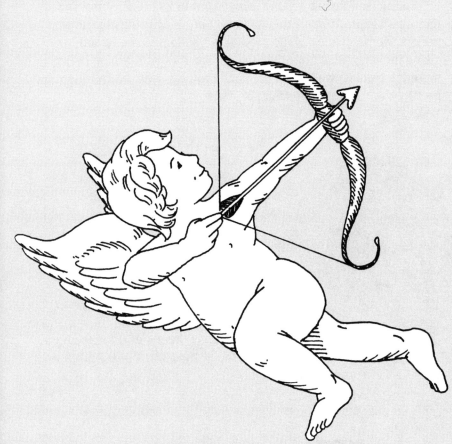

Throughout this book we have stressed the importance of having fun and relaxing during your dates. We've discussed the joys of meeting new people, engaging in scintillating conversation, and experiencing endless new activities. Now we turn our attention to a more serious side of dating—a side that most people would rather not deal with. The issue of safety is an important one and should never be dismissed in the name of having a good time.

We've all heard the horror stories of dates gone very bad. The fact of the matter is that, unless you subscribe to the "stranger danger" philosophy, many of your dates will be virtual strangers. Of course, everyone is not out to get you, and there's no need to get so hung up on the risks that you forgo your love life. But while the last thing we want is to overwhelm you with paranoid fears, you should become aware of the hazardous side of dating.

When it comes to keeping yourself out of trouble, the key word is "precaution." Taking steps to minimize your risk of encountering danger is smart. Avoiding meeting new people or going outside after dark is overly cautious, while picking up random strangers and taking them home is downright dangerous. As with anything in life, there are gradations of safety measures you can take. So be smart, be savvy, and, most importantly, be alert.

The Screening Process

Smart singles know the importance of running background checks on their admirers. That doesn't mean you should go out and spend hundreds of dollars on a private investigator every time you meet someone new. What it does mean is that you'll have to become a dating sleuth who hunts out the facts for yourself.

There are many ways to get the goods on someone without coming off like a paranoid schizophrenic. All it takes is some initiative and a little know-how.

Be Inquisitive

When you first meet someone new, make a pointed effort to grill them about their background. Instead of allowing your mind to wander as the person drones on in response, make a mental note of the answers. When talking to this person over the phone, ask the same questions again to see whether there are any holes in his or her stories.

If you should discover any discrepancies, the best thing to do is to steer clear. Because if your date-to-be can't so much as keep the name of his or her hometown straight, then he or she is hiding something you want no part of. At this point you should inform this person that you will have to think about going on the date. Wait several days before calling back with a good excuse—you're either too busy or getting back together with your ex. Who knows what kind of person you're dealing with here. This may not be someone you want to upset. So play by the rules and let them down as gently as possible.

Using Connections

Another good way to scope out the truth on your new beau/belle is to question his or her friends and acquaintances. Ask your date about setting up an outing with his or her friends. Once everyone is assembled, use the opportunity to subtly ask these people about your date. His or her job, personal history, and family life are all fair game. If their answers match your date's, you can breathe easier. If your beloved's friends are as clueless as you are, you may have to keep digging.

Should your date refuse your request to meet his/her friends, you may want to ask about his or her reasons. If your date simply has no friends to speak of, think twice before agreeing to a meeting. A person without close friends or associations can be classified in the high-risk group. Unless they've just moved from out of town—and have proof in the form of a driver's license—people with little or no close ties are cause for concern.

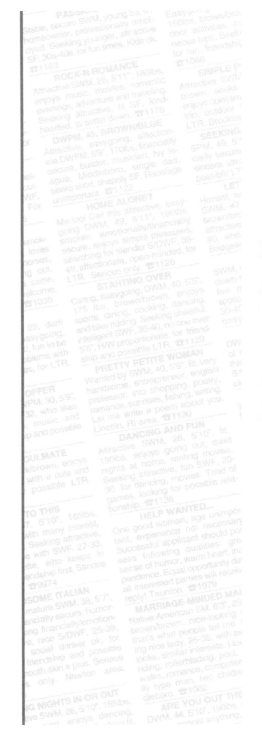

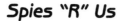
Spies "R" Us

While we don't condone stalking as a means of getting closer to someone, you can, on occasion, try to verify your date's identity via surveillance. This measure should only be taken if you are harboring major suspicions as to who your date really is. Sometimes it's as easy as popping into an office and inviting him or her out to lunch.

When you first meet your date, make sure you get a business card. Then, once you're ready to make your move, stop by his or her office building and announce your presence. If he or she is snugly tucked away behind a desk, you can say you were in the area and wanted an impromptu lunch. If your potential date is not where he or she is supposed to be, and never was, then all bets are automatically off.

Do Not Date These People

Liars and frauds are not the only types worth watching out for. The truth is that most potentially toxic personalities are forthright and honest about everything save the flaws in their character. But as no one can hide their nature for long, it is up to you to keep your eyes peeled for the true colors. Forget about concentrating on the positive—anyone can lay on the charm whenever they so desire. Whether it's as early as the first date or as late as the twentieth, the telltale warning signals will eventually trickle through. Those who value their peace of mind should avoid consorting with people matching the following descriptions at all costs.

The Short Fuse

Weeding out short-tempered suitors can be the easiest task of all. In fact, many who suffer from this lack of self-restraint will admit the flaw as freely as they fess up to biting their fingernails. But hot-tempered partners are far more dangerous than messy cuticles. In the heat of the moment, they believe that they are not responsible for their words and deeds, which can often be quite violent.

Signs that your date's temper is prone to flare-ups are snappishness, a tendency to overreact, extreme impatience, and obvious displays of temper such as yelling and/or physical aggression. Quick-tempered people belong in anger management seminars, not in relationships.

> *Chris and I met in college. Our relationship had gone on for months before I realized how mean he could be. If we weren't getting along, he'd fly off the handle and say really hurtful things or put me down in front of his friends. I broke up with him, but we ended up getting back together. I thought he'd changed, so we moved in together and got engaged. I was so afraid of loneliness that I didn't do anything the first time he hit me. I thought it was okay, because it seemed as though he hadn't meant to hurt me. But then he did it again, and this time he used his fist. I never thought that people from good families could act this way. After he refused to go to counseling, I canceled the wedding. I've been on my own for over a year now. A few months ago, I met someone who is kind, considerate and makes me happy, yet I'm still somewhat leery. Women have to learn that men with bad tempers have no reason to change as long as their girlfriends accept their behavior.*

—LISSA, 27, MORTGAGE BROKER

The Sexual Predator

When two people find each other irresistible, innuendo-charged banter is bound to ensue. Sometimes, neither can wait to be alone and both break out in a public display of affection. As long as this breach of etiquette is committed by two consenting adults, all is right with the world and your love life. If, on the other hand, your date is touching you in what you deem to be all the wrong places, you have a problem on your hands.

Sexual aggressiveness isn't always a sign of a potential rapist. But if you're feeling uncomfortable with your companion's physical advances, and find that their persistence is deterred by neither your

What's Your Sign? Romance According to the Zodiac

Libra
Libras are drawn to beauty, whatever its form. The only thing they enjoy as much as beauty is harmony. Even when a relationship has gone sour, a Libra hesitates to be the one who ends it. They can't stand hurting anyone's feelings; emotional rawness is one of those ugly realities that they don't like to see. As a result, they may remain in a relationship longer than they should just because disharmony is so distasteful. Libras seek harmony because in their heart they know that enlightenment lies at the calm dead center of the storm.

nonverbal hints nor your outright admonitions, chances are high that you're dealing with a dangerous person who is likely to believe that while your lips are saying "no," your eyes are saying "yes." Run, don't walk, away from this person.

The Green-Eyed Monster

In the first bloom of romance, signs of a possessive nature can be mistaken for ardor. It's all too tempting to overlook the jealousy for the assurances of affection that it represents. The reality, however, is something altogether different. Possessiveness is more a sign of low self-esteem and an inability to trust than it is of undying devotion. In the long run, jealous lovers invariably ruin any chance of a happy union. Whether their possessiveness will manifest itself in violence is hard to tell. However, it's safe to say that this is one dénouement you don't want to stick around for.

There is one sure way to spot a jealous streak in your dates. Watch how they react to your opposite-sex friends and acquaintances. When they come upon you chatting it up with an attractive stranger, check their reaction. If they're clenching their jaw, acting tense, and then giving you the third degree on the way home, make this date your last.

The Power-Tripper

The golden age of the sensitive man has ushered in a nostalgia for the John Waynes of yesteryear. Many women are tired of going Dutch, doing all the driving, and making all the arrangements. A female's desire to kick back and let someone take care of her is understandable, as is her wish to be pursued instead of doing all the wooing herself. Yet it is precisely this type of attitude that can blind women to the domineering male.

Overly dominant male personalities are happy to take all the responsibility for the romance. To them a woman is little more than an object. They will bombard her with phone calls, fancy dinners, and gifts. They will open all the doors, pull out all the chairs, and take care of all the coats. They will do all of this with the

vengeance of a Stepford boyfriend, until there is a difference of opinion. Then and only then will Dr. Jekyll finally step aside to reveal the Mr. Hyde who believes that he's earned the right to think and make decisions for you. While not all gents are monsters-in-hiding, men who pursue women so forcefully should be held suspect.

The Barbarian

Common sense dictates that violent people are not relationship material. Unreasonable, frightening and altogether toxic, the pugilistic contingent is best left to Don King. Intellectually, everybody knows this to be true. Why then do so many women wind up in the position of battered wife/girlfriend? Low self-esteem is only one explanation.

The fact is that many women don't recognize the warning signals until it is too late. Bar-brawling, hurting small animals, and putting their fists through walls are obvious signs of a dangerous personality. But, sadly, men prone to violence know how to hide their dark side and can appear very charismatic in social situations. Often, it is not until time has passed that you can figure out exactly who you're dealing with. Trust your instincts. If you so much as suspect that you're dealing with a potentially hazardous personality, cut the romance short before you get too involved.

When I first met my ex-husband, Andy, I thought he was the perfect man. I was only eighteen and he was an attractive professional boxer who lavished me with gifts and attention. Although he fought for a living, I never thought that he would ever raise his hand to me. So after dating for five months, we got married. As it turned out, I was wrong to jump into the marriage so soon. While we had one beautiful daughter, my husband's temper was out of control. He began to hit me. Whenever I threatened to leave, he would undergo a complete turnaround. But it never did last. Eventually, he would hit me again. Finally, I left. Since we have a daughter together, I am still in contact with him. It's not easy, I have had to get restraining

Safe Dating Zones

The one sure-fire way to avoid all manner of mischief is to meet in public places. The more people you have around you, the less chance you'll have of encountering any real danger.

Restaurants, movie theaters, and bars are ideally suited for your plans. Choose an establishment you've been to before and suggest that you meet your date there. Once you get there, park your car in a well-lit area close to the entrance.

When you're finished with your date, make your exit alone. If your date tries to follow you to your car, tell them that you will be fine on your own—something along the lines of, "Oh, you don't need to help little old me. That's what this here pepper spray is for." If they still want to accompany you, chances are they're just in it for the good-night kiss. You'll have to decide how to proceed from here on out.

orders against him for threatening my life, and I believe he had someone slash the tires of my car. His boxing career was also undermined by his temper—when he got his shot at the title, he was reprimanded for punching his opponent in the groin. Had I been more mature at the outset of this relationship and taken some time to get to know this man better, I would not have married him.

—MARIANNA, 29, ATTORNEY

Precautionary Measures

Feeling unsafe can make us feel small. It can stop us in our tracks and prevent us from fully enjoying our lives. When thinking about all the dangers posed by the world at large, it's easy to understand why so many people develop irrational fears. Since we can counteract most hazards by learning how to deal with them, there is no excuse for living in fear. Preparation is key to feeling powerful and in control.

While signing up for a self-defense class, meeting in public places, and verifying the safety of your destination may seem like one hassle after another, taking these steps will ensure that your date is safe and worry-free. So if a little effort is all that's standing between you and your peace of mind, why not start taking control right now?

Developing Your Sixth Sense

One of the crucial factors in keeping you from harm's way is your ability to spot signs of impending danger. Intuition is another term for this sixth sense, and we all have our fair share of it, regardless of whether we use it or not.

Much like ESP, a keen intuition can help you study your surroundings with more accuracy and precision. Most people are trained to use reason and logic to form perceptions and solve problems. But your emotions, or what is often called your gut instinct, can tell you much more about any situation than you ever thought possible.

Where to Strengthen Yourself

Whether or not you choose to go so far as to enroll in a basic self-defense class, it's always a good idea to be fit and strong. Working with a personal trainer at your local gym can help you work your muscles evenly and develop your strength, agility, and reflexes—all of which will make you feel much more confident in safety or in danger. Here are some of the best gyms and what they offer.

YMCA
http://www.ymca.net

So much more than just a great Village People tune, the YMCAs bills itself "the largest nonprofit community service organization in America," serving 16 million men, women and children. They go far beyond barbells and treadmills, offering a wide array of facilities, fitness classes ranging from step aerobics to tae kwon do, community outreach programs, and more. they pride themselves on their focus on values and community, and have a policy of not turning anyone away for inability to pay. Joining your neighborhood Y can make you feel more like a part of your community, and that's not such a bad thing either. Visit their website to find a Y near you.

World Gym
http://www.worldgym.com

If you're looking to pump yourself up, World Gym is a good place to start. Founded by a renowned bodybuilder, it has a fairly macho image as primarily a bodybuilding gym.

The Fitness Zone Gyms Locator
http://www.fitnesszone.com/

If you haven't found anything satisfactory yet, here's a great website that will surely solve your problems. FitnessZone's Gym Locator lists by region over 13,000 U.S. gyms and health clubs.

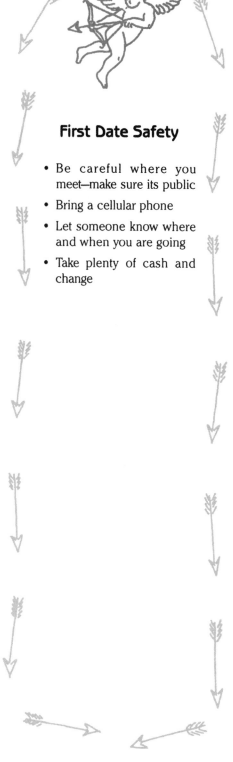

First Date Safety

- Be careful where you meet—make sure its public
- Bring a cellular phone
- Let someone know where and when you are going
- Take plenty of cash and change

Four Steps to Harnessing Your Intuitive Awareness

1. **Be Open to New Sensations.**

   The ability to remain open to new ideas and impressions is key to self-preservation. All too often we tend to become rigid and inflexible in our beliefs. But that is exactly the tendency you want to avoid. The best way to keep your mind expanded and open to new concepts is to avoid falling into a routine for any extended period of time. Celebrate the extraordinary by inviting new events, people, and sensations into your life. The best way to do that is to try something new every day, whether it be driving a different route to your office or switching your brand of tea. Breaking your routine will keep your mind fresh and alert.

2. **Identify Your Feelings.**

   When you're in a difficult situation and are having a hard time determining exactly how you feel, excuse yourself and find a quiet area where you can think about your feelings. Take deep breaths and clear your mind. Try to think of empty space as you bring your focus slowly on your feelings. Then, begin assigning words to your feelings, like "scared," "excited," or "angry." Once you have a vocabulary of feelings, you can sort them out and make a more informed decision.

3. **Trust Your Instincts.**

   It is important for you not to doubt yourself when you have a premonition or a strange idea. There is a reason behind every thought or fear. So if you find yourself in a situation that makes you feel strange or uncomfortable, make sure you listen to your instinct.

4. **Act with Confidence.**

   Following through is an important step to harnessing your intuitive powers. Unless you take action and act on your instincts, you will never be able to measure their accuracy. But taking decisive steps to avoid conflict can be difficult, especially if you're not sure what you feel. So when in doubt, take the plunge and make your escape. And if it turns out that your instincts were off, you'll be able to learn from your mistakes.

Bring a Cellular

A cellular phone is a great way to signal someone for help. If you want to get out of a situation fast, then your trusty phone may end up being your closest ally. Before heading out for your date, make sure your phone is fully charged and preprogrammed to speed-dial the police or a trusted friend. That way you can get your message across in a hurry when you don't have a minute to waste.

Leave a Trail of Bread Crumbs

When Hansel and Gretel got into hot water in the forest, a trail of bread crumbs led them to safety, and it can do the same for you. But while bread crumbs will most likely fall prey to the pigeon population or the whim of the wind, you should try telling someone close to you where you will be going. Give your trusted friend the address and name of your destination, as well as a time when you will be expected to return. If anything unusual happens, you will have someone waiting in the wings to save you. But don't shirk your responsibility to call. If you're having a great time and run late, make sure to inform your friend lest they stay up all night and worry—or worse yet, sic the authorities on your free-wheelin' fanny.

Take Plenty of Cash and Change

When accepting an invitation for a date, many people expect to be paid for and as a result neglect to bring emergency cash. Believe you us, there is nothing more unfortunate than getting stuck in a bad date situation without so much as a ten spot to call your own. What if you need to duck out in a hurry? Nothing beats cash money when hailing a cab. Even a phone card is a hassle compared to the quick and easy spare change method of pay phone access, if you have yet to invest in the wireless variety. Do not rely on credit or ATM cards to lead you safely home. You never know if some backward company doesn't accept credit cards or when a cash machine will be out of order.

Transport Yourself

Yes, we know, we've made mention of this before, but driving your own car cannot be stressed enough. While having someone pick you up on your first date may sound convenient, you may want to rethink that plan. Your safest course of action is to take your own car to meet your date. If you don't happen to own a car, or if it's in the shop, make alternate arrangements. You can borrow a friend's, ask for a ride from someone close to you, or take public transport. The last thing you want to do is rely on someone you barely know to get you home. Take matters into your own hands and find your own way.

Look Smart

While no one wants to be told what to wear, you should reconsider any outfit that is too revealing or suggestive. Appropriate attire will not only go a long way towards making the right first date impression, but it will also keep you from sending any mixed signals. The way we dress has a tendency to affect our personality. If your dress is prim and proper, your attitude will be as well. Needless to say, this cautious mindset is the best way to enter into a first date.

Defense Mechanisms

Once in a while, we all have to think about matters of self-defense. Whether it's because someone you know has been mugged, or there's a maniac on the loose in your neighborhood, or even if you yourself have been caught in a life-threatening situation, defending your life is an issue that cannot be denied for long.

The Fast Getaway

If you're in an uncomfortable or even dangerous situation, you'll have to keep calm and collected. There's no reason to bust out the cell phone and dial 911 as soon as you feel a little unsafe. You may actually push your date into a threatening action or insult someone who isn't at all dangerous. Take the following advice, and make your exit as smooth as possible.

1. **Claim to be sick**
   If you're in an uncomfortable situation and can't find a way out, just feign illness. Pretend that you have horrible stomach cramps, but don't overdo it. Be convincing, and then beat it.

2. **Suggest that someone is waiting for you**
   When in doubt, make sure that your date believes that someone is awaiting your arrival and will alert the police if you don't show. This way, the chances of them trying anything funny drastically decrease. So even before your date begins, mention that you have to meet someone back at your house at a certain time. Even if your date is just boring, this excuse will help you get away before you fall asleep.

3. **Alert someone**
   If the situation becomes unmanageable, it's wise to inform someone of your predicament. Anyone from a waitress to a gas attendant will do. You can even tell them to notify the police if things are getting out of hand.

4. **Run like the wind, grasshopper**
   If your date has got you thoroughly freaked out, pull the old ditcheroo. Say you need to go to the bathroom and beat a hasty retreat out the back exit.

Fortunately, thinking about self-defense is also the first step to discouraging unbecoming behavior on the part of your date. You'll gain an air of confidence that will deter any unwelcome advances. And don't worry, even the most petite of people can take action to keep themselves from harm's way. And while nothing replaces a standard self-defense course, some of the following tips should, at the very least, start you thinking about your safety.

Choose Your Weapon

The most effective weapons may not be the ones we would normally think of during nonviolent situations. Sitting around playing Scattergories in the living room, weapons that start with "K" would usually yield the same answer from all Scattergories parties—you guessed it, knife. However, the most powerful means of protection may actually be your everyday household items, such as keys or knitting needles (in keeping with the Scattergories "K" analogy). The most important thing to remember about protecting yourself with a weapon is to choose something that can be easily transported and that you use every day. That way you will never be without some form of defense, whether you're on a date or just going about your everyday business.

Keys

Most people use keys on a daily basis. Whether it be walking to your car or walking in your house, keys are a permanent fixture in everyone's lives. That is why using keys to defend yourself is so practical. Whatever your situation, you can bring your keys to your defense. Scratching someone or poking at someone with your keys should let them know, in no uncertain terms, that you're no sitting duck. In fact, feel free to go right for the eyes. There's no reason to be squeamish—after all, it's your life we're talking about.

Feet

Whether you're wearing stiletto heels or flats, you can use your feet to really kick up a storm. If grabbed from behind, your best recourse is to stomp your heel right into the attacker's foot. Bear down as hard you can, and when they reach down on impulse to protect their feet, you can run like mad. Use this opportunity of freedom wisely by running into a crowded zone.

Fingers

Poking someone in the eye may be unpleasant, but sometimes it may be your only chance. If you're left without any protection, you'll always have your fingers to protect you. But make sure to take aim and fire quickly. Any hesitation may cost you.

Teeth

A good bite can disarm the most aggressive date rapist. If someone grabs you from the back and wraps their arm around your neck, you're in the perfect position to give them a hefty bite. Just open your mouth wide and dig deep. They will most likely loosen their grip, and that's your cue to get the hell out of there.

Voice

A powerful voice can be all it takes to show someone that you mean business. If you're approached in a hostile or violent manner, back off slightly and say "no" in your most authoritative voice. Because attackers look for easy targets, a strong voice and a determined stance may stop them in their tracks.

Stride

Most policemen will tell you that most victims fit a certain profile. The classic victim posture involves a slow, relaxed gait with the head and eyes pointing directly to the ground. Make sure that you don't fit the bill by keeping your posture erect and your stride determined and brisk.

Whistle

Strapping a whistle onto your key chain or a necklace can deter an attacker. It's relatively small, so it's easy to hide. And with the regulation rape whistle, you can make enough noise to wake up an entire neighborhood. But don't abuse your whistling privileges. They are only to be used in a dire emergency.

Pepper Spray

Now that Mace is illegal in so many states, you'll have to rely on pepper spray to temporarily blindside your attacker. Since pepper spray has also been banned in certain parts of the country, you should check with your local police station to see where the authorities stand on this issue in your neck of the

Unsafe Dating Zones

Any place where you will be out of sight is strictly off limits for the mysterious first date. Again, it's best not to get into the car with your first date regardless of where you two choose to go. Also, avoid straying from the beaten path at all costs. If your date suggests going to a cabin in the woods or driving out to some unknown destination, simply refuse to go. Often your companion will want to surprise you with a destination. Chances are their surprises are harmless, but we still suggest you stick to the safe side by claiming that you hate surprises. If he or she can't understand your need to feel safe, than maybe your date's first priority is not your security.

woods. If used properly, a good splash of this stuff can impair your attacker's motor functions, opening up a sizable escape hatch. But make sure to keep your spray in your purse or jacket pocket where you have quick access to it. You should also try to avoid spraying into the wind, since this will most likely cause your strategy to backfire.

A Word About Guns and Knives

The reason we would not recommend the use of guns or knives is mainly because they can be turned against you if you're not careful. For instance, if you're wielding a knife and are up against someone stronger and more skilled at fighting (of course, we're assuming you didn't major in knife throwing in college), you are at great risk of being disarmed. Of course, there's a lower chance of this happening with a gun. But if you're not trained in the proper use of firearms, a gun can also turn on you. It can be wrestled out of your hands or go off at the wrong time. If you carry a gun, you must be ready to use it.

Thinking Fast

Sharpening your reflexes will serve you well in any situation. Oftentimes, it's not how clever you are but how fast you think that determines your success. This rule holds true for protecting yourself during a date.

If you panic, your mind automatically begins to cloud over, obstructing your ability to make good decisions. The key to staying on the ball is to avoid the "what if" frame of mind. If you start thinking the worst about the future, you will divert your concentration from where you need it most—the present. So if by some horrible chance you find yourself having to fend for your life, thinking positively and constructively will help you make effective choices that can save your life.

Self-Defense 101

The basics of self-defense are as follows: never be caught off guard and use anything you can to maim your attacker. While we're

not going to try and instruct you on how to deliver death kicks to the groin or the best way to perform lethal combat combinations, a self-defense course can equip you with some simple and amazingly effective self-preservation skills.

Self-defense classes are your best bet if you're looking for a crash course in disarming potential assailants. But any exercise that physically empowers you is also worth checking into. Kickboxing, karate, judo, tai-chi, take your pick, they're all designed to help you defend yourself.

Date Rape Prevention Tactics

Date rape is not an issue anyone should approach lightly. Many women will at some point be confronted with this issue, whether it happens to them or to a friend. But too many women think that date rape is still something that only happens to other people. While this attitude may help you sleep better at night, it won't prepare you to defend yourself.

The most common misconception about date rape is that the rapist has to fit a certain physical profile. So whatever picture you have of the typical date rapist, you can bet that few rapists will meet those standards. Actually, a date rapist could be anyone. It could be a guy wearing a business suit, and it could even be your next door neighbor. The problem is you'll never know who it is until it happens. Take comfort in the fact that you don't have to be a victim; you can protect yourself from attack.

Watch the Booze

Getting too drunk on your date is not only unattractive, it can also weaken your defenses and cloud your judgment. The majority of date rape cases involve alcohol, either when one or both people had been drinking. Lower the odds by eliminating drinking from your date. You can also drink non-alcoholic beer and other beverages to quench your thirst.

Should your date have consumed too much alcohol, do not prolong the date. You should also avoid telling your date to stop drinking. He or she will only become upset and defensive at being told what to do. Simply excuse yourself and go home—alone.

Fitness Centers

Bally Total Fitness
http://www.ballyfitness.com
Bally Total Fitness is one of the largest commercial health club chains in the country, offering aerobic programs, personal trainers, and sophisticated cardiovascular and strength training equipment.

24 Hour Fitness
http://www.24hourfitness.com/
Though not as widespread as some of the other chains mentioned here, 24 Hour Fitness is very big west of the Mississippi. Like the Y, they pride themselves on being accessible to all kinds of people, regardless of age, background, and fitness level. And as the name implies, they're open all the time—24 hours a day, seven days a week.

Go Public

Moonlight drives and walks on the beach are prime areas for date rape incidents. The problem is that you don't know whether your date is just trying to be romantic or looking to set the trap. Just to be safe, stay near others and don't wander off into any secluded locales. You can have many long walks and scenic drives once you've gotten to know each other better.

Skip the Nightcaps

No matter how attracted you are to someone, unless you are well-acquainted with his family and friends, and it is your intention to have sex, avoid going into his apartment or taking him into yours unchaperoned. While you may feel the heady excitement of being with someone you like for the first time, you just never know what's waiting for you behind closed doors—especially on the first date. The most perfect gentleman can just be putting on an act to lure you into his chambers, whereupon he will turn into a monster in a split second. So never give your dates the opportunity to show their dark side.

The Monthly Friend or the VD Defense

If you find yourself in a situation where your date will simply not listen to reason or the word "no," your most effective recourse is to claim that you're only stalling until you've stopped menstruating or until the doctors finish treating your herpes or crabs. In a high percentage of date rape attempts, these types of excuses proved effective in stopping date rapists in their tracks. Remember, it doesn't matter what you say to get away because chances are that you'll never see this person again.

Stressing the Legal Ramifications

Sometimes a good kick in the pants is all it takes, and other times you'll have to pull out the heavy artillery. Screaming "no" over and over is not going to get you out of a bad situation. But if

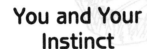

You and Your Instinct

One night I was out with a guy from school. I had met him on the quad; he was cute and seemed nice enough. He met me at my dorm and told me he had picked out a great restaurant for us to try. Since I didn't know him that well, I suggested that we go to my friend's party first. When we got there, he refused to talk to anyone, and when I asked him about school, he wouldn't give me any straight answers. Right when we were about to leave, he mentioned something about college kids being very annoying. But then I laughed and told him that he was a college student also. Then, when he mumbled "whatever," I got this strong feeling that this was a case of mistaken identity. I decided that maybe it wasn't such a good idea to go out with him. And I told him to go ahead without me, claiming to have a stomachache. It was a good thing I did that, because two weeks later I read a police report about a man matching his description who was arrested for indecent exposure. I'm not saying it was him for sure, but I was glad I chose to listen to my instinct nonetheless.

—LIZA, 28, CIVIL ENGINEER

you calmly explain that what your date is about to do is illegal and he will be prosecuted, your date will most likely stop. Because date rape happens in the heat of the moment, most people don't think about what they've done until it's too late. Reminding him in advance can help your date see that what he is doing is punishable by law.

Other Dating Calamities

While date rape is one of the most serious crimes that can be committed on a date, you should be aware of and prepared for other forms of abuse as well. It is unfortunate that dating and danger may sometimes go hand in hand. But if you keep a sharp eye out for trouble, you can make dating the fun and exciting experience that it deserves to be.

Stranded at the Drive-In

If you should be out with someone who is obnoxious enough to leave you stranded somewhere, you should immediately try to locate a phone. This is where a cellular phone or spare change would come in very handy.

Should your date threaten to leave you in the lurch during an argument, do not try to pacify the ruffian. Make your own arrangements to get home immediately. Because if your date is cruel enough to leave you on the side of the road, you just don't know what else they're capable of doing. So leave the situation and then figure out what to do next.

If Someone Hits You

Hitting someone is never acceptable. Should your date even lightly hit you, get away from him as soon as possible. Express your anger gently and inform him that his behavior is unacceptable. Never try to rationalize the behavior by accepting the blame for the situation. No matter what you said or did, no one has the right to hit you. So cut your losses and get home on the double.

Dealing with Verbal Abuse

There are times when words can hurt more than anything. Some people have a habit of being verbally abusive even around people they hardly know. It can be a power game or an attempt to make you feel bad about yourself. But whatever your date's reasons are, you should not take any form of verbal abuse, however slight. If your date insults you or in any way makes you feel less than perfect, that's your cue to get out of that date and move on to better things.

Never Fear

If, after reading this chapter, you're ready to sign up for the cocoon lifestyle and sever all ties with the outside world, you've read too much into it. In all likelihood, your dating career will proceed without incident and you may never get the chance to put your self-defense skills to the test. But isn't it better to err on the side of caution where safety is concerned?

Think of this chapter as drivers' ed for daters. Just as you can't always count on other drivers to stay out of your way, you can't count on your companions to protect you. It's about being a defensive dater and taking personal responsibility for your own safety. Hopefully, you are coming away with an awareness of the potential hazards and the means to avoid them. There's no reason to panic, indulge any latent paranoia, or cancel your plans—as long as you understand that you're in full control of your dating destiny, you've got nothing to fear.

Chapter 8
Sex, Love, and Intimacy

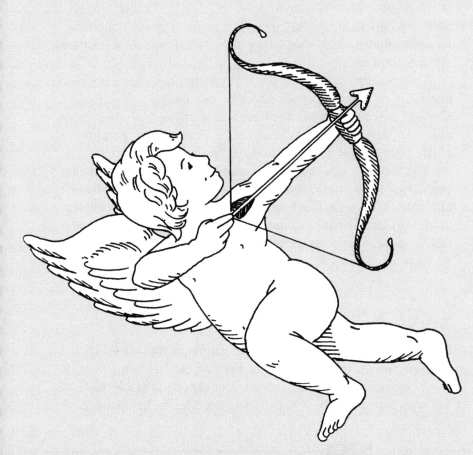

The Beatles clearly hit a chord when they said "All you need is love." Many people are still quick to second that motion, claiming that love makes the world go round. According to the prevailing wisdom, love is the only thing that keeps us from taking a leap right off the Golden Gate Bridge. And since billions of people can't be wrong, then love must really be all it's cracked up to be. Yet the real question still remains unanswered: How can we find and keep true love in our lives?

Philosophers have been on the horns of this very dilemma for centuries. Scientists have even tried to pin down this powerful emotion to a series of chemical reactions in our bodies. But to this day no one has ever been able to bottle or explain the concept of love. Simply put: Love is magical and, as a result, defies all attempts at logic and explanation.

But what about sex? It seems like a much easier concept to explain away. Or is it? Ask ten random friends what sex means to them, and you're likely to come up with ten different answers. Some people believe sex is a dangerous weapon, others believe it to be a form of procreation, and still more just see it as a very good time. So what's the answer? What is sex, what is lust, and how are they different from love?

The relationship between sex and love has always been a complicated one. Take the gender issue, for example. Since the beginning of time, men and women have waged private and not-so-private wars over this very issue. When to do it, how to do it, and how often; these are just some of the struggles surrounding sex.

The bottom line is that no one should ever feel bad about being befuddled by the issue of sex. Sometimes it can take years to figure out where to draw the line between physical and emotional intimacy. That's why this section is so important. Because it is only when you realize what love and sex mean to you that you can begin to form strong relationships that can bring you happiness in the years to come.

Solving The Mystery Of Love

Crush, lust, admiration, respect. Love can mean different things to different people. The filial love you feel for your family, for example, is very different from the passionate, Eros-Greek-god-of-love feelings you have for your mate. You can love your friends, but that sort of platonic affection is much different from what you feel for your boyfriend or girlfriend.

Yet some maintain that there is no difference, that all forms of love spring from the same human desire to connect with another being. And while this may be true, how can you determine that what you feel is love and not something else, like sexual attraction?

And what if you happen to find someone you're in love with but decide to ignore your feelings because the timing is off? Does true love only come around once, or can it happen many times throughout one's life? Is there really such a thing as love at first sight, or can you only fall in love with someone you've known for a long time? There are a million questions to answer, so let's get started.

What's the Difference Between a Crush and True Love?

Crushes usually occur when you first meet someone and feel a special connection. Most are based on sexual chemistry and are accompanied by a rapid heartbeat, sweaty palms, and for an unfortunate few, drooling. A crush has more to do with lust and infatuation than with enduring love. It could stem from both a physical and a mental attraction.

The main difference between crushes and love is that crushes often happen when there is little chance of forming a relationship. These types of crushes are a safe way to explore your feelings for someone who you may think is unattainable. But sometimes the strongest variety of crushes occur when the person is not completely outside one's reach. These can closely resemble love, and if your feelings don't fizzle after you've snagged the object of your crush, they can lead to love.

Can You Fall in Love with Someone You Don't Know?

Yes, you can. But whether you can have a relationship is another matter altogether. Usually, this type of love involves a fantasy. The person who falls in love projects his or her feelings and ideas of happiness onto the love interest. And since a fantasy can often be as strong as any true-life situation, love in these types of scenarios is not out of the question. But be careful. Should you meet that person and they turn out to be very different from the person you imagined,

What's Your Sign? Romance According to the Zodiac

Scorpio

You don't know the meaning of the word intensity unless you've been involved with a Scorpio. No other sign brings such raw power to romance. The rawness probably isn't something you understand or even like very much, but there's no question that it's intricately woven through the fabric of your relationship.

The odd part is that you're never quite sure how the intensity is going to manifest: jealousy, fury, endless questions, or unbridled passion. Sometimes, the intensity doesn't have anything to do with the relationship, but with the personal dramas in the Scorpio's life. So don't try to figure it out. If you're in for the long haul, then accept your Scorpio the way he or she is. If you're not in for the long haul, then hit the road.

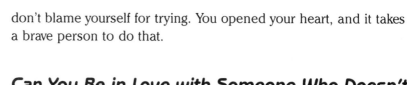
don't blame yourself for trying. You opened your heart, and it takes a brave person to do that.

Can You Be in Love with Someone Who Doesn't Love You?

Unrequited love is very common. And while the nineteenth century poets may have made it sound romantic, the problem with this situation is that it can quickly turn into an obsession if you're not careful. You see, most people are programmed to want what they cannot have. So by simply being denied someone's love, they form feelings of attachment, which can turn into obsession if left uncontrolled.

Another problem with love not reciprocated is that it can quickly become more of a challenge than a real emotion. Being rejected can rob someone of their ego, and in turn, this person may try to prove that he or she is worthy of love. Seeking to win the love that was denied can then become almost like a game, and real love is never about playing games. On the other hand, if you feel strongly attached to someone because you respect and admire who they are, you may actually be in love. So assess your situation carefully and put your feelings to the test.

Is There Such a Thing as Love at First Sight?

Some people are true believers in this phenomenon. These are usually the ones whose love at first sight led to a happy and satisfying relationship. Others, who felt this connection only to be let down as soon as the introduction was made, believe that love at first sight is nothing short of lust at first sight. Nonetheless, love at first sight does happen more than you think. If you spot a person across a crowded room and feel a rush of emotions, don't be so quick to dismiss your feelings as fleeting. When someone falls in love at first sight, it's usually an indication that the love interest has evoked some pleasant memory from the past. Maybe they remind you of a your parents, your first love, or even someone you used to love from afar. There is a strange familiarity that is difficult to describe. Many couples who have fallen in love at first sight have gone on to live happily ever after. So the lesson is you never know when Cupid's arrow will strike gold, so go with it and enjoy the ride.

Can You Love Someone Much Older or Younger Than You?

Often we cannot control with whom we fall in love. But if the person you love is not legally ready to receive your advances, our only advice to you is to write "good things come to those who wait" one thousand times, and look for love elsewhere.

Provided you're both legal, there's no reason why love can't unite two people of very different ages. Whether or not your relationship can withstand the criticism of others is something time will tell. But if you're confident about your feelings, the opinions of others should not play a significant factor in the relationship.

Delusions Of Love

The two of you have shared several great dates, you've talked on the phone nonstop for several weeks, you've even shared a toothbrush. Everything is going great, but there's one thing on your mind: Is this love or just a passing fling?

Good question. The love question has boggled the minds of many singles. It seems that no matter how much fun you're having with your new friend, you're always plagued by doubts as to whether he or she is a keeper or a temporary pastime. As we all wish to understand our emotions, this is only natural. We don't want to be led astray and try to prepare ourselves for good-byes or long, lingering hellos. Guessing about the future is all well and good, provided you don't forget to enjoy the present moment. So if you're having a hard time coming up with the solution to your question it may be that you are asking too much of yourself. Under these circumstances it's wise to close your eyes and let the wheel of fortune spin its course. When the time comes, you will know how you truly feel without having to second-guess yourself.

But let's be realistic. There will be many of you who want to know if they're in love right now, or at least have a vague idea about what your feelings mean. Patience can be overrated. So if you don't have any to spare, the following love clues will give some indication about where your relationship is heading.

Lust vs. Love

In the beginning stages of your relationship you may feel those special feelings around your newfound companion. You may feel like calling all the time, kissing or touching every time you meet, or think about this person nonstop. This could very well be love, or it could be that you simply have the hots for someone and admire his or her physical prowess.

It's no wonder you're having such a hard time. The line between love and lust can be very thin, if it's visible at all. So read on to find out if what you feel is real or if it's just sexual.

What words come to mind?

Everyone talks with friends about their dates from time to time. Come on, admit it; you know you have. Think back to your last conversation. What words did you use to describe your new companion? Did most have to do with this person's physical appearance or did you discuss other qualities such as a great sense of humor and other favorable personality traits? While commenting on your date's looks is expected to a degree, it can point to one thing if that's all you tend to do. And while being attracted to someone is great in its own right, you may not be smitten with the love bug just yet.

Love Them or Leave Them?

Suppose your date informed you that he or she could not have sex before marriage. Would you bolt in a nanosecond or stick around to see what developed? In order to analyze the strength of your feelings, you must imagine that this hypothetical scenario is a probability.

Visualize yourself receiving the news and try to determine your first reaction. If you're horrified at the prospect, you may be involved in a strictly sexual liaison. But if you feel calm, relaxed, and anxious for the wedding day, you're clearly harboring some serious emotions. Once again, having a purely sexual relationship is not the end of the world, provided that it's what you're really looking for.

Is it in the Kiss?

When kissing your date, do you find your mind wandering about what sexual phase you will enter into next, or do you simply get caught up in the moment? Too much sex on the mind whenever

Lifestyle Quiz

Now that you are one with your rationale, you'll have to decide which lifestyle matches your personality. Are you a taker or a giver? How do you deal with compromise and rejection? Figuring out if you have what it takes to stay single or get hitched will put you on the right track.

1. Your boy- or girlfriend is away on business almost every weekend. How do you feel?
   a) You are thrilled.
   b) You are upset and spend your weekends waiting by the phone.
   c) You are disappointed but use the time to catch up with old friends.

2. You and a group of friends are deciding where to eat dinner. You want Italian; they're set on Thai. What do you do?
   a) Insist on Italian. You are not about to waste your money on sprouts and bamboo shoots.
   b) Agree to Thai. If your friends are big fans, maybe you should join the club.
   c) Consent to Thai but complain throughout the whole dinner.

3. An old flame pops into town and wants to meet for drinks.
   There is just one hitch: you're already involved. What do you do?
   a) Go anyway—"What they don't know won't hurt them."
   b) Decline because you don't want your boyfriend/girlfriend to get jealous.
   c) Accept the invitation by saying, "We'd love to be there."

4. Your sister asks you to baby-sit her two-year-old but you have a date. What do you do?
   a) Pretend you didn't hear her.
   b) Agree to help, and reschedule your date.
   c) Baby-sit but tell her that she owes you one.

Scoring:
If you selected option a three or more times, you should run from any and all relationships. You won't have a difficult time escaping; your stubborn and selfish ways will keep most people at bay. If option b was your most frequently picked response, you are compatible with neither lifestyle. You're bound to run into problems whether you're in a relationship or hanging out on your own. How can you forge your own path when you're too busy following the crowd? If you selected option c three or more times, you can rest assured that any relationship you're in will be a success. Compromise isn't synonymous with sacrifice; but you probably already knew that.

you're around your date is a clear sign that you may be in lust rather than in love.

If you enjoy the dating process—the long walks, lingering kisses, stimulating conversations, warm embraces—as much as the prospect of sexual relations, then you may be suffering from the first pangs of true love.

Love vs. Like

In the film *When Harry Met Sally*, Billy Crystal's character labors under the delusion that men and women can't be friends. Yet how many times have you gone out with someone only to realize that the two of you would probably make for better friends than lovers?

Then, there are those occasions when it becomes difficult to tell if what you feel is friendship or love. And since many couples attribute their staying power to a close bond of friendship, what role does friendship play in love?

To make things simpler, try thinking of love and friendship as a pair of socks. When paired together, the socks make a perfect combination. But when torn apart, you can try to match each sock with another, but you will never again be able to recreate the magic of that matching pair. All analogies aside, love isn't friendship, and friendship isn't love. Yet both have the power to forge strong bonds. Still confused? Well, look no further, because we've got the answer.

> *Me and my friends have hung out since high school. Every year we take a spouseless, significant other less hiking trip together. We've always had the best time, but this year something changed. My friend, Rob, has always teased me about everything—my hair, my choice of boyfriends, and even my job. But this last year, he was acting very strange around me. He was really putting a damper on the trip, so I asked him what was wrong. That's when he told me he had separated from his wife, because he still loved me. I never knew he ever loved me. I couldn't deal with it, especially with everything going so well with my boyfriend. So I basically told him to put his feelings on hold. Recently, I broke up with my boyfriend and called Rob on a whim. He was really*

*happy to hear from me, and we went on several dates
after that. I could see how such relationships can work
out for many people, but Rob and I only realized that we
worked best as friends.*

—GWEN, 32, FLORIST

Love vs. Self-Love

The power of vanity is very strong. So strong that it can sometimes trick us into believing we love someone we don't. When
Narcissus fell in love with the boy in the lake, he thought his feelings were real, until it turned out that he had fallen in love with his
own reflection. Let his story be a lesson to you.

There will be times when you will experience a strong emotion
towards someone who simply adores you and can't stop praising
your many virtues. Falling for these types of people may be fun at
first, but in the end you are just letting them stroke your ego.
Actually, what you end up doing is falling in love with someone's
image of you, and not that person. To determine if your love is
directed at the right person, try to focus on how you feel about
them as opposed to how they feel about you.

Love vs. Trophy Love

It's a sad fact of life, but some people use the attractiveness of
their boyfriend or girlfriend to earn respect from their peers. At
business engagements and group outings, having an attractive date
is definitely a bonus. But true love has nothing to do with
someone's looks.

To determine whether you're truly, madly, and deeply in love or
just love the idea of showing off before your friends or business
associates, go back and analyze your past dates. If most of them
involved large groups of people, such as parties or corporate functions, it may be that you are more interested in putting your date on
display than in getting to know them. But if you've tried to probe
beneath your companion's lovely surface, and have even enjoyed
their company in private and out of the way places, you are probably just dating someone attractive and not falling victim to the
trophy collector's mentality.

You Know You're Just Friends When...

1. You call him/her to discuss how your date went.

2. You can tell him or her
to lose weight without
sounding odious.

3. You burp without hesitation.

4. You show him or her
pictures from your awk-
ward days as a teen.

5. You set each other up
with your most attractive
friends.

6. You devour your food
with no consideration
for appearances.

7. You don't get jealous
when meeting his or
her ex.

8. You call only after being
stood up.

9. You don't expect a gift
on Valentine's Day.

10. One of you is gay.

The Date Doctor Is In

Q: My boyfriend told me that I dress too provocatively. I don't get it. Don't guys like that?

A: *You're right; guys do like that, until they become your boyfriend. This is the perfect example of the male ego. When he first met you he loved your sexy spirit, but because of his need to have you all to himself he is threatened when other men look at you. My suggestion would be to reassure him that you're only interested in him and he should not worry. If he still can't handle it, let him know that you're not going to change only for the sake of accommodating his immature insecurities.*

"I hate to admit it, but for about six months, I dated a girl from my office just because she was really attractive and all of the guys wanted to date her. I was really flattered when she singled me out for special attention, because every guy was after her. Unfortunately, when we went out, I was pretty bored the whole time. All she wanted to do was talk about her exercise and diet habits. But when my friends found out that we were dating, they were so jealous and I fell into the trap. I told them we had a great time, and even went so far as too ask for a second date to prove my point. I'm not proud of it, but it took me leaving my job to realize that I would have never dated her if my friends hadn't made such a big deal about the whole thing. The worst part of it all was knowing that I had only been leading her on. She ended up taking the breakup really hard.

—GREG, 36, FINANCIAL PLANNER

Love vs. The Love of Credit

While your new sweetheart may think nothing of showering you with expensive gifts and lavish outings, you should think long and hard on whether your new cohort is the apple of your eye or if those are just dollar signs in there. While it may be nice to enjoy the favors of a generous date, convincing yourself that you are truly in love would be ill-conceived.

In many of these situations, the person on the receiving end feels obligated to fall in love as a return on the investment made in them, or simply to keep from feeling bought and paid for. So examine your feelings and ask yourself if they would be the same regardless of your date's spending habits. If you're even slightly unsure, try to remember that gratitude is the kiss of death where love is concerned. Next thing you know you'll be stuck in a loveless marriage, with a great big house that is only eclipsed by the gaping hole in your heart. Take our advice—the next time you feel indebted to your date, try saying no to their offers of gifts. In the end, when you're free to find your true love, you'll have only yourself to thank.

In Love With Love

Some things are beyond your control, right? Like the mascara that runs freely down your cheeks, or that lump that rises up your throat unrestrained after you've sat through your millionth romantic movie. You know, the one that never fails to end with a beautiful couple sharing a perfectly staged kiss that's destined to send them into an equally idyllic future. There, there, it's okay. After all, who wouldn't want a little piece of that for themselves? From day one, we are pounded with the notion that love will save us, enrich us, and make us whole. So the question becomes not who *is* but who *isn't* in love with the concept of love?

While most us long to feel our heart pound with anticipation of our loved one's arrival, pushing ourselves to feel something we don't for the sake of a dream isn't a good idea on any level. There are a myriad of problems that can crop up if you choose to delude yourself into thinking that wanting love and having love are the same thing.

To guard yourself from this all too common fate, you should try to figure out what the two of you have in common. Focus on the person rather than the relationship, and you may find your answer in no time.

The Compatibility Report

All right, now that you have some idea about what love is and isn't, you can start your quest for truth by taking a closer look at what is involved in your new relationship. If you spend too much time thinking about your feelings, you may waste precious moments that would be better spent in evaluating your compatibility as a couple.

So what is compatibility? Contrary to popular belief, compatibility is not sharing one brain, being two peas in a pod, or finishing each other's sentences. And while to be compatible you must have the same basic principles and values in life, a little opposition never hurt anyone.

Being compatible is not only about finding common ground, but also about becoming the person you want to be by balancing each other. The most successful relationships are ones where each person brings something unique into the equation. For example, if you have a tendency to be on the morose or depressive side, then someone who is more cheerful and animated may be just what you're looking for. Or, if you have a tendency to be irresponsible and flighty, finding someone who has their feet planted firmly on planet Earth is bound to do wonders for your life.

If you're getting tired of all our analogies, brace yourself—this next one's a doozie. Compatibility is much like a coloring book. As long as you're both working on the same page, using different colors to fill in the picture will create a more dynamic and exciting composition.

Do Opposites Attract?

While balancing each other is important, a couple that is too different may create some great sparks in the beginning, but these will eventually diminish. Singles looking for short-term fun will benefit from this fiery combination; however, those looking for something a bit more permanent would do better to find someone who shares their interests and opinions. True, brief flings can be a whole lot of fun, but constantly looking for someone who is different from you can be a signal of bigger issues.

Those who consistently reject people similar to themselves may be suffering from self-esteem issues. Instead of looking for a good match, they seek out those people who are outwardly different. Unfortunately, this apparent polar opposite usually has an equally low self-esteem, as they too are drawn to people bearing no resemblance to themselves. Such relationships rarely achieve the intimacy that is so crucial to successful unions and so terrifying for people with a negative self-image. So if you're prone to want only that which is different, try to analyze what it is you don't like about yourself and relationships before getting involved with people you'll never truly connect with.

A Match Made in Heaven

Finding out whether your tryst has all the makings of a great romance or nothing more than a brief dating encounter hardly qualifies as rocket science. While it may be good to balance each other on smaller points, you'll have to agree on the basic tenets in order to create a lasting bond.

We've created a compatibility assessment worksheet in order to help you match your personal beliefs with those of your partner. Your first order of business should be to decide what's important to you and fill in your responses. Then, as you get to know your new play pal better, you can fill in their responses. Of course, don't let them in on your plan. No one likes to feel like they're being tested. Casually ask your date about the following subjects, and you'll have more than enough information upon which to base your decision.

1. **Religion.** Religion plays an important role in people's lives. Whether you're Catholic, Jewish, Protestant, Muslim, or an atheist, religion can affect your decision and even your behaviors. Do you consider yourself observant? Is celebrating religious holidays and including religion in major life events important to you? In the following space please note your religious beliefs and the impact they have on your life.

Your Religious Beliefs:_____

_____

Your Date's Religious Beliefs: _____

_____

2. **Marriage.** Some people are out to destroy the institution, while others shed sentimental tears at the mere mention of an altar. Where do you fit in? Do you wish to be married, and soon? What do you consider a good marriage? Do you want to have children, and if so, when? Are you looking for a life partner who would just as gladly do away with the legal mumbo jumbo? Or is merrymaking (the more the merrier style) your main priority?

Your Views on Marriage: _____

_____

Your Date's Views on Marriage:_____

_____

3. **Career.** Career is an important issue for many people. Some people go to great lengths, prioritizing career over the three F's family, friends, and fun. Have you ever considered giving up your chances of having a family for a successful career? Or would you drink the midnight oil rather than burn it and skip a night out on the town as a result? Think about your answer carefully, and try to think about how your current career affects your personal life. Do you rarely have time for friends and family, or do you make a pointed effort to schedule some free time?

Your Views on Career: _____

_____

Your Date's Views on Career: _____

_____

4. **Money.** Your relationship to money can say a lot about the kind of person you are. Do you contribute money to charities? Do you spend freely and enjoy the good life money can buy, or are you the type who takes all that "penny saved is a penny earned" stuff literally? Maybe you're somewhere in the middle, so think carefully about how you spend and view money before responding.

Your Views on Money: _____

_____

Your Date's Views on Money: _____

_____

5. **Lifestyle.** The way in which you choose to live your life is key to assessing compatibility. If you're an outdoorsy type who is active and full of zest, you're not going to stick around a couch potato for long—no matter how much you like his rock band. And if you're a coffee, cigarettes, and red meat kind of guy, a caffeine- and smoke-free gal whose stomach does flip-flops at the sight of a "chicken abortion" (a.k.a. an egg) could push you to drink in no time.

Your Lifestyle: _____

_____

Your Date's Lifestyle: _____

_____

6. **Basic Personality.** Are you outgoing or introspective? Are you artistic or analytical? Are you unconventional or traditional? Stubborn or willing to compromise? Slight variations in traits will keep things exciting, but stray too much from your own path and you're looking at conflict down the road. Figuring out who you are will help you determine your match. The work you did during Chapter 1 should prove to be of some assistance in this area, so feel free to think back to what you learned.

Your Basic Personality: _____

_____

_____

Your Date's Basic Personality: _____

_____

_____

7. **Ethics and Morals.** As much as we would like to think that all people value honesty, consideration, and justice, this simply doesn't hold true. Some people think that honesty is overrated, that considering the feelings of others only cramps their style, and that justice is an unrealistic idea. Better you find out now than discover the truth once you're in too deep.

Your Ethics and Morals: _____

_____

_____

Your Date's Ethics and Morals: _____

_____

_____

Now that you've completed your compatibility worksheet, you can begin to evaluate how well you and your honey bunny match up. When looking over your responses, try to see the big picture. Just because the two of you may differ on some points doesn't mean your relationship won't last. Use this worksheet as a guideline, and remember that nothing guarantees success. It is only from working out conflicts and compromising that great romances are born.

Express Yourself

Because not everyone can boast the ability to sum up their feelings as eloquently as Shakespeare, you may experience a time when you feel awkward or strange about telling your new companion how you feel. Many people fear the commitment that may arise from their confession and the risk of rejection should their beloved not feel the same.

Once the words are said and done, there's no taking them back. So those who fear speaking before thinking have a legitimate reason to do so. Of course, people who take words very lightly have no problem saying "I love you" to everyone they meet. The worst offenders are usually found in entertainment industry circles, where the phrase "I love you" now carries as much weight as, say, "Thank you" does in the rest of the country. Still, uttering those three little words like you mean them to somebody who actually cares never fails to inspire dread. The following primer should help you combat the fear of such raw honesty.

Words of Love

If after thinking it through you are still convinced that the time is ripe for the big proclamation, try to be as spontaneous or as romantic as possible. The worst thing you can do is make it look like you've planned this moment all along. There are many ways to tell a person that you love him or her. Spur-of-the-moment declarations can be blurted out while watching TV, whispered during dinner, or slipped in during a hot and heavy pillow talk session. Romantic ways to profess your ardor can range from skywriting to song dedications on the radio.

If you're especially nervous, you could try testing the waters by casually asking your date how he or she feels about you. If your date tries to equivocate, ask point blank if he or she loves you. Whatever your date says can be your cue. While this may seem like a cop-out, getting past the first "I love you" can be very difficult, so make it as easy on yourself as possible.

Another way of proclaiming your love is to simply send a message in a bottle. While it may not be as brave a tactic as speaking your mind come what may, a good love letter has been known to melt a heart or two. While not everyone has the innate ability to write a first-rate love letter, honesty can work just as well. Should

your date judge you on such trifles as penmanship and grammar, you'll know to continue your search for the true love of your life.

Back when I was first going out with my wife, we were always joking around with each other. Part of the way we communicated was by playfully making fun of one another. Pretty soon, our feelings began to grow more serious. And I realized that I was truly 100 percent head over heels in love with her. So one day, when she invited me to go to a picnic, she made my favorite dish, lasagna. She had me taste it, and it was really good. So when she asked me if I liked it, I told her there was only one thing that I loved more than her lasagna—her. At first she laughed—she thought I was joking. But when she realized that I was telling the truth, she told me that she also loved me. It's become somewhat of a tradition, because now every time she makes her lasagna, I tell her that I love her.

—KURT, 29, PASTRY CHEF

The Love That Dare Not Speak Its Name

While saying "I love you" to someone is a big step, people who have a big fear of speaking their mind should try to think about what they are so afraid of.

In some families, displays of affection are strictly frowned upon. If yours was just such an undemonstrative family, a long-standing tradition of staying mum may be at the root of your problem. To change this behavior, you should realize that there's nothing wrong with telling someone how you feel. Being honest is not a sign of weakness. On the contrary, it takes a lot of courage to express yourself.

You First

This is a battle that can occur in any relationship. Two people get together, share the same feelings, but silently insist that the other reveal themselves first. This game is like an adult version of the staring contest—whoever blinks or laughs first loses the game.

If you're locked in this battle of wills, you should first try to realize that love is about two mature people getting together, not

The Date Doctor Is In

Q: What's the best way to get your date in the mood?

A: *The thing that's always worked for me is to plan a surprise. My personal favorite has to be the song dedication. Before the date, pester the DJ at your local radio station until he or she agrees to dedicate a song from you to your date at a specific time. Then make sure that you're in the car when the song is set to air. After your date hears the dedication, there's no way he or she can resist you.*

some variation on the clash of the titans. Provided you're really in love, try to be the bigger person and don't let pride dictate your behavior. Think of it like this: Whoever says "I love you" first, wins.

When to Keep Quiet

Letting your words of love flow is all well and good, provided you mean what you are saying. Just like those times when you want to say something but can't, there are times when you want to say something but shouldn't.

One of these times is during or right after sex. While you may be feeling especially intimate, you shouldn't say anything you may want to take back once you're in a less passionate state of mind. Sex has the power to make us feel transported, like we're the king or queen of the world. Sadly, when dawn breaks, the light of reality will hit you like a cold shower. Having to take back your words is no easy feat. Guilt the likes of which you never knew existed will come out of the shadows to haunt you. If your partner takes the news to heart, the conversation can even get ugly. So if you really want to say the magic words, wait till morning when your thinking is clear and sober.

On the flip side, you should abstain from telling people you love them just to get sex. Sex should never be attained through manipulation or lies. Only the most desperate bottom-feeders would so callously toy with another's emotions. Anyone who dissembles for the sake of lust had better get ready to be prosecuted to the full extent of the karma police. Luckily, 99 percent of humanity has caught on to this truth. If you've yet to get with the program, try imagining how you'd feel if someone you truly cared for boosted your expectations one minute only to shatter them the next.

Finally, the most important time to stay silent is when someone tells you they love you, but you don't return their feelings. The majority of people have fallen into this trap at one time or another. You've been seeing someone for awhile, and they finally get up the nerve to tell you how they feel. The stage is set for you two to make beautiful music together, but there's just one hitch—you're not quite sure how you feel. For fear of hurting your paramour's feelings you do what comes naturally—say the words as quickly as possible and proceed to pretend that the exchange never took place. Pretty soon you're called upon to repeat the phrase. Repeat it enough times, and

you're liable to believe your own fibs. Next thing you know, you've got a Shamoo-sized sham on your hands, and it's the basis of your entire relationship. So be wary, because words are just that powerful.

The best way to sidestep this snare is to simply tell your date that while you like them immensely and enjoy every minute spent in their company, you need time to consider your feelings. And while your date may feel hurt and suffer internal bleeding of the ego at first, this pain will pale in comparison to the one he or she would feel if you waited months or years to reveal the truth.

All About Sex

Let's be honest—if you needed to learn about the birds and the bees, or the best positions, you could have bought a sex manual. So we won't bore you with any anatomically correct lingo or astound you by going into graphic detail. Sorry to disappoint, but giving tips on how to drive your man or woman wild with desire also falls outside the rubric of a dating book.

However, we are free to discuss the role of sex in the wild world of dating. As we all know, sex can be a terrifying and exciting time in a relationship. And unless you're under the legal age or planning on waiting until marriage, there will come a time when you too will plan on taking the plunge.

While sex and dating seem to go hand in hand, the whole thing can be very complicated and confusing. You will be forced to ask yourself some tough questions, and, sometimes, you may not have all the answers. For example, is the third date really the best time to initiate contact? What are some romantic tunes that will set the mood? What to wear during your first encounter? And what to expect once you've gone the distance?

No matter how many notches you've got marring your bedpost, a time will come when you will want to make sure that everything goes according to plan. Whether it's because you're finally in love or close to the verge of falling, sex can sometimes make or break a relationship. And while the issue should be approached in a somber frame of mind, you should never forget that having a good time is your foremost priority. No matter how much is riding on your first encounter, staying calm and relaxed will ensure that yours will be an affair to remember.

Show Your Love

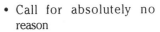

Words can be a great way to show someone your true feelings. Some of the greatest love poems on record were inspired by romantic love. But if words just don't come easy, you can always show your new companion how you feel about them through pantomime. Actions speak louder than words. So in lieu of sweet nothings, try the following romantic gestures on for size:

- Call for absolutely no reason
- Surprise him with a home-cooked meal, candles and all
- Buy new lingerie
- Send a flower every day
- Carve your names in a tree
- Make her breakfast in bed
- Serenade her with a love song
- Wash each other's hair
- Perform a full-body massage
- Present her with the first edition of their favorite book
- Have a food fight
- Pick him up from work
- Bake your famous home-made brownies

Perfect Timing

Sex does not come with an automatic timer; that is, there is no perfect time to have sex. The time you wait before partaking in the act will depend entirely on you and your partner. Whether you're on your first, third, or thirtieth date doesn't make one bit of difference. The only factor to consider is that you feel comfortable around the person.

Yet there are definite pros and cons to jumping in too early or waiting too long. Should you decide to pluck a fruit from the tree of sexual knowledge prematurely, you may be cheating yourself and your companion of a fully ripe sexual experience. If you're not entirely comfortable sleeping with someone you've just met, the encounter is in danger of becoming awkward and strained.

Waiting too long also comes with its own share of headaches. If, once ready to leap into the throes of passion, you hesitate, a disappointment is likely to follow. Waiting for someone or something can breed great expectations, so don't be surprised if the first experience ends up falling short of satisfactory. But there is a bright side to playing the waiting game. While the initial exposures may buckle under the pressure of performance anxiety, once you're past this stage, you'll be sharing the most deeply intimate moments of your life with one of your closest friends. All because you cared to wait.

Setting the Mood

Before we begin, put away the oysters, the black lights, and the Artist formerly known as Prince soundtrack. The first night of lovemaking should be a pleasant and sensual experience, not a seedy seduction. Don't insult your date's intelligence with these predictable sex trappings. You'll end up looking corny and, even worse, alone.

Setting the mood for your interlude will require subtlety, taste, and skill. The key is to make the evening seem as spontaneous as humanly possible. Because no one wants to feel manipulated or cajoled, this approach is really your only chance of scoring. So whether you have a couple of hours to prepare or a few minutes, the following steps should get both of you in the mood in no time.

Lighting

While pitch darkness may hide some flaws, a little romantic lighting never hurt anyone. But don't overdo it by covering every available surface with lighted candles. While these may add ambience, you don't want your partner to feel like they've just stepped into a love trap. Two candles or dimmed lighting should give you just enough visibility to make the experience exciting.

Music

Anything too loud or blaring can distract you and your partner from the moment. Try to keep the music in the background. We also have to warn you against putting on anything too suggestive such as Snoop Doggy Dog, Prince, or Ravel's "Bolero." Your date should feel relaxed and comfortable. If you're really pressed for musical selections, jazz should do just fine (statistically speaking, jazz listeners have sex more frequently than any other group).

Between the Sheets

When you're talking linen, save the satin leopard prints for another occasion. While it may be fun to explore your animal instincts once you know each other better, this type of bedding can make your date feel like a hunted animal. For your first time, we strongly recommend flannel sheets or good old-fashioned cotton. (Tip: Your date's willingness to go to bed may increase in direct proportion to your sheets' thread count.)

Dressing the Part

Playing around with sexy attire can be a fun idea for couples who need to spice up their love life. But if this is your first time, you should keep your lingerie and underwear as basic as possible. For any ladies who are into the French Maid bit, we suggest a more simple yet still sexy approach like a black lace bra and matching underwear. Men should also stick to either briefs or boxers. And while going au naturel is rarely discouraged, anything resembling a Speedo is a major turnoff for many women.

Keep It Clean

Since no one wants to make love for the first time in a pig sty, consider yourself advised to clean your place before the moment of truth. If you're going out for the evening and aren't sure where the

Ten Things Not to Do After Having Sex

1. Forget your money on the nightstand.
2. Invite your date to visit your parents.
3. Compare your date's assets with your ex's.
4. Take a thirty-minute shower and clean the house.
5. Call your friends to tell them the good news while your date is still there.
6. Say anything akin to "I take it you know how to find the door."
7. Give your partner a silly nickname (i.e. "snookums") and beg him or her to stay the night.
8. Push "play" on your camcorder and replay the highlights for your partner in slow motion.
9. Introduce your date to your stuffed animals.
10. Thank your partner for deflowering you (that trick is so old you'll immediately go down in your partner's memory as the date who cried virgin).

night will end, try to make the place look as clean as possible. And since scent plays a critical role in arousal, we suggest you pick a seductive air freshener (i.e. vanilla) to really further your cause.

I had been going out with Danny for a couple of weeks, but aside from some snogging sessions, we had yet to consummate the relationship. Just as I was beginning to wonder if he was ever going to make the big move, he asked me back to his flat. Still, I didn't think anything of it until we walked through the door. It was just so obvious! He had taken out this ridiculous lava lamp, turned his artificial fireplace on high, scattered brightly colored pillows all over the floor, and had even been so bold as to prominently display a bottle of champagne in a bucket of ice. If all this wasn't bad enough, he quickly put Enigma into the CD player. It was like watching a bad movie. The worst part of it was that he kept asking me if I thought it was romantic. I finally told him that I was feeling sick and had to get home. It was no lie—his creepy idea of romance really did nauseate me. Needless to say, I haven't been back since.

—TRACY, 24, ASSISTANT EDITOR

A Word about Safe Sex

With the HIV virus and countless other sexually transmitted diseases still going strong, safe sex is more a requirement than it is an option. When confronted with condoms, many people still react by clenching their fists and stomping their feet. And while both genders have been known to complain about this basic precaution, abstinence aside, it is still the only way to protect yourself against disease. Spermicides, sponges, and pills can go a long way to keep babies at bay, but when it comes to life-threatening illnesses, condoms are your only hope.

Safe sex should not take away from the sexual experience. On the contrary, it can only enhance the pleasure. After all, how can you have any fun when you're worrying about contracting a disease? Unless you're totally unaware of the risks involved, keeping it safe is your only chance to relax and truly enjoy the moment.

The biggest concern singles have about safe sex is broaching the subject. Gone are the days when people have to hide condoms underneath their mattress. Today, Sheik, Trojans, and Lifestyles are the buzzwords of all careful singles. Both men and women are responsible for buying condoms. So if you're unsure as to how to go about bringing up the condom issue, don't be. Just whip it out and be proud. Your partner will not judge and will only be relieved that you prepared yourself for the moment.

Safe Sex and Alcohol

In order to have a thoroughly safe carnal experience, you'll need to keep your wits about you. If you need alcohol to lower your inhibitions, chances are you're not ready for a torrid tryst just yet. Alcohol also poses a safety concern in that it has a tendency to cloud one's judgment. While using a condom is hardly neurosurgery, intoxication can make you feel like it's a chore not worth bothering with. So if you're nervous and want to get in the mood, try letting your CD collection set the tone but limit your alcohol intake to a bare minimum.

The Aftermath

Sex can be a very revealing and exciting experience. But what do you do once the sex is over, and you're lying in bed together? Many people would argue that a good cuddling match (the type where both parties assume the spoon position and disclose all their deep, dark secrets) is in order, while others would rather nod off undisturbed.

You who admire your wee hours companion, but would love to do away with cuddling altogether, can suggest an alternative. There's that late-late-movie, or what about that video rental you two were so quick to neglect earlier in the evening? Use your date's immersion in the on-screen plot line as your opportunity to get some shut-eye, and no one will be the wiser. In fact, if you want to treat your date well and make them feel secure, pretty much anything is better than picking up and stomping off.

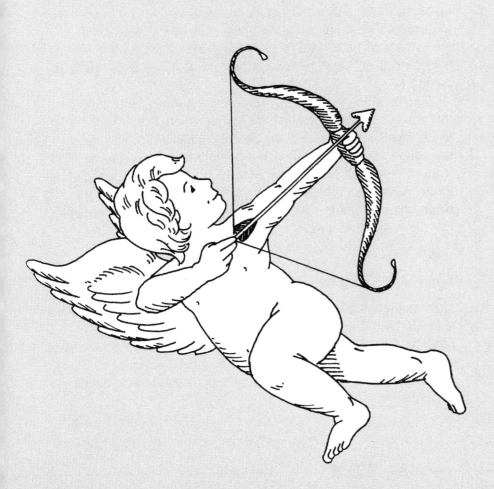

Chapter 9

Breaking Up Is Hard to Do

Breaking up is probably the single toughest problem any dater will ever have to face. Whether you're the one who's calling it quits or the one who's being hung out to dry, the death of a relationship can be a tumultuous time to weather.

No matter how often you've done it before, severing ties with somebody special continues to traumatize otherwise healthy singles worldwide. With all the time invested in the relationship and all the shared good times, how could putting a stop to the rapport be anything other than an ordeal? Chances of going through the basic withdrawal symptoms are high, as you will most likely experience denial, anger, grief—in short, the whole bean burrito.

Yet all your post-breakup trials and tribulations should not be taken as undisputed proof of your undying love. In fact, simple growing pains are the most common cause of such post-parting depression. In order to proceed with your life, you are breaking yourself of a most comfortable habit. And if you've tried to quit smoking or eating between meals, you probably know that old habits die hard. What's even more disconcerting is that relatively short relationships can also be a chore to drop cold turkey.

The most important thing to remember about parting ways is that it is an inevitable part of the dating experience. Like life and death, breakups are part of the natural order. While no one is suggesting that you forgo grieving for your lost loves, you could learn to take it all in stride by adopting the right attitude. Leaving a relationship isn't the end of the world; in fact, it can be the beginning of a whole new life. Just think what an adventure you may have in store, and remember, time heals all heartaches.

Quitting Time

Most people just don't know when to blow the whistle on a relationship. Maybe it's the fear of the unknown or the reluctance to revert back to the singular pronoun after having spent months referring to yourself as "we." Whatever your particular reason, it's probably rooted in the fact that no human being enjoys drastic change and upheaval.

Of course, there is that breed of person who hates to be called a quitter. Rather than blame their relationship problems on a mismatch, they choose to bear the brunt of the guilt. So instead of composing a Dear John/Jane letter and skulking off in the middle of the night, they, in their infinite wisdom, choose to stick around in hopes of one day mending a situation full of holes.

But we don't need to tell you that staying in unsatisfying relationships for any of these reasons is nothing short of putting off the inevitable. Sooner or later the ax will fall, so why drag out the suffering? Put an end to the misery, because life is too short to be unhappy for long.

Yet being torn about whether to stay or go never fails to stump the ambivalent single. One day you decide that you've had it with your comrade, and the next you're clinging to him or her like latex. So what's the best way to make this toughest of calls? Read on, and you'll discover all the options you have to weigh and all the factors you need to consider before casting the die.

The Fun Factor

While relationships aren't all fun and games, you have a right to expect a certain amount of enjoyment. Ask yourself: When was the last time the two of you had a good laugh together? Do you still look forward to spending a quiet evening just watching videos? If you aren't sure on both counts, then either you're a somber and hyperactive type of person, or you're on the horns of a major slump.

Almost all couples get into a slump from time to time. The question is how long your slump has lasted. All things being relative, a six-month relationship need not end because of a two-week slump. If, on the other hand, two full months of your three-month affair have been spent down in the dumps of a slump, cut your losses because, believe you us, the grass *is* greener. Once again, every couple experiences times when fun takes a backseat to gravity and hard work. But if your relationship is always demanding that you make a gargantuan effort, you may not have the energy to pull this locomotive off its collision course. And that's a definite sign of a train wreck in the making.

What's Your Sign? Romance According to the Zodiac

Sagittarius
Remember the movie *Two for the Road* with Audrey Hepburn and Albert Finney? The romance between Hepburn and Finney definitely fell under a Sagittarian influence. The exotic place, their individual searches for truth, and the truths they ultimately found in each other are Sagittarian themes. No matter who a Sagittarian loves or marries, a part of him or her is always slightly separate and singular, aware of the larger picture.

Ten Good Books About Breaking Up

1. *Get Rid of Him*, by Joyce Vedral

2. *100 Reasons to Keep Him, 100 Reasons to Dump Him*, by Sharon Naylor

3. *50 Ways to Break Up With Your Lover*, by Lori Salkin and Rob Sperry

4. *Bad Boys: Why We Love Them, How to Live With Them, and When to Leave Them*, by Carole Lieberman and Lisa Collier Cool

5. *Coming Apart: Why Relationships End and How to Live Through the Ending of Yours*, by Daphne Rose Kingma

6. *Uncoupling: Turning Points in Intimate Relationships*, by Diane Vaughan

R-e-s-p-e-c-t

Mutual respect is crucial to a happy and healthy coupling. So if you're not getting your fair share, then you may want to seek it elsewhere. If your partner has a habit of putting you down and making you feel inferior, take matters into your own hands before you wind up in divorce court. "But I love *(name of belligerent louse here)*!" is no excuse. What kind of person belittles someone who loves them, anyway? Every second that you remain is a shameless waste of the valuable love and time that can be spent on more caring and sensitive individuals.

Of course, if you've changed dramatically and are even having a hard time respecting yourself, you may not want to lay all the blame at your partner's feet. Sometimes, people change throughout the relationship. They can lose their motivation, fall into a funk, and deplete their reserve of personality. If you've been feeling especially vulnerable and are having a hard time getting back on your feet, tell your partner that they should bear with you. If your self-improvement efforts don't inspire them to become more supportive, you had best get your act together on your own.

Holding Out

Since the human being in no way resembles an amoeba, you shouldn't have to put up with an asexual partner. While things may have gotten pretty steamy at the beginning of the relationship, as you get to know one another, sex can taper off somewhat. But if your partner continually refuses to engage in sexual activity, you may want to ask what is bothering him or her. If your partner still refuses, you have three options: couples counseling, terminal celibacy, or a speedy breakup.

While sex is not the be-all and end-all of a romantic union, it is a critical part of any relationship. Withholding sex from a partner is either a sign of aggression, a loss of interest, or some deep-seated dysfunction. Talking through your feelings should shed some light on the issue and help to decide your future course of action. If, on the other hand, you are the one who loses that loving feeling, you may want to reignite the flames of your passion with someone else.

Change of Heart

Although we don't condone seeing other people while in a relationship, you may chance upon someone who turns your head. Your next step depends on how long you've been in your present relationship and how happy you are within it. If you've been in a fulfilling relationship for quite some time, meeting someone you like doesn't mean you're ready to dump all over the person who has made you so happy in the past. All it means is that you are captivated by the concept of something new. If that's the case, you can flirt all you want, but don't give up a perfectly great relationship for a brief, meaningless fling.

If you've been seeing someone on the side, and have been in your current relationship for only a short while, you may want to consider switching sides. If your present companion can't even hold your interest in the first blush of romance, when things should be going most swimmingly, consider what will happen down the line. In this case, your interest in meeting new people can signal an unwillingness to forsake all others and a disinterest in pursuing the relationship.

Irreconcilable Differences

Sometimes the best reason to break up is that you simply do not get along. Constant fighting, bickering, and nagging can get on anyone's nerves after a while. Think about the times when you're together. Can you calmly enjoy one another's company or are you perpetually walking on eggshells for fear of a fight breaking out? It may be that the two of you are simply incompatible. Or it could be that both of you thrive on challenge and drama and wouldn't think of abandoning a perfectly juicy argument for the sake of plain old peace and security.

Those of you who chose the latter option should not be so anxious to call it quits, since your next relationship will probably bear a striking resemblance to your current one. Loving a good fight is different from being unable to stop fighting. Your feelings for one another may be real, so try to limit the fireworks as much as possible—or take them for what they're worth and enjoy.

(continued)

7. *Too Good to Leave, Too Bad to Stay: A Step-By-Step Guide to Helping You Decide Whether to Stay in or Get Out of Your Relationship*, by Mira Kirshenbaum

8. *Exorcising Your Ex: How to Get Rid of the Demons of Relationships Past*, by Elizabeth Kuster

9. *Dumped: A Survival Guide for the Woman Who's Been Left by the Man She Loved*, By Sally Warren and Andrea Thompson

10. *Breaking Up: From Heartache to Happiness in 48 Pages*, by Yolanda Nave

However, if you're truly incompatible, your fighting is probably brought on by a heartfelt dislike for one another. In that case, finding a new, more suitable partner may eliminate the fighting and bickering once and for all.

When I met Beth, it seemed that we had so much in common. We attended the same church, enjoyed outdoor sports, and worshiped sushi. For a time, we really clicked and I couldn't think of being with a cooler person. But after the first two months, Beth became more and more difficult to deal with. She would make unfair demands, interrogate my friends, and started shopping with my mom. I don't know whether it was because she started getting so serious, but slowly I became more and more annoyed with everything she did. It was like one day everything was great, and the next I couldn't even watch her eat her food. The slightest thing would get me aggravated, and finally I had to break it off. When she asked my why, I really didn't know what to tell her. It wasn't anything she did in particular, it was that we just weren't meant to be together.

—JERRY, 32, WEB DESIGNER

A Clean Break

Deciding whether you're ready to break up is the first step. But once you're sure of your decision, stick to it, lest you find yourself right back where you started come next year.

For the sake of both you and your former snuggle bunny, try to make your exit as smooth as possible. To avoid the theatrics, the long conversations, and the tedious explanations, some people are partial to the hit-and-run approach to breaking up. But when all is said and done, breaking up too quickly may lead to even more troubles than you imagined.

While you may want nothing more than a quick getaway, your partner may not see things your way. In their eyes, everything was probably just peachy. News of your sudden turnaround may hit them like a ton of bricks. So be extra sensitive in dealing with your

partner. Try to do everything that's within your power to ensure their well-being. You may even have to bend the truth to keep them from taking the rupture personally (i.e., any variation of "it's not you, it's me" should do the trick.)

While you're being Mr/s. Sensitive, don't forget to be firm. You don't want to give your companion any indication that they still have a chance. Betray even the slightest hint of weakness and you're just begging for a torrent of supplications, all intended to do one thing—persuade you to change your mind and stay put. Watching an otherwise dignified person go to pieces can make even the most sadistic person relent, so take care to hold your ground. To keep you from spending a lifetime with the wrong person, we've compiled some tried-and-true breakup strategies. Now your biggest problem should be deciding which one to use.

Guerrilla Breakup Tactics

Every relationship is different. You and your companion are individuals with unique traits, tastes, and desires. You may be tempted to go at this breakup routine alone. While you may have it in you to pull a Christopher Columbus and discover unchartered splitsville territories, we highly recommend sticking to the time-tested methods disclosed herein. You have much to learn from those who came before you, and you'd be wise to follow in their retreating footsteps.

Some of these guerrilla breakup tactics may not be the ones your mother used during her single days, but others are as old as the years back in high school were long. While you may be shocked by the fact that almost all of these tactics require you to lie, if you swallow the moral outrage long enough, you'll realize that this approach was developed with the express purpose of diminishing your partner's pain.

By making you appear as loathsome as possible, these strategies will make your companion wonder what they ever saw in you to begin with. And if they have any sense, they will beat you to the punch, thus sparing you the emotional turmoil of having to initiate the breakup process. So if you have their best interests in mind, and don't mind playing the bad guy, a potent combination of the following tactics may just be your only hope.

Bite Your Tongue!

The best way to avoid trampling on your soon-to-be-ex's feelings is to tell the plain truth, provided it's not too brutal, or come up with some creative little white lies. Any combination of the following five lines will fall woefully short of the originality requirement.

1. It's not you, it's me: Not only will you fail at sparing your partner's feelings, but you will add insult to injury by underestimating their intelligence with this thin-worn cliché.
2. I want to see other people: Unless you're breaking up to join the nunnery/monastery, this goes without saying.
3. I'm not ready for a commitment: Anyone with an IQ over 60 shouldn't have any problem seeing through this bald-faced lie.
4. You're too good for me: Yeah, right!
5. Let's be friends: After you've reduced your ex to a sniveling mess, them's fighting words.

Rule 1: Limit Phone Calls

It may not be ethical or right, but establishing your distance prior to the big adieu is very important. The telephone affords you the simplest and most convenient means of establishing boundaries.

However long you used to talk on the phone, start limiting that amount of time. If you would have two-hour conversations while curled up in bed, cut that number down to half. Then cut it again. But do it gradually so your partner has a chance to get accustomed to the new way of life.

Eventually, you should start calling less and less. If you used to call three times a week, switch to once a week. And should your partner try to set his or her own phone pace, excuse yourself politely and get off the phone. It may be hard at first, but it's for your partner's own good.

Rule 2: Start Fights and Nag

Constant fighting and nagging can make your partner more anxious to see you off. You should start picking fights about minor things, like not calling as promised or forgetting to put the toilet seat back down. Anything minor will do. You'll have to keep the bickering up for several weeks.

Should your partner show no desire to dump you, start in on more serious issues, such as general values and personality traits. The more offensive you are, the more happy your partner will be to bid you farewell. After you've carried on the quarreling for some weeks, you can begin the denouement by simply asking, "Have you noticed that all we seem to do is fight these days?" And with that, you're as good as gone.

Rule 3: Start Talking Marriage

Dreams of a picket fence and the pitter-patter of 4.2 little feet around the white clapboard house may not scare off everybody, so be careful. Make sure that what you have is a full-blown commitment-phobe on your hands before you launch into a telling of your homespun fantasies. Male or female, you can start by pointing out the engagement rings you like (men should pick the ridiculously gaudy, while women should always go for the obscenely expensive). You can even go so far as to proudly show off the picture of a family that you drew in first grade and have been storing in your

hope chest ever since. (Draw a picture and put it into an old shoe box labeled "hope chest"—they'll never know the difference.) While it may be cold and calculating, you will finally have the walking papers you so desired.

On the flip side, if you know for a fact that your companion wants to get more serious, you can do the opposite by bashing the institution of marriage every chance you get. Talk about how you would rather die than get married and how all children are the devil's spawn. If your partner is eager to tie the knot, your not so subtle hints will have him or her running for the door in no time.

Rule 4: Become a Religious Fanatic

Pretending that you're a born-again anything can help you smoothly exit any relationship. For some reason, the idea of a scripture-thumping zealot appeals to a very small percentage of the population. While having some religion is all well and good, having too much can put a major scare into your partner.

Begin the charade by talking about how you joined some new religious order. Make it sound as cultish as possible by giving yourself a new name more in keeping with your belief system. Then, gradually start to pepper your conversation with dogmatic quotes and short bouts of chanting. You can also institute a mandatory pre-sex prayer ritual. This should prove to be the last straw, getting your companion out of your hair once and for all. Unless, that is, your partner decides to up and join your imaginary religion. In that case, refer to any of the other rules for Plan B.

Rule 5: Withhold Sex

Claiming you have a headache all the time works on two levels when trying to spurn a lover. If you persistently deny your partner sex, you will eventually be able to use the excuse that you would make better friends than lovers. And considering the dry spell your partner has had to endure, he or she will definitely second that motion. In fact, if you keep up the boycott on sex, your partner may spare you the trouble of explaining yourself and simply request that you forget his or her number.

Withholding sex works best when you've lost all romantic interest and would rather eat live worms than endure another evening of forced passion. It can get tricky if you're still very

Tearjerker Movies

Need a good cry after breaking up? Rent one of these tearjerkers:

1. *Fools Rush In*
2. *What Dreams May Come*
3. *Field of Dreams*
4. *Terms of Endearment*
5. *Love Story*

attracted, so steel yourself against temptation. You should also avoid cheating on your boy/girlfriend. You may be easily enticed during this enforced period of abstinence, but remember that cheating does not qualify as a guerrilla dating tactic. It is an act of treason that should be avoided at all costs. In order to get through this trying time, take lots of cold showers and know that you will soon be put out of your misery.

Rule 6: Break Dates

Standing up your date may be a foul thing to do, but so is kicking your date to the curb. The only difference is that by doing the former you will be making your partner's fall from your good graces that much less painful. To achieve this goal, you'll have to come up with at least marginally plausible excuses to make it seem like you're not out to hurt your boy/girlfriend. Whenever you break an engagement, claim that you forgot, that you were tied up at work, or, to steal the old Greg Brady standby, that "something suddenly came up."

You should also refrain from breaking every date you make. If you flake out just enough times, your partner will realize that while you may have good intentions, you are not a reliable person. This epiphany may just be what it takes to break off the relationship.

Rule 7: Seeing Other People

No one in a committed relationship takes kindly to the idea of seeing other people, especially if your boy/girlfriend is the jealous type to begin with. By telling your companion that you are anxious to expand your circle of intimate friends you are warning him or her to shape up or ship out. Prepare to heap on the charm if your partner makes a scene, refusing to share you with others. Tell your companion that it's for his or her own good and not to waste his or her time on someone as undeserving as yourself.

And who knows? Your partner may have been hoping for this arrangement all along. Your partner may just be thrilled at the prospect of taking you up on your offer. If that is indeed the case, go with the flow and encourage your partner to whoop it up with more suitable companions.

Dream Symbols

Having doubts about your relationship and mysterious dreams at the same time? Here are some sure signs that you've got a serious case of bad vibes.

Actor or Actress

Perhaps you're only seeing your own or someone else's persona, the side the person shows to the world. Seeing yourself as an actor in the spotlight suggests a desire for publicity or a more public life. Such a dream can also suggest that you're acting out a role or "putting on an act" for someone else.

Arch

Passing under an arch in a dream may symbolize a transition in your life, a move from one phase to another. If you avoid walking under the arch, the indication is that you are resisting transition or change. Note the shape of the arch, whether it's adorned in any way, or whether other people are also using it. This will flesh out the symbol for you.

Car

A moving car may mean you are headed toward a goal or moving ahead. If you're in the driver's seat, a car can symbolize taking charge of your life. Is there a "backseat driver" in the vehicle? Or are you taking the backseat in some situation in your life? Being a passenger indicates that someone else might be controlling a situation. A stolen or lost car could indicate that you are losing control of your life. Cars sometimes represent the physical body, so take not of the car's condition. Is it rusting? Does the exterior shine? How does the interior look?

Escaping

If you dream of making an escape, consider whether you are avoiding something in your life, or whether you need to get away from something.

Photograph

Since a photograph is an image of a person or object rather than the real thing, a dream of a photograph hints of deception. If you recognize a person in a dream photo, be careful in your dealings with the person and look for hidden meaning in the person's actions. To dream of having your own photograph made suggests that you may unwittingly be the cause of your own troubles.

Trial

A dream of being on trial suggests that you are being judged, or are afraid of being judged. Alternately, a trail in a dream could indicate that you are judging others too harshly.

Rule 8: Pretend You're Clinically Insane

This guerrilla breakup tactic should only be used in dire emergencies. If you've tried every alternate strategy only to find them wanting, this may be your last resort for breaking your ill-fated union.

For many of you, feigning clinical insanity may be a bit of an acting stretch. Success in this matter requires that you take your new diagnosis with the utmost seriousness. And while you will not be required to spend most of your waking hours in a straightjacket, you will be expected to engage in the following behaviors until you've officially broken up.

1. Talk to yourself about the demons trying to steal your socks.
2. Wake up in the middle of the night and paint his or her toenails green.
3. Lick your partner's furniture, while he or she is in the room.
4. Make googly-eyes with your eyes closed.
5. Serve boiled washcloths for dinner.
6. Insist that your boy/girlfriend drive you to the airport, and then calmly ask when his or her flight leaves.
7. Pretend you're on the phone with Pauly Shore for two hours.
8. Say you have something in your mouth, and then refuse to open it.
9. Swear at your partner, then apologize. Repeat.
10. Throw a sheet over your head and demand to be addressed as Casper.

Mending A Broken Heart

Now that you've read about how to put a stop to a prematurely accelerated relationship, you're ready for the next step. While leaving someone in the dust isn't easy, you'll find that being the ditched party is even more difficult. Unfortunately, at one point or another, all of us (yes, even the heartbreakers) will have to go through the humbling experience of getting dumped. It's a rite of passage that actually makes you a more sensitive person next time you feel like cutting someone loose.

We're not going to sugarcoat heartbreak. While it can do wonders for those of you who are professional poets and songwriters, on the whole, it pretty much sucks. Any way you slice the humble pie, being the dumpee is much worse than being the dumper. It doesn't even matter how much you liked the other person. Your ego is bound to get a thorough lashing.

Time is the only panacea to heartbreak. And much like mourning the death of a loved one, you'll have to go through several stages of grief before you can begin on the road to recovery.

Denial

When you first hear the news you may feel shocked, numb, or nothing at all. That is because you do not yet understand what has happened. Your brain is literally unable to process this information. One minute you're a couple, the next, friends. Pretty hard to stomach no matter how you look at it.

The disbelief stage can last anywhere from one minute to a whole lifetime. Some people simply refuse to believe what has happened, fearing that they will never recover. Don't let this happen to you. Your goal is to accept your fate and move on. Being dumped is not the end of the world, so try to think through what has happened as quickly as possible so you can begin the healing process.

Anger

As long as you don't try to beat your boy/girlfriend to a pulp, pot boil his or her favorite pet, or slash your companion's tires, expressing your anger is a healthy outlet for all those negative emotions welling up inside you. If you want to tell your ex how you feel, go ahead and do it. If you feel slighted or jaded, speak your mind and let him or her deal with the fallout.

Another way of dealing with your anger is to write a poem, song, or even paint a picture expressing your anguish. Feel free to write a long and hurtful letter to your ex, being sure to pick apart all of his or her insecurities, and then burn it. In short, do everything necessary to keep yourself from acting on any immature impulses towards aggression. Losing control over your actions may feel good for a split second, but it will only make you feel worse down the line.

Places Not to Break Up

1. Your apartment
2. During a movie
3. On a vacation
4. On a train
5. While driving
6. On the phone
7. At parent's house
8. At a wedding
9. During an expensive dinner
10. After sex

Twelve Tips for a Quick Recovery

There are many factors that can help you quickly recover from any breakup, casual or messy. The best therapy has little do with antidepressants, binge eating, or crying yourself to sleep every night. No, you can wash that (wo)man right out of your hair in no time, provided you do the following:

1. Remove any trace of your ex (pictures, clothes, gifts) from your house.
2. Write a list of everything he or she ever did to annoy you.
3. Go out with someone new, every week.
4. Get together with the girls/boys for a wild night out.
5. Look the other way if you spot your ex with someone new.
6. Throw yourself into your work.
7. Change your look by cutting your hair or getting in shape.
8. Take him/her off speed dial.
9. Sever all ties with his/her family and friends.
10. Prohibit your friends from mentioning your ex.
11. Find a new favorite restaurant the two of you never frequented.
12. Have a good time!

Guilt

The guilt stage should dawn right around the time you're done venting your frustrations. In this phase, you may find yourself turning the anger inward. This turning of the tables will manifest itself as the idea that you are the one to blame for having ruined the relationship. See it for what it is, and do not linger in this stage for too long. People who indulge themselves and spend countless hours rehashing the minutiae of the liaison can drive themselves insane.

In order to get through this trying stage, you'll have to remember that it takes two to tango. Meaning nothing you could have done on your own contributed to the demise of the relationship, unless you cheated on your partner or ran off with all of his or her loot. But if you abstained from causing your boy/girlfriend any harm, then you're in the clear. So if you decide to turn on yourself for some minor infraction, like not helping enough with the chores, flirting too much, or even nagging, think twice about putting too much credence into these theories. Better you chalk it up to a serious case of incompatibility and start getting on with your life.

Grief

If you start getting moody—buying stock in Ben & Jerry's, missing work, or crying during antiperspirant commercials—then you're probably entering the grief stage of the recovery process. Many people feel the loss of a loved one deeply, so don't get down on yourself for pining away for Mr./Ms. Wrong. No matter how badly you were treated or how shocked you were about the breakup, you will still feel the pangs of unrequited love for some months to come. Some say that it takes a full three months to recover for every six months you were together, but, of course, the time varies for every individual.

Remember, your attitude can have a tremendous impact on how long it takes for you to get back in the swing of things. You can sit around the house moping and feeling sorry for yourself, or you can get out there and force yourself to enjoy what life has to offer. While a certain amount of grief is expected, it is ultimately your responsibility to decide how long it lasts.

Acceptance

Coming to terms with a breakup isn't easy, but if you're willing to give it your all, you'll enter the final acceptance stage sooner than you think. When you've had your heart broken, it can feel like you'll never get over the pain. But you will. The funny thing about accepting the breakup is that you never know when it will happen. You may be out on a date and realize that you didn't think about your ex during the whole night. Or you may wake up one morning only to discover that the ache in the pit of your stomach has magically disappeared.

When you do reach this critical stage, be grateful that you withstood the grueling experience. Think about how much stronger you've become and never, ever get embittered by the situation. Focusing on the positive side of recovery will make you a more confident person and prepare you for any obstacle that may arise in the future. Finally, do something to celebrate. A moment like this should be remembered forever.

When my boyfriend of five months broke up with me, I was devastated. It turns out he had been cheating on me for a whole month. I became very depressed and got down on myself for many reasons. I told myself I wasn't attractive enough or smart enough to keep him. For three months, I refused to go out, was fired from my job, and didn't return any of my friends' phone calls. I was a real mess. My parents were also getting really worried, and were even talking about taking me to see a psychologist. I couldn't blame them. For months, I kept calling my ex and hanging up. I thought that I would never get over him. And then one day, I saw him across the street with a new girlfriend. But instead of feeling jealous, I discovered that I was no longer in love with him. It hit me like a bolt of lightning. Ever since that day, I started thinking about him less and less. And today, I wouldn't go out with him even if he begged me—which he has.

—BLYTHE, 24, RECEPTIONIST

Taking Revenge

Take a moment to imagine your ex in this scenario: He/she wakes up in the morning, probably in the arms of a new boy/girlfriend, takes a shower, eats breakfast, and walks out to the car to leave for work. But your ex is not going anywhere as, screaming in horror, he or she discovers that all four tires have been slashed. How does it feel? If you answered good, great, or glorious, wipe that smile off your face immediately. No matter how much he/she deserves it, revenge has a funny way of backfiring on you. And we're not even talking about the legal ramifications.

Revenge has become a very popular sport in recent years. There are books, seminars, movies, and even private avengers that will do the dirty work for you. So it's easy to see why so many people fall prey to the vendetta virus. You are probably angry with your ex, who may even have had the audacity to treat you abominably. Regardless, the moment for retaliation has passed. If you didn't think of standing up for yourself while the relationship lasted, take a lesson and perform better next time. Now that all has been said and done, we recommend you let sleeping dogs lie. The following reasons should give you a clue as to why.

You Can Lose Your Dignity

Contrary to popular belief, there is very little dignity in pouring sugar into your ex's perfectly innocent gas tank or in collecting cockroaches to throw through the window while your ex is out. While you may be successful in carrying out your reign of terror, your ex will always have the upper hand in knowing that you can be driven to such extreme measures. Hey, there's something really flattering about a jaded ex being so torn up about the breakup that they have to resort to childish antics for attention. You don't want your ex feeling superior, so refrain from doing anything that may make him or her feel more loved than necessary. A little apathy on your part will make your ex feel like the relationship meant very little to you, and isn't that the best possible revenge?

Another reason to hang up your Avenger hat is because you can lose the respect of your friends, your community, and even your family. If word gets out about you pulling some ridiculous prank, how will people feel about you then? Since you've already lost your

boy/girlfriend, the last thing you want to do is alienate your support network. After all, they're the ones who will help you get through this time.

Finally, you should think about how you will feel about yourself if you perform an act of revenge. Most acts of retaliation are followed by remorse and a lowered self-esteem on the part of the revenge seeker. You can't possibly respect yourself knowing that you lost control over your ability to use reason and restraint. Once you've sunk this low, God help you.

You Can Get Arrested

While you may be able to plead temporary insanity to get off the hook, you're better off avoiding the whole legal mess altogether. But crimes of passion are still crimes, and premeditated revenge will not go unpunished simply because someone broke up with you. You will have to adhere to the law, regardless of how bad you feel. So if you're really hung up and are just imploding from the need to redress the wrongs your ex has dealt you, try something relatively innocuous like writing his or her name and number on every bathroom wall you encounter. No matter how much you want to stick it to the evildoer, your first priority should always be to avoid landing in a holding cell.

You Can Get Hurt

The most common reason people act on their need for revenge is to get their ex's attention. Those of you who have never so much as contemplated any vengeful misdeeds may see this as a loopy way of going about things, but many people unconsciously hope that by doing something outrageous they will be able to win their ex's affections. They are basically saying, "Look what I'm willing to do to prove that I still love you." But what their ex boy/girlfriend is hearing is, "Look at how pathetic I am!"

The miscommunication inherent in all schemes of revenge can contribute to a lot of pain on both sides. You may not know it, but what you're after is impossible to get via pranks, manipulation, or trickery. What you're looking for is love, and nobody ever found it by hurting the object of his or her affection. In the end, you'll just end up feeling more lonely and depressed than ever.

Videos to Rent After a Bad Break-Up

1. *Fatal Attraction*
2. *Single White Female*
3. *Misery*
4. *I Know What You Did Last Summer*
5. *Carrie*
6. Any Pink Panther film
7. *Ishtar*
8. *Sleepers*
9. *Meatballs*
10. *Airplane*

What's most important here is that you be honest with yourself and accept that you may still have unresolved feelings. Stop laying the blame for the breakup on your ex. Take responsibility for the role you played, and you may not feel so desperate to get even.

> *When I found out that my girlfriend had been thinking about moving to another city to be with her old boyfriend, I totally freaked. It's not like she even cheated on me, but I still felt betrayed when I found out she loved someone more than me. When I heard, I immediately kicked her out. She had no place to go and ended up crashing on a friend's couch. The next day, I was still so mad that I packed up all her stuff and called in the Salvation Army. When the guys came to pick up my generous donation, I realized how stupid I was acting. I took back her things and called her to apologize. We never did patch things up completely, but I'm happy knowing that I kept my head in a terrible situation."*

—GREG, 36, DENTIST

On The Rebound

Coming out of a relationship is a miserable time. And since misery loves nothing so much as company, it is difficult to withstand the temptation to forget about what ails you by jumping into another relationship. The problem with using other people as heartbreak menders is that it can turn into a pattern. Next thing you know, you've got a list of busted relationships a mile long and no idea as to why your love life seems destined for failure.

As anyone who has ever been there will tell you, be sure to stay away from any new relationships until you are good and ready. When you're on the rebound, you are especially vulnerable and could put yourself in situations or relationships that you normally wouldn't be caught dead in. Better you clear your plate of all liaisons and concentrate on yourself for a while. Think about your past relationship issues and learn from them. Because, as the saying goes, those who do not learn from history are doomed to repeat it. So if you truly want to enjoy what the future has in store, give yourself time to come to terms with your past.

Consider Yourself Lucky: True Love Gone Awry

The history of love is littered with bad breakups and unhappy endings; for every Cinderella and Prince Charming, there is also an Amy Fisher and Joey Buttafuoco. If you're feeling depressed about your breakup, consider these star-crossed lovers:

Oedipus and Jocasta

Boy meets girl, they fall in love and get married; girl turns out to be his mother.

Romeo and Juliet

Boy meets girl, they fall in love, then they tragically kill themselves after societal pressures drive them nuts.

Carmen and Escamillo, from Bizet's Carmen

Bohemian temptress falls for handsome toreador, only to be killed by a spurned lover—a timid bureaucrat, no less.

Porgy and Bess

A kindly handicapped man falls in love with a big-hearted but wayward prostitute, who eventually leaves him for a good-for-nothing pimp named Sportin' Life.

Scarlett and Rhett

Two of the antebellum South's proudest and most charismatic souls fall in love and are dragged apart by equal doses of war, hardship, and personal shortcomings.

Tony and Maria

Before there was the comedy wedding, there was West Side Story—Romeo and Juliet of 20th-century New York. One minute Maria feels pretty, the next she's caught in a tragic crossfire.

Deanie and Bud, Splendor in the Grass

A midwestern high school couple, mad with desire, fall apart when society won't let them have sex; ultimately, Deanie recovers from mental illness and Bud becomes a dirt farmer with a large family.

Jenny and Oliver, Love Story

Rich boy and poor girl fall in love and have lots of long conversations; she dies.

Diane and Bobby; Andy and Sylvia

It's not Shakespeare, but the cast of NYPD Blue has had more romantic trauma and pratfalls than Hamlet and Falstaff rolled into one.

The Ex Factor

Upon breaking up, many a couple fantasizes about getting back together. Long nights spent alone can wreak havoc on anyone's psyche, especially if you don't have the first clue about how to work that Eric's Solitaire icon on your computer. So be forewarned: The urge to reconcile will be strong, but you must be stronger. After all, you did have a perfectly good reason for breaking up, right?

If the temptation to call your ex or show up at his or her house is just too overwhelming, head straight for your daily planner and make an appointment to call the next day. Yes, go ahead and write it down in permanent marker. This will allow you to rest easy for the time being. And chances are that come sunup you'll be looking at your agenda and shaking your head in bewilderment or disgust.

The more times you resist the impulse to come crawling back, the better you'll get at spending time without an escort. Once you're not so desperate for company and thinking more clearly, you'll finally be able to judge whether you did the right thing. Until that time comes, you should stock up on some serious willpower if you don't want to get into a vicious cycle of an on-again, off-again love affair.

Too Soon to Tell

If, in spite of all our warnings, your belief in the theory that the best way to forget a spoiled romance is to start a fresh one remains unshaken, go ahead and do what comes naturally. But at least try to gain a little perspective before you fall head over heels in love with the first man or woman who shows the slightest bit of interest. Understand that you are, in fact, on the rebound and keep a casual and light-hearted attitude about all of your dates.

If, perchance, you should find yourself falling deeply in love with someone you've just met, understand that it may just be the rebound talking. While seeing new people can distract you from your woes and confirm that there is life after you know who, then by all means, date away. But if you're beginning to get serious about someone new too soon after the separation, you may be getting in over your head.

The best way to deal with intense, rebound-related emotions is to reason your way out of them. Admit to yourself that you may be in dire need of affection and try to see your new flame from an objective perspective. If you still feel that you are deeply in love, then hold off on saying anything. You don't want to lead someone on, only to realize months later that you were never truly in love to begin with.

Heart to Heart

There's no harm in rebound relationships if you take them for what they're worth. They can reaffirm the fact that you are still as desirable and vied-after a catch as ever there was. Staying single for a year or longer is also par for the course. You can use this time to get back in touch with yourself. And don't worry if all your dates fail to measure up to the one that got away. That's only to be expected. After all, how can mere strangers ever compare to someone you once called "cookie toes." Eventually, as you put more and more experiences between the time of your breakup and the present day, you'll be ready for a new, and hopefully improved, relationship—one which may just force you to retire the phrase "on the rebound" from your vocabulary altogether.

Fighting Dream Symbols

Quarrel

A dream of a quarrel may indicate that an inner turmoil is plaguing you. If the person you're quarreling with is identifiable, look at your relationship with the person and see if you can identify the area of disagreement. There could be clues in the dream that indicate a way to resolve the differences.

Thorn

A thorn may represent an annoyance of some sort, "a thorn in your side."

Chapter 10

Let's Stay Together

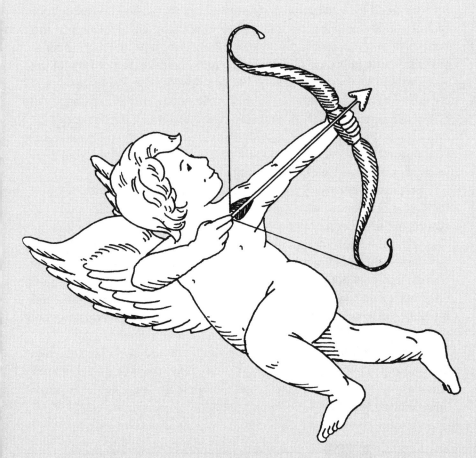

Now let's consider a much sunnier scenario: as a couple, you've cleared the hurdles of starting a new relationship admirably. You exchanged a first kiss, you made each other laugh, you even met each other's parents. It seems like there's nothing the two of you can't do, or is there? Right around this time, you happy lovebirds may start wanting something new. You've had your months of "I wonder if s/he likes me?" fun and are ready to enter the secure stage of "S/he likes me! S/he really likes me!" Once this happens, you may, in all likelihood, begin itching for a commitment. After all, doesn't a mature, committed relationship naturally follow meeting someone and falling in love? Maybe and maybe not.

Couples do many things together, but rarely do they agree on the right time to take the relationship to the next level. While you may be interested in getting a ring, a drawer, or anything in between to solidify your relationship, your partner may be worried and anxious about moving too fast.

Unfortunately, there is little agreement as to the right time to bring up your need for greater intimacy and exclusivity. There are two schools of thought on this one. The let-nature-take-its-course-ists hold firm to the belief that commitment has to evolve on its own, and that any discussion about the future can be damaging and disruptive to the flow of the relationship. Yet the other school, better known as the five-year-planners, believes that it is important to express your needs and feelings regardless of the outcome in case you end up wasting too much time in a dead-end liaison. In other words, if you're anxious to start a family, make sure your partner feels the same so you don't end up squandering your fertile years on someone completely incompatible.

As a single person, you probably wished to be in a relationship, thinking every person with a matched pair lucky, comfortable, and secure. Yet many committed people feel the same way about singles. They envy their carefree, independent ways and yearn for a time that has passed. Bottom line: Both lifestyles have their ups and downs. Living with someone is not an indication of future happiness, while living alone does not mean that your fate is cursed by the powers that be. Ultimately, it will be up to you to decide whether you're ready for the world of couplehood or wish to remain a lone ranger for a little longer.

Whether or not you're ready to commit, you are bound to face new trials and tribulations with the one you love. No one ever said that commitment was going to be easy or fun. So while getting together is one thing, staying together is the real challenge.

Mi Casa, Su Casa

Everything is going great: you practically live together and see each other every day. Then one day your partner tells you that maybe it's time you thought about splitting the rent. After all, it doesn't make much sense to be paying for two apartments while practically living in one.

Whether you were ambushed or made the suggestion yourself, living together for the first time can take some getting used to. While it's not as final as getting married, it's great practice for the real thing. Cohabitation is the best possible opportunity for two people to learn all about each other's habits, quirks, and temperament before finally tying the knot. The dating stage only takes you so far by letting you see your boy/girlfriend on his or her best behavior. Living together, on the other hand, can actually bring your partner's true colors to light. And, if you find that the two of you are truly compatible in every department, moving in together can be a wonderful experience.

Of course, you may have gotten used to the single lifestyle. There's the issue of privacy to contend with, money matters, and even the dreaded chores. You may have mastered the daily grind of living on your own, but now that you're part of a twosome there may be some changes afoot.

Private Property: No Trespassing

Just because the two of you have decided to share a roof doesn't mean that you will all of a sudden become one person. Each of you has individual needs and you will have to learn to respect your live-in lovee's personal space. That means no reading his mail, no listening to her phone calls, and no waiting up for one another in the middle of the night. The two of you will come and go as you please, provided you're not coming or going with someone else.

When moving in together, establish the rules of privacy right away. That way there won't be any spats or crossed wires. If your boyfriend insists that you stay away from his computer, you should try to do so, even when he's not around to catch you. And gentlemen, if your lady insists that you stay out of her medicine cabinets, lingerie drawers, and journal, make sure you respect these wishes.

In the beginning of your "playing house" experiment, you will also be tempted to spend all your time together. Make sure you don't make a habit out of it. Separate lives, friends, and interests are just as important now as they were at the beginning of your alliance. A variety of social outlets will keep both of you from getting cabin fever and will give your relationship that extra spark. And should your roommate decide to traipse off to enjoy a boys'/girls' night out, make sure he or she feels supported and understood. Realizing that separate interests will fuel mutual happiness should help you ward off any feelings of jealousy and insecurity.

Cleaning House

When it comes to housework, it makes little difference which of you is staying put and which is moving in. Claiming, "it's your place, you clean it" won't score you any points, and neither will, "washing the dishes is the least you can do as my guest!" Repeat after us: A live-in lover is not the same as a live-in maid. Cleaning up after yourself and doing the dishes as well the laundry will not stop even if your partner is a neat freak. If you're hoping to effect a diffusion of domestic responsibilities, whereby your constant companion will end up doing most of the work, think again. The two of you will have to come to a mutual agreement about these pesky but necessary details if you want to keep trouble out of paradise.

There are three ways of handling this division of menial labor. The two of you can decide who handles which chores. For example, you vacuum the rugs while s/he takes out the garbage. That's one option. If there is one chore that both you find especially detestable, taking turns can work wonders. One night you perform the hideous task, and the next night you gleefully watch your partner do it. Finally, the two of you can do each chore together. You can wash the dishes while s/he dries them. This kind of camaraderie will not only help you get things done faster, but you can whistle while you work and have fun all the while.

When my husband and I decided to live together for the first time, we had a lot of arguments about cleaning the house. I am a very neat person, and he doesn't care what the place looks like as long as he has enough free space to put his feet on the table. Whenever I tried to get

him to clean, he would complain and shirk his responsibility. Since he loved sports, I decided to turn the cleaning experience into a fun competition. Every time the house needed a good scrub, I would put on really fast music and we'd race around picking things up. We would score one point for every item we hung up or threw away. At the end, the one who earned the least amount of points would have to cook a full-course meal for the other. And since he hates to cook and loves anything I make, he's always motivated to win. Not only do we have fun doing the cleaning race, we have the most spotless house of all our friends.

—Sue, 29, Kindergarten Teacher

Paying the Bills

Not only will you have to figure out who pays which bill, you'll also have to split everything right down the middle. Regardless of your incomes, breaking everything down fifty-fifty will prevent arguments and inequality. And don't even think about pooling your funds via a joint bank account. There will be plenty of time for that once you are married. Unless your partner's fortune and the rent on his or her penthouse apartment rivals that of Donald Trump—in which case you could still find a way to pay your way by contributing to the house staff fund—insist that you split everything despite any protests.

Going Dutch on living expenses is the only way to avoid feeling either mightier-than-thou or lower than dirt. No matter what the two of you tell yourselves and each other, the person riding the gravy train is bound to feel indebted, while the one pulling it may acquire a superiority complex, replete with an entire gaggle of unsavory control issues. At this crucial formative stage of your relationship, even the slightest imbalance of power is bound to sow seeds of discontent. Even if your relationship isn't financially motivated, toe this line now and avoid problems in the future.

Too much talk of who owes what and how much can suck the romance out of any relationship. If you're concerned about how to split everything without forsaking that loving feeling, don't worry; where there's a will there's a way. You should first appoint one of you the designated buyer/payer. Each time the buyer purchases anything for the two of you, like groceries, housewares, or dinner, the

What to Do With the Things You Can't Live With

1. Hide them in the back of a closet.
2. Lend to someone who will appreciate their value.
3. Have them appraised for resale.
4. Put them all in one box and let your partner pick "just two."
5. Mention them to a best friend in hopes of creating an embarrassing situation.

nonbuyer should stash away half of that amount in a separate box. At the end of each month, the nonbuyer can simply give that money to the buyer. Feel free to reverse the roles every month just to keep things interesting. This way, you won't have to deal with the question of who paid for what or feel like you've just come from the cleaners. Most importantly, you'll be able to keep money issues from becoming a major factor in your relationship.

Padding the Love Nest

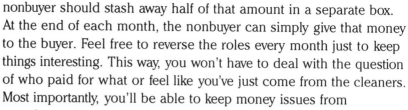

Different tastes call for different settings, but when two people put their heads together, there's simply no telling what they will come up with. The key to transforming your pad into one you could both appreciate is compromise. Many women may balk at the black leather La-Z-Boy recliners and minimalist styling tactics that are the signature props of red-blooded males everywhere. What's even worse is that many men will hold their ground, unable to tolerate the gossamer curtains and flower-print wallpaper that scream home to millions of modern women. While this conflict of interests may deal a crushing blow to your confidence in future bliss, there is no cause for worry just yet. This is where compromise comes in and saves the day.

The two of you can decide which items are absolutely indispensable and then draw up a floor plan, specifying where each item should be placed. Don't be surprised if a heated debate ensues, and don't burst into tears at the thought of having to spend many of your waking hours staring at a hideous pair of matching beanbag chairs. Flip a coin and resolve to live with the outcome.

Whatever personal effects are left over can go straight into a storage bin until you decide to stage a yard sale, go your separate ways, or invest in a larger house. Now is not the time to put your worldly possessions out with the trash, since you never know when and how your living arrangements will change. Keep your booty safely tucked away until you are sure of your future plans.

In terms of decor, try to strike a balance. You want to achieve a unisex look, so make sure that both genders are evenly represented. If you're planning on shopping together, try to pick neutral colors and solid patterns for the furniture and walls. That way, you'll both be pleased to call your new space "home."

Deciding whose television, VCR, or stereo to use shouldn't be difficult. All you have to do is figure out who has the most updated technology. And if you're really bogged down by this debate, put the extra telly and hi-fi in another room, just in case you don't agree with your partner's choice of music or televised programming.

Making It Work

Saying "I do" or "Let's move in together" may be hard, but sticking it out with the person you've chosen can be even more difficult. Once you make a commitment, you will feel obligated to make things work. Don't shake your head; this is a good thing. All relationships require a certain amount of work and effort.

Many people have a hard time swallowing this fact. They think that once you've selected the love of your life, it will be smooth sailing from here on out. Actually, nothing could be further from the truth. Finding someone to love may have its degree of difficulty, but the real challenge is in maintaining your staying power—sticking it out when most people would probably have thrown in the His and Hers monogrammed towels.

Relationships may be all fun and games at first, but to keep the spark alive you'll have to dig in your heels and prepare to work overtime. And while this line of work can be exciting, it's not going to be easy. If you make a concerted effort to stay together, the two of you may just come out stronger, closer, and even more in love than when you first got together.

Cheating Hearts

Now that you've taken the bold step of moving in together, you are expected to abide by certain rules. Rule #1: You will not have any other partners. By agreeing to live together, you decided to give up any other dalliances, no matter how tempting. The stress of moving into a new place or in with a new person is mind-boggling enough without the added pressure of one partner going through a delayed cold-feet reaction. Old leases will have to be shredded and new ones signed, furniture and clothes will have to be packed up and removed—in short, endless headaches will ensue. So if you're

Romantic Videos

Have a romantic night in your new-we're-living-together pad. Rent one of these videos:

1. *Titantic*
2. *Brief Encounter*
3. *Notting Hill*
4. *Mrs. Brown*
5. *Dr. Zhivago*

intent on settling in, make sure you're fully invested in the future of this relationship.

Staying true to your sweetie shouldn't be difficult, especially now that you're in cahoots. Hopefully, your love for your partner has blinded you to the charms of all others. But if you're still tempted to stray or have difficulty sticking with one person no matter how much you love them, the following tips should help keep you in line and out of the doghouse.

Keep the flirting to a minimum

A little harmless flirting has never hurt anyone. But if you're the type who's easily aroused, you may want to lay off the witty repartee and suggestive word play until you've battled the sex demon within.

There's nothing like a picture of your honey dumpling to keep the savage beast at bay. If you find yourself drawn to someone, whip out your wallet-sized photo and gaze into your baby's eyes to your heart's content. Pretending that the alluring stranger is your brother or sister is another efficient line of defense. Instead of flirting with the object of your lustful fancies, try to imagine how you would like your sibling to be treated. Using this more familial approach when meeting new people may just keep you from doing something you'll regret later on.

On company business

Conventions are hotbeds of vice and iniquity. When away on business, people tend to lose many of their cares and inhibitions. If your job requires extensive travel, you are at high risk of losing your virtue. While out from under your partner's vigilant watch, you may feel like cheating with a coworker or even a random bystander.

To avoid jeopardizing your relationship, bring extra work on all your business trips, just to make sure you won't have any time for fooling around. You can also plan activities like sightseeing to make sure you don't wander around with too much free time on your hands. By focusing only on company business or day excursions, you will be able to avoid dreaming up new and exotic ways to spend your free time.

Be upfront

If you don't want to make like a cat and stray, you should learn to be honest about your relationship status with new acquaintances.

More likely than not, people will stay away from you when they hear about your companion or spouse.

But take heed: there are people out there who thrive on doomed attractions, targeting those of you in committed relationships just for the fun of it. So, if you've been frank and up front but are still getting a serious vibe from some chip or chippie, take this cue to stay away. Not only does this person have no respect for you or your relationship, he or she is obviously trying to prove something to himself or herself. Simply walking away will spare him or her this unnecessary effort.

Bring more life to your own party

By paying closer attention to your companion and going out of your way to orchestrate fun activities that both of you can enjoy, you will single-handedly squash dead the cheating bug. When couples stop trying to have fun with one another, they sometimes turn to other people to recapture the spark that they themselves have lost. Taking responsibility for the down cycles in your relationship and turning bad times into good times may just keep you from seeking affection elsewhere. Not only will you avoid cheating on your companion, you will bring your relationship to a new level of excitement and mutual consideration.

Dealing with Betrayal

Finding out your partner has been unfaithful has got to be the worst feeling ever. After all, it was understood that neither of you would see other people. But then one day, when you least expect it, you find out that you were played for a fool as your partner flagrantly defiled the sanctity of your agreement.

Whether your boy/girlfriend just came out and told you or whether you discovered the horrid truth on your own doesn't matter. What does matter is how you and your companion feel about the future of your relationship. If your partner has fallen deeply in love with someone else, you may not have much of a say in what happens next. Or you may be the one who's unwilling to let the matter drop and may choose to end the relationship right then and there. But if you're both still madly in love and are willing to chalk up this incident to bad judgment, then there are things you can do to repair the damage.

What's Your Sign? Romance According to the Zodiac

Capricorn

At times, Capricorns need a partner who is serious, while other times they need the comic, the lighthearted innocent who makes them laugh. Which mate they end up with depends on where they are in life. That may be true for all of us to one extent or another, but it's especially true for the Capricorn.

Ultimately, the Capricorn's path is always serious business. No matter how hard you make them laugh, their path always leads back to the same riddle. Regardless of how hard they work, how far they climb, or how emotionally or physically rich they become, it's never enough. It only leads back to the solitude of self.

Get it out of your system

Anger is a healthy way to express your disappointment with your partner. There is no better time to get really mad than right after you find out what has been going on behind your back. If you have to throw pillows or even throw all of his or her clothes out the window, go ahead. Do anything that will help you vent your frustration. In the long run, you will feel better having expressed your emotions.

A place of your own

If you want to patch things up, the worst thing you can do is dwell on the situation ad infinitum. Instead, you should set aside a period of time in which to vent your anger. You can schedule a brief separation or even go out of town for a few days. Putting some distance between yourself and your partner will help you sort through your feelings and come to terms with the betrayal. Only after your thinking is clear can you decide whether to stay put or go with the wind.

When I found out my boyfriend had cheated on me with someone at work, I was furious. One night when we were coming home from an office party, he told me that he had slept with one of the secretaries. He insisted that it didn't mean anything, and that he loved me very much. But I was so mad, I told him I never wanted to see him again, and ran away to stay with my dad for two weeks without telling him where I was going. Eventually, he figured out where I was and started sending me flowers and candy every day. While none of these tactics to win me back worked, after spending some time on my own, I realized that I wasn't really mad at him. I was angry because I felt I had cheated myself by rejecting many great guys just to be with him. I then tried to go out with other people just to prove that I too could have fun. But when I was out with them, all I could think of was my boyfriend. The time I spent by myself helped me realize that I still loved him, and was ready to forgive him.

—SANDRA, 38, REGISTERED NURSE

Let bygones be bygones

If you have chosen to forge ahead with the relationship, you should avoid bringing up the betrayal every time you need a bargaining chip. While your partner may be sorry, constantly throwing the incident back in your partner's face will make him or her resentful and angry. Better to have several long discussions about the affair in private or with a counselor than to spend a lifetime rehashing the graphic details.

Doing Battle with the Green-Eyed Monster

At one point or another, even the most secure people have had a bout with jealousy. A little of this possessiveness is natural. It can make your partner feel loved and make you realize the depth of your feelings for your partner. But this is one case where a little goes a long way, because the results of too much jealousy are insecurity, hostility, and even criminal action. Some people get so consumed by the green-eyed monster that they get into the habit of accusing their partners of infidelity without so much as an ounce of proof. Needless to say, this type of jealous behavior can force the once-innocent consort to seek solace in the arms of strangers, and thereby pound the final nail into the coffin of what was once a beautiful romance.

There are many reasons why people feel jealous. They may have a bad cheating-chum experience in their past, they may fear being abandoned, or they may get queasy at the thought of their beloved preferring the company of another. Neither does jealousy restrict its dirty work to those times when one partner is hanging with members of the opposite sex. Some people get jealous when their partner spends time with friends, family, coworkers, or even a newborn child. There is no telling what catalyst will trigger these feelings.

Jealousy is as old as time itself, but there's no reason why you can't tame the green-eyed monster. Even the most jealous people have learned to live with their affliction without letting it destroy their lives. And even if you only get a wee bit insecure from time to time, the following coping mechanisms may help you curb the base urge to snoop, snipe, or otherwise let jealousy make a mockery of your relationship.

Eight Things You Should Never Do if Your Partner Cheats

1. Turn the other cheek
2. Call your partner's parents to give them a play-by-play rundown
3. Contact your partner's mister or mistress to schedule a duel
4. Tie your partner to the bed to make sure this kind of thing never happens again
5. Eat a gallon of ice cream every night
6. Drink lots of alcohol
7. Start smoking cigarettes
8. Blame yourself

Separate Lives

People who invest too much time in their partner have a higher chance of becoming jealous. If you are lacking hobbies, a full social life, and interests of your own, you may come to rely on your partner to keep you entertained and amused. But what happens when s/he makes other plans? If your only options now are to either rent a movie or to read yourself to sleep, you're in trouble. With so little resources, it's no wonder you automatically feel abandoned, lost, and jealous of all the people spending time with your partner as you sulk.

The best way to combat the jealousy of a dependent personality is to get a full and thriving life of your own, a life that does not depend on your partner's participation. You can take a class, learn to rollerblade, or get back in touch with old friends. Instead of sitting at home worrying about what your partner is doing, let your partner worry for a change by going out to have a little fun of your own.

Playing What If

Never underestimate the power of the imagination. Thinking about or visualizing your partner having fun with members of the opposite sex is not only a form of self-flagellation, but it can lead to misdirected anxiety and aggression.

To keep a rein on your imagination, try to recognize when and where these flights of fancy begin. Maybe these ideas pop into your mind during times of stress or when you're feeling depressed. Try to come to grips with the fact that while your imagination may be all-powerful, its creations have nothing to do with the reality of your situation. When your imagination does get out of hand, try to think about your situation as logically as possible. Think about the love you share as a couple and what you can do to make the relationship even better. Recalling the many times your imagination has led you astray should also help you see the error of your ways.

Guess Who's Coming to Dinner?

Experiencing pangs of jealousy over your boy/girlfriend's life B.Y. (Before You) is not uncommon. Few living, breathing people can measure up to the mystery and allure of the past. Those who find themselves obsessed with a partner's former life and love are bound to feel pale in comparison. The truth is that no one can beat out the ghost of good times past, so stop trying. Instead, get to the

bottom of your problem by finding out who it is that has got you running so scared.

While this may not work in all situations, getting the real goods on a specter from your partner's past may allay a lot of fears. If s/he is still palling it up with a former flame, the best thing you can do is to join in. While your imagination may have built the dreaded ex into a superior being, once you meet the face behind the name, you'll be able to tell for certain. Chances are your mind has been playing tricks on you, and there was nothing to worry about.

Conflicts of Interest

Do you remember your first fight? Many couples do. If you recall anything at all about that first altercation, it's probably not the cause of the uproar but the reconciliation that you remember. Yes, those were the days, times nearly forgotten, when quarreling actually seemed like a novelty or even a sign of increased comfort in the relationship. You probably fought about issues that were important to both of you, as opposed to trivial arguments such as whose turn it was to cook dinner. Now that you're living together, prepare to argue on a whole new playing field. Not that lovers' spats are all bad. Actually, couples who never fight have a much greater chance of landing on the skids in the future. Depending on your methods, a good fracas can be a positive way to express frustration and concern.

At an early age, we pick up our habits and styles of conflict resolution by watching our parents. As an adult, you may begin recognizing patterns in your family's fighting styles. Once again, fighting on its own is not a negative thing. It's just that most people never learned the right and wrong ways to clash wills. Becoming an apt fighter can be easier than you think, provided you simultaneously help your partner improve his or her ability to manage conflict. Once the two of you have learned the ropes, there will be no problem you can't solve.

Harboring Grudges

Constructive fighters know that any feelings that are repressed for long periods of time can turn into potential problems down the line. If your partner does something to upset you, make sure you point out what has offended you. Be as specific as possible. Many people believe that their partner should be a mind-reader. Unfortunately,

Best Movies for Fighting Couples

1. *Who's Afraid of Virginia Woolf?*
2. *When Harry Met Sally*
3. *The Goodbye Girl*
4. *Rocky*
5. *The Odd Couple*
6. *The Taming of the Shrew*
7. *The War of the Roses*

most people don't have that ability. It's up to you to air your griev-
ances, concerns, and disappointments, lest your needs go unnoticed
and you end up harboring feelings of hostility and anger.

Time Out

In the heat of passion, people can say and do things they're
likely to regret later on. Oftentimes the best course of action is no
action at all. If you find yourself getting very angry, extricate yourself
from the situation until you've calmed down. But since leaving the
scene of the crime can anger your partner, try explaining the reasons behind your quick exit to avoid upsetting each other further.
You can then take a walk, run an errand, or go out with some
friends. Once the two of you have some perspective on the situation,
you may not feel so angry with one another and will be able to
come up with a solution.

Keep a Lid on It

Too much anger during a fight can be counterproductive. If you're
discussing a sticky situation, make sure to keep your voices down and
the household accessories intact. Anger has a domino effect—the
more hostile you become, the angrier you will make your partner.

If you feel out of control, take a step back and evaluate the situation. Try to freeze-frame the moment and evaluate the situation
from an objective perspective. People sometimes fight about the sil-
liest things and feel ridiculous about it the next day. Performing this
technique will speed up this realization and will have you reunited
and laughing about your foibles in no time.

No Low Blows

Doubtless, many of you have heard the following variation on an
old saying: "Sticks and stones can break my bones, but words cause
permanent damage." People can and will say the most horrendous
things, and those who are closest to us can be the worst offenders.
As a couple, you learn about each other's most intimate fears and
vulnerabilities. But using these to hurt your partner in times of conflict is strictly off limits.

This type of fighting style can create a feeling of distrust, and
your partner will have a hard time confiding in you because of the
fear that you will use the privileged knowledge as a weapon. If

you're about to use something very personal against your partner, try to think about these consequences. Once lost, trust is a difficult thing to regain.

Idle Threats

Threatening to leave your partner during a fight is a very immature way of handling conflict. You may feel like packing up and leaving right there and then, but in reality the two of you will probably stay together long after you've cooled off. By threatening abandonment you are putting your partner on the defensive. Your partner may either call your bluff and force you to evacuate the premises, or repress his or her feelings of anger to keep you from walking away. Either way, both of you lose.

The best way of dealing with this impulse is to remind yourself of the other fights you survived. Realizing that fighting is normal and not grounds for premature evacuation will help both of you stick it out long enough to resolve the problem.

Take Responsibility

Blaming others for your problems is easier than looking within yourself. But sometimes, admitting that you may have had something to do with the argument is the only way to solve it. If you constantly insist that your partner apologize or admit that s/he is wrong, don't be surprised when your partner ends up resenting you. Arguments are all based on the simple action-reaction combination. Someone does something; someone else reacts and voila! You've now got all the makings of an argument. As you can see, it's well near impossible to cause an argument on your own. Just like the tango, it takes two to start a fight. So if you refuse to say you're sorry and you won't budge an inch until your partner gives in, you should try to figure out what you're so afraid of.

Some people fear that by admitting fault they will be admitting to not being perfect and will, in turn, lose their partner's admiration and respect. But what you have to remember is that your partner loves you, flaws and all. Contrary to what you may have told yourself, your partner doesn't think you're perfect by any means—especially if you have a hard time taking responsibility. So go ahead and say it, "I was wrong." The experience may be liberating.

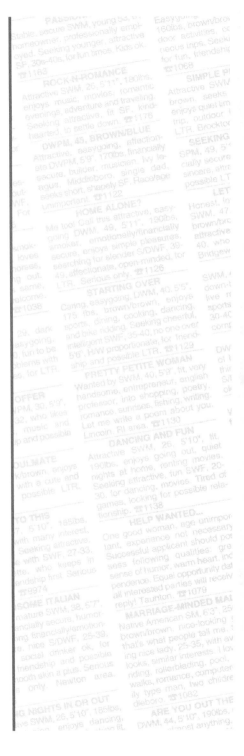

Chapter 11
Big Firsts

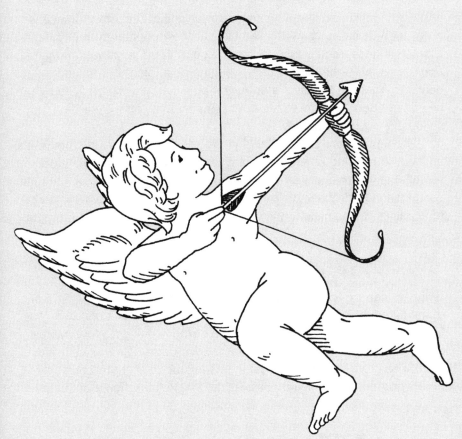

In any burgeoning relationship there is a plethora of gut-wrenching, stomach-turning moments—they're called firsts.

You'll have your first fight, and find yourself feeling confused as to how you should proceed. Should you storm out, slam the door behind you and wait for a conciliatory phone call, or should you stick around lest you leave and never hear from your beloved again?

You'll also have the disquieting pleasure of celebrating your first Valentine's Day. Woe to those who have to undergo the dreaded gift exchange ceremony after only two weeks together. Should you, for instance, splurge on expensive perfume, or play it low-key with a designer imposter? Must you plan an elaborate evening that includes a five star dining experience and a carriage ride through the park, or can you stick to a date that won't require a tuxedo rental? Believe it or not, these are the questions that will keep you awake at night.

When it comes to relationship milestones, we all have a tendency to create problems where none exist. The truth is that while you may be destined for each other, you're still virtual strangers. Thus, you're dealing with the unknown and being confronted by an infinite realm of possibilities. Every word and gesture is laden with significance, every silence is pregnant with meaning. When she laughed after opening your birthday gift, was it because she found your choice of *The Everything Dating Book* amusing, or because she was beginning to plan your untimely demise? When he frowned after unwrapping that new stereo system, was he just pondering where to put it, or thinking that you were getting too serious? You never can tell.

Of course, there is a way to circumvent all such moral dilemmas. It's a little known thing called protocol. This all-purpose code of conduct will enable you to handle every discomforting moment with just the right combination of delicacy, diplomacy, and tact. If you want to avoid hours of needless consternation, we suggest you learn it, love it, and live by it.

You Say It's Your Birthday, Already?

Birthdays can be a difficult time for those of us who live in mortal fear of the aging process. That's a given. But what many don't realize is that birthdays take just as great a toll on the birthday boy/girl's love interest. Most people in relationships feel as if they're on trial and awaiting judgement when giving a gift. Fortunately, picking the perfect present would be a whole lot easier if you consider the single, most important deter-

mining factor—relationship duration. The amount of time you two have spent in the throes of snuggling bliss should have a direct impact on the two variables of cost and creativity. In other words, as time spent together increases so should the amount of cash spent and/or creative energy expended on gift selection.

The Birthday Fundamentals

If you're so unfortunate as to have only had three dates before a birthday arrives, the general rule is to acknowledge the occasion without going overboard. It is never appropriate to completely disregard a friend's birthday, even if they've only recently walked into your life. However, spending hundreds of dollars on someone you're just getting to know is no solution. After you've shared a few dates, a token of your affection, be it ever so humble, will suffice to say that you cared enough to give something—even if it isn't the very best.

Now suppose you've been dating each other for about three or four months, and can easily point him/her out in a crowded room. In this case you should put a little more time and effort into picking out that perfect gift. Let the type of present you bestow onto your boy/girlfriend be a reflection of how much you relish the times you've spent together. A more personal gift is in order, something that says I know you better than most people and my gift will stand out.

Finally, for those lucky couples who have stayed together above and beyond the six-month high-water mark (or have verbally acknowledged their burning love for one another), thinking up a birthday gift should be taken very seriously. You should find yourself cogitating long and hard about a meaningful gift, something that tells your significant other (s.o.) that they are truly significant. Upon receiving your gift, the birthday boy/girl should recognize it as something special, something that you'd never dream of giving anyone other than him/her. In this case try to balance a certain degree of creativity with monetary value, but be advised: nothing creative ever came out of the local K-mart.

Helpful Hints

If you're still stuck for ideas, you've stumbled upon the right page. Here's where we turn the theory of birthday gifts into practice. Short of going out and actually buying the gift for you, there's little else we can do.

What's Your Sign? Romance According to the Zodiac

Aquarius
Aquarians need the same space and freedom in a relationship that they crave in every other area of their lives. Even when they commit, the need doesn't evaporate. They must follow the dictates of their individuality above all else. This stubbornness can work against them if they aren't careful. Aquarians usually are attracted to people who are unusual or eccentric in some way. Their most intimate relationships are marked by uniqueness.

The Car Rental Companies

- Alamo (800) 354-2322
- Avis (800) 331-1212
- Budget (800) 527-0700
- Dollar (800) 800-4000
- Enterprise (800) 736-8227/ (800) RENT-A-CAR
- E-Z Rent-A-Car (888) 755-4555
- Hertz (800) 654-3131
- Hertz Gold Club Reservations (800) CAR-GOLD
- National (800) 227-7368
- Payless Car Rental (800) PAY-LESS
- Rent A Wreck (407) 823-8388
- Thrifty (800) 367-2277

Third or fourth date: If you've had two or three dates with a person before his/her birthday arrives, chances are you've covered banal territories such as favorite type of movie or music of choice. Get some mileage out of these vital stats by procuring a book, video or CD that you know your date will enjoy. If, per chance, s/he happens to be an avid viewer of the televised *Felicity* saga, it might be a good idea to purchase a copy of the *Felicity* soundtrack. They don't have to listen to it to understand that you're keeping track of their likes and habits. In regards to planning an event for a third date birthday, no special design for the evening is necessary, a dinner and a movie will more than suffice.

Third or fourth month (or the emotional equivalent thereof): Time to get more personal. In this case, nothing says "I like you" like an article of clothing that you know will flatter your date's appearance. A note to men: this is not the time to buy yourself a gift, for those guys who've already made the woman-gift-clothing-sexy lingerie connection, forget it, its probably too early for a "bad girl kit." As far as planning an event goes, a romantic candle-light dinner, made with your own two hands, should do the trick. Just make sure you prepare the kind of dishes that you both know how to cook and know that your date will appreciate. Don't let burned and bitter experience teach you that home-cooked birthday meals do not lend themselves to culinary experimentation.

Six months or more (or the emotional equivalent): By this time you should plan a truly unique event in honor of your aging darling. A weekend getaway to his/her favorite nearby vacation spot (since most birthdays don't fall on national holidays time spent away will be a factor) comes highly recommended. The same can be said of dinners at impossible-to-get-reservations restaurants and popular theatrical productions. Whether you decide to go out of town or remain local, a hot-oil-massage-by-candle-light nightcap will end your special evening on a high note.

Foregoing the above is alright only for those who are monetarily or back-rub challenged. If such is your situation, planning a surprise party should be an excellent alternative. Not only will this go to show that you know all of your date's friends and family members, but it will also express the depth of your emotion and your commitment to a shared future.

At Last: Valentine's Day

After spending a spate of Valentine's Days alone, with nothing but a variety of 900-numbers to console you, the idea of sharing this magical time with a special someone can be quite exhilarating. No longer will you have to seethe in silence as other, less deserving, guys and gals prance smugly about town, with their Valentine's flowers and heart-shaped boxes of candy in hand. All your hard work has paid off. You are now ready to observe the one day reserved solely for the celebration of love and join the throngs of happy Valentine's Day couples everywhere.

Testing the Waters

Whether you've celebrated your fair share of V-Days or are a novice, there are a few ground rules to follow from the get go. The most important rule (and this applies to both of the sexes) is that no matter how you feel about the occasion—whether you beam at very mention of the word or are a veritable Valentine's Day abolitionist—Murphy's Law will guarantee that your date will see things a little differently.

Here's how it works: Should you decide to chuck the Hallmark convention, explaining to your date that you don't need an excuse to celebrate your relationship, they will probably think that you've forgotten to buy them a present. Worse yet, they may chalk your balk up to penny-pinching. If, on the other hand, you decide to go all out, splurging on everything from stuffed animals, to candy, to flowers only to realize that your date doesn't particularly care for this annual event, you will probably feel as if all of your hard work was for naught.

Part of preparing for Valentine's Day means having a talk with your s.o. about your plans. Don't get too specific, you don't want to ruin a surprise, but do try to hold a general conversation about the holiday well in advance. The issue shouldn't be too hard to broach. Simply come right out and ask whether your date's experiences with Valentine's Day have been positive. If he/she grumbles and tries to avoid the discussion, you can rest assured that your coupon for a free make-out session won't meet with the appropriate level of excitement. However, if your partner seems genuinely pleased with the notion, you have your green light to let all systems go.

Dare to Be Different

From day one in kindergarten, we are taught that all Valentine Day presents are created equal. Think back to those plenty-card packs, where all you have to do was write in the lucky person's name and slip it into their locker or desk. When you consider the uniformity of our earliest gift-giving experiences, is it any wonder that we can't make heads or tails of what to get our special someone on Valetine's Day. Sure, you can head out to the store and stand in the candy/flower aisle with the rest of the pack, or you can try something different for a change.

Just because we associate Valentine's Day with flowers and candy, doesn't mean you can't break the rules a bit. Okay, so you can't resist splurging on a huge red box of candy that screams "Happy Valentines Day" or a dozen long-stemmed red roses for your Valentine. Who can? But ask yourself, is it really the gifts, or is it the color red that gets you in the holiday spirit? An enduring symbol of romantic love, red can cause bulls to charge and traffic to halt. Without the red badge of fiery passion, flowers and candy are just so much flora and calories—totally powerless.

The key to keeping the spirit of Valentines Day alive is to incorporate the color red with a totally unique gift idea. The possibilities are endless when you consider red boxers, red T-shirts, red hats, red photo frames, red ear muffs, red—or rather rose-colored—glasses, even red bookmarks for those of you who've just met. If all this fails, you can always go for a red alert: get a red beer/coffee mug, fill it with red candy and complete the presentation with a big, red bow.

Women can also have some fun by turning the tables on their boyfriends. Buy him the red box of chocolates and the red roses for a change. Believe you us, no one can deny the pull of a sweet craving, and ladies aren't the only ones who need to stop and smell the roses. Don't worry, the last thing he'll be seeing is red.

"You Go First." "No, You." "But I Insist."

When we say "gift exchange," we're not suggesting you trade the fruits of your dates' hard labor into cold, hard cash (especially as this maneuver can backfire when they ask you about that watch they bought you last Valentine's Day). No, we're simply talking about an oft-neglected custom that has managed to retain its importance

despite centuries of abuse. In days of yore, when feudal lords still roamed the earth, the exchange of gifts was never just about "I'll show you mine, if you show me yours." It used to be that paying homage and receiving gifts were sacred acts, requiring much pomp and circumstance for their proper execution.

Of course, that's not to say that you should bore your date senseless by prolonging the gift-giving ceremony. But you should understand that exchanging gifts is a far more serious matter than our cynical society will have you believe.

Consider this scenario: You buy your date a large, heart-shaped cookie, because you know how much s/he loves that chocolate chips. Just as you finish patting yourself on the back, you learn that s/he got you that expensive Mont Blanc pen you've been eyeing for eons, but would have never bought for yourself. Uh-oh.

Should your gift exchange resemble the foregoing, you have recourse to two strategies. The first is to pretend that your gift was but the peak of a far greater iceberg—naturally, you have something special in store for your thoughtful companion. To pull this off, you'll have to generate a quick game plan like a carriage ride through the park or booking a hotel room and telling the concierge to stock it with champagne and caviar at the last possible minute. For those of you who squirm at such underhanded tactics, there is option two. As much as it may pain you to go through with this, you'll have to take your lumps like a wo/man and vow to do better next time.

Think you have it all figured out by now? Don't be so sure. What if the opposite happens, and you're the one who has spent countless hours in the pursuit of a perfect gift, only to find out that your special someone has recycled the old vase given to him/her by Aunt Lucy last Christmas. Do you A) scream in horror, B) cry all over your romantic candlelit dinner, C) simply accept the gift and vow to get revenge next Valentines, or D) none of the above?

The mature adults who chose answer D can skip on to the next section. As for the rest of you cry babies, we have only one thing to say, grin and bear it. No matter how terrible the person's gift turns out to be, you can still salvage the evening by faking it. Even if you're in no mood to be romantic and are even on the verge of tears, by all means try to smile through them. Multiply your own mortification by ten, and maybe you'll have some idea of how your date feels at this very moment.

Friend-Meeting No Nos

- Drinking too much.
- Revealing secrets about your sex life.
- Showing off about job or money.
- Flirting with them.
- Taking about yourself too much.
- Trying to dig up dirt about your date.
- Flaunting your relationship in their face.
- Criticizing your date in front of them.

Major Airlines

American Airlines
(800) 433-7300

AmericaWest Airlines
(800) 235-9292

Bahamasair (800) 222-4262

British Airways
(800) 247-8726

ComAir (800) 354-9822

Continental (800) 523-3273

Delta Airlines/Delta Express
(800) 221-1212

Northwest Airlines
(800) 225-2525

Southwest Airlines
(800) 435-9792

TWA (800) 221-2000

United (800) 241-6522

US Airways (800) 428-4322

US Airways Vacation
Packages (800) 455-0123

Virgin Atlantic
(800) 862-8621

Western Pacific
(800) 930-3030

Friends or Foes?

Meeting your significant others' friends for the first time is much like being the new kid in town. No matter how cool, good looking or successful you may be, you feel as if you're somehow presumed guilty until proven innocent. If this seems unfair, it's only because you've yet to hear the accusations. You are hereby charged with the theft of a best friend and the disruption of a once peaceful equilibrium between single allies.

Here's the rub: You can't possibly defend yourself against any of these charges. The best you can do at a first meeting is to keep an open mind and remain cool, calm and collected. Just because you can't determine the actions of your s.o.'s friends doesn't mean that you're powerless to control your own reactions. Understand that these people have been around long before you came along, and their hostility is not aimed at you, but at the potential loss of their friend. This stoic approach will help you pass the first meeting test with flying colors, and, most importantly, save you from any unnecessary aggravation.

Mind Your Manners

In all likelihood, your girl/boyfriend's clique is just as eager to be liked as you are. Still, good friends are like loyal dogs, their initial instinct is to defend their territory. As the trespasser, you are in no position to get snippy. Just stay cool, and try to deflect the attention away from yourself. If you look for common interests and ask his/her friends about their jobs and backgrounds, you just may find that any friend of your steady is a friend of yours.

Conversely, should you find that your tolerance is running dangerously low, the standard operating procedure is to make as hasty an exit as possible without causing a spectacle. Instead of dragging your date with you, and certifying yourself as a bona fide friend-stealer, try to leave on your own. You can make a quick phone call, and come up with an excuse about an emergency at home. No matter what happens, being considered a flake is much better than getting into verbal fisticuffs with people you barely know.

Letting Your Guard Down

Even the fortunate few, those who meet with a warm reception at the hands of their partners' friends, should not be so quick to consider themselves in the clear. While your date's confidantes may seem like the most open-hearted of people, you should remain wary. You are, after all, still trying to make a good first impression.

Being embraced by your partner's peers may give you a warm feeling, perhaps too warm. Heady with the power of your own charisma, you stand in danger of getting too comfortable and forgetting that your actions have consequences. Even if your date's comrades are falling all over themselves trying to be nice to you, remember that you are still being judged. Since these people don't know you, their concept of you is being formed and amended with every word you utter and every gesture you make, so be on guard and on your best behavior.

The Parent Trap

After passing the dreaded friend-test, many of you will feel as if you're home free. What you don't realize, poor dears, is that the greatest test of your relationship still lies ahead. No matter what you do to avoid it, no matter how you try to escape it, meeting your partner's parents is as inevitable as death and taxes.

First meeting with parents can be tricky. If they love you too much, you may come out feeling that you are being primed for the big "M"—marriage. Should they not embrace you with open arms, your relationship with your s.o. may become a thing of the past. So what is a person to do?

Show No Fear

In the war between parents and potential suitors, there is only one line of defense—confidence. Most parents are dying to see you sweat. Well aware that they are in the driver's seat, parents will undoubtedly relish their authority with undue zeal. They will ask you questions, grill you under the hot lights of the living room chandelier, and then watch happily as you crack under the pressure of their

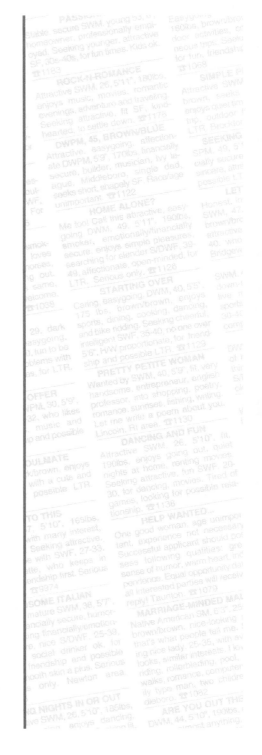

scrutiny. Okay, okay, it's never quite that bad, but by preparing for the worst, you will be ready for any situation.

By bolstering your confidence before the big meeting, you will be able to disarm even the most belligerent set of parents. Tell yourself that it is they that will have to make a good impression on you, and not the other way around. Then, remind yourself of all your best qualities. Your confidence is bound to shine through, and make you seem smarter, funnier, and more engaging than all those who came before you.

A Small Token

Whether you're stopping by for ten minutes or staying for dinner, bringing a gift will make you seem thoughtful and considerate. Even if you end up breaking a precious family heirloom, you will not be judged as severely if you've come bearing gifts.

Selecting the proper gift shouldn't be too hard. All you need to do is try to find something the whole family can enjoy, like a bottle of wine for dinner, a pie for dessert, or a board game for entertainment. The last thing you'll want to do is neglect any member of the family or overspend.

Act Your Age

Think back to when you were a teenager. Didn't you hate when adults tried to be hip or talk on your level. Not only is talking down to someone patronizing, it's also annoying. The same is true of talking up to someone. In doing so, you will come off haughty and insincere, two qualities that won't sit well with the people you're trying to impress.

Instead of scrambling to find topics of conversations that you think will appeal to them, let them lead the repartee. If no chit chat is forthcoming, ask Mom or Dad about their neighborhood, how long they've been married, their jobs, interests, and so forth. Once you get them to open up, you can launch into your own spiel. Just don't pretend to be someone you're not. If Mom is an avid golfer, and you've never played a round in your life, don't act as if you know what a nine iron is. Be honest. It works almost every time. And if it doesn't? Well, at least you'll respect yourself in the morning.

Bon Voyage!

Escaping the daily grind as a couple can be a thrilling experience. You can leave the entirety of your worries at the departure gate, you can put a do-not-disturb sign on your door and do what comes naturally all day long, you can even indulge your Bonnie-and-Clyde fantasies by pretending you've gone on the lam with your illicit affair. To go or not to go, however, isn't always the question.

The processes of analyzing your expectations and making your travel arrangements can usher in a vast array of unexpected concerns and pesky details. By the time you're through, you might actually find yourself thinking up new and inventive put-downs for whichever Martha Stewart-ancestor that said "getting there is half the fun." Still, if you want your vacation to have its optimum restorative effect, you'll have to face a host of issues head on.

High, Apple-Pie-in-the-Sky Hopes

All people, at some point in their lives, have had the misfortune of buying a movie ticket or renting a video that exposes them to what we call the "happy couple montage." In this sequence, a director usually has the beautiful and lithesome actors engage in a series of behaviors that could only be described as preposterously happy. See the happy couple laughing and making love over their morning coffee, see the happy couple splashing at the beach, see the happy couple playing at the amusement park, in fact, see the happy couple breaking into spontaneous fits of laughter over just about anything at all.

Later that night, the once contented movie-goers come home from their dinner-and-a-movie date, and act out a montage of their very own making. See the movie-goers reflecting on their relationships. See the movie-goers bursting into uncontrollable tears.

Moral of the story? Relationships are not all about good times and burning love, and neither are romantic getaways. If uncomfortable silences, annoying habits, and petty squabbles find their way into your interaction at home, chances are they'll follow you on vacation. Even if your relationship is nothing short of coupled bliss, you may find that travel, with all its drastic changes of circumstance, can put undue pressure on a once stable rapport. Those are the plain facts, not reasons to avoid the travel agency. Because, as many

The Laws of Meeting Your Potential In-laws

1. Proper attire is a must. No down-to-there necklines or cut-off jean shorts.

2. Muster every ounce of sincerity to compliment the family home

3. Bring a small gift for the hosts

4. Don't overstay your welcome

5. Take interest in their family history

6. Never engage in PDA in front of parents

7. Avoid Mama and Papa bears' favorite chairs at all costs

can attest, the bright side of a shared journey is that it truly can bring two people closer together.

The thing to keep in mind is that if you go into your vacation with realistic expectations, you'll not be disappointed. Better yet, prepare for the worst case scenarios (lost luggage, cancelled reservations, round-the-clock rain, the works), and see if you don't wind up having the time of your life. A vacation is not necessarily going to intensify or sour your romance. And be prepared, because your relationship can go either way.

Ready or Not

If you're two weeks into a relationship, and you've yet to ascertain whether your s.o. has quit playing the field, this is not the time to be dropping hints and sending away for B&B catalogs. Neither should you propose taking a trip if your sole intention is to get your date into bed (very naughty). Sadly, when it comes to romantic excursions, both men and women are guilty of jumping the gun for their own selfish reasons.

When the urge to splurge on a vacation with your s.o. strikes, may we suggest that you analyze your motivation prior to spilling the big news. If pressuring your partner into a commitment or a compromising position figures anywhere on your list, you're better off holding your tongue. Your s.o. will quickly see through your subterfuge and recoil before you can so much as say, "I only meant that . . . "

A certain level of commitment must be established before you can make the dinner companion-to-travel companion transition. Time will have to be spent, trust earned, mutual affection determined and sexual issues resolved. Then, and only then, will you finally be ready to say "Where to?"

Let Me Take You to the Casbah, Please?

Broaching the issue of a romantic getaway should not pose a problem. Most people will jump for joy at the prospect of vacationing with someone for whom they harbor deep feelings. Let's face it, there comes a time in all our lives when tagging along on our parents' vacations no longer inspires the same childlike wonder that it did when we were, say, four. The orgiastic spring break ritual may also lose its grip on the imagination after four consecutive years of flying Mexicana to Cancun. And while Big Chill-style retreats can still entice us, nothing gets the juices flowing like a romantic getaway.

Once you decide that a joint vacation is the way to go, you can test the waters by asking, "What do you think about you and me taking a trip together?" Or you can take the authoritative approach, and say "Let's take a trip together." If the thought of making either of these innocuous propositions leaves you with sweaty palms and knots in your stomach, it's fair to say that your relationship has not progressed to the point where you'd be comfortable spending several days together.

Who's Got the Time?

After agreeing to hop the holiday express as a pair, you'll need to address some practical concerns, the first of these being scheduling. Unless you and your s.o. are both retirees, royalty or heirs to ancestral fortunes, your fun-filled plans are probably going to have some rigid work schedules to contend with. You may think that love conquers all, but try telling that to your employer and see which wins out, your source of money or a good time with your honey.

Since taking your laptop, cell phone and beeper with you is ill-advised, you may need to put off the travel until your two-weeks of freedom rolls around. To synchronize your vacation time, expect to delay the journey for a minimum of one month. Even if you and snuggle bunny both have weeks and weeks of unused vacation time, you'll still have to give your employer some notice if your scheme is to skip out for one or more work weeks. Depending on your professional environment, you may have to wait anywhere from three weeks to three months.

Unacceptable, is it? Well, short of walking out on your job, there's little you can do. And we mean "little" in the most literal sense of the word. A mini-trip, which lasts a mere two or three days, can be just as much fun as a full-blown vacation. Better yet, these short spurts of constant togetherness can be a great way to ease yourself into the notion that you've crossed the great divide, the dating equivalent of the Cumberland Gap—you're now part of a couple that travels together. Make no mistake, once you start traveling as a duo, the altar, or talk thereof, is only minutes away.

Surprise! We're Going to Vegas!

If the spark in your relationship is grounded wholly in the element of surprise, you may well be able to get away with presenting your beau/belle with a plane ticket at the very last moment. In fact, you may

Priceline Is a New Type of Travel Agent

If you're looking to save money on your airfare and have some flexibility in your travel schedule, contact Priceline at (800) PRICELINE or www.priceline.com. Priceline works with the major airlines to sell unsold seats. What's great about this service is that you decide how much you want to pay for your tickets and Priceline will locate an airline that has seats available and that will accept your offer. There are some restrictions, but the goal of Priceline is to provide travelers with the airline tickets they want at the price they want to pay. Tickets can be purchased hours, days, weeks, or even months in advance.

even rack up bonus points in the spontaneity department. Otherwise, you're not to make any crucial decisions (i.e. destination, accommodation, mode of transportation) without your partner's input. Unless, of course, your intention is to tick them off good and proper.

You might find this hard to believe, and we beg you to brace yourself for the shock fast approaching, but not everyone enjoys lying out in the sun. Gambling is yet another activity that doesn't interest all the people, all the time. While your best memories may be of a cruise line, those prone to motion sickness (yes, even the claustrophobic ones) may opt to spend an hour suspended between floors in a crowded elevator rather than a day on any vessel bearing a proper name.

To be effective in pleasantly surprising your s.o., you have to know them very well. You will have had to discuss past travels, preferred accommodations, dream destinations, and the like. No surprise, however, is completely fool proof. After meeting every conceivable contingency and running yourself ragged to make all the arrangements, you may still find that you've bungled the timing. How could you have known about that unavoidable bachelor/bachelorette party, scheduled to kick off only twenty-four hours after your departure? Oh the humanity, oh the exercise in futility.

Take heart. In time, you will be able to make the surprise vacation a reality, if that is indeed your ultimate dream. When it comes to the first trip, however, two heads are better than one. You'll have to decide on your destination, your travel arrangements, and the length of your stay. Choosing a hotel, a motel, or a camp ground should also be done as a team. Remember, making all the arrangements alone is just as unfair to you as it is to your would-be companion.

After you've come to some semblance of a compromise, have fun talking about all the things you'll do together, while revealing to your companion just the type of tourist persona s/he can expect to encounter on the trip. Since this is your first vacation together, there's still so much that you don't know. Travel brings out odd qualities in people—some want to take in every view, gaze at every national treasure and turn over every stone, others are content to watch Spectravision in their hotel rooms from dusk till dawn and emerge only for snack breaks. Hopefully, you two will be able to meet somewhere in the middle.

Your All-Purpose Packing List

Cross out the items that don't apply. Then check off each remaining item as you place it in your suitcase.

- ❏ Airline tickets and travel itinerary (confirmation numbers for your airline, hotel and car rental reservations)
- ❏ Bathing suits
- ❏ Beach towels
- ❏ Books
- ❏ Cash or traveler's checks
- ❏ Camera, camcorder, film, batteries
- ❏ Coat(s) (light or heavy depending on destination)
- ❏ Cosmetics
- ❏ Credit & ATM cards
- ❏ Day clothes
- ❏ Drivers' Lisence, passport and/or photo ID
- ❏ Evening wear
- ❏ First-Aid kit
- ❏ Fashion accessories (ties, belts, hats)
- ❏ Handbag/pocketbook
- ❏ Hair care products (blow-dryer, curling iron, shampoo, conditioner, etc.)
- ❏ Jeans

- ❏ Jewelry
- ❏ Magazines
- ❏ Medications
- ❏ Playing cards
- ❏ Sandals/dress shoes/beach shoes
- ❏ Sleeping clothes/pajamas
- ❏ Sneakers/comfortable walking shoes
- ❏ Socks/pantyhose
- ❏ Sporting gear (tennis rackets, gold clubs, rollerblades, etc.)
- ❏ Suits/Skirts/Dresses
- ❏ Sunglasses
- ❏ Sunscreen
- ❏ Sweaters/sweatshirts
- ❏ Toiletries
- ❏ Trousers/Slacks
- ❏ Underwear
- ❏ Wallet
- ❏ Workout clothes

Paying the Piper

Those couples who have waited for just the right moment to take a holiday together are all but guaranteed a good time, provided they resolve the issue of finances to their mutual satisfaction. Unfortunately, money is the dark, or rather the green, underbelly of all things exciting and new. Only the most stringent ascetics will dispute the fact that credit and ATM cards have become our only lifeline to the finer things and experiences. From plane tickets, to hotel rooms, to taxi cabs, to restaurants, you can't go one waking hour, on vacation, without parting with greenbacks—even if it's only to buy a two-dollar bottle of designer H2O.

The sooner you settle the question of money, the better. To avoid a miscommunication, you should explain your financial intentions to your companion right after asking him/her to go on a trip. If you're planning to play the generous host/esse, make it clear to your s.o. that your wish is to take them on vacation, so they don't spend hours wondering whether or not you meant to treat them. If, however, you're playing the Pauper to your partner's Prince, and you would like them to take you on vacation, go ahead and say so—if you must (remember, soliciting gifts can be construed as terminally uncouth). Don't act as if you'll be paying for half if you expect your boy/girlfriend to cover your losses, they may get the wrong impression and wind up resenting you for tricking them into spending too much money. The best way to go about your first vacation, if you and your partner share an income-tax bracket, is to split the bills.

Unless you want to keep a running tally of every last expenditure, be prepared to throw your calculator to the wind and divvy the expenses according to categories. For example, you can arrange to pay for the flight and let your s.o. pay for the hotel. Once you're at your destination, the two of you can alternate paying for meals and transportation. Try not to get carried away by this spirit of equality, lest you find your cross-country vacation ruined by an argument over whose turn it is to spring for the toll tax.

A Trip for all Relationship Seasons

Since the type of getaway you decide to pursue will determine much of the planning, we've broken this section into a variety of travel circumstances. The logistics of packing and finances will vary,

but you can be sure that if you've got the will, you'll find your way with the following guidelines.

A Hasty Retreat: Spending two to four days with the object of your affection is a great way to prepare for the grand-scale vacations that are bound to spice up your future together. Short trips are heavy on fun and light on emotional and time commitments. Best of all, their cost pales in comparison to what you'd spend on a week or more of romantic revelry.

In terms of packing, one bag will do. Remember to pack for the weather and keep your agenda in mind. Comfortable shoes are a must if you plan on doing a lot of walking. For spending time at the beach or poolside, you don't have to be a fashionista to know that swimsuits/trunks are de riguer. Since you'll be gone only for a few days, two to three evening ensembles, two pairs of pants/jeans, three sweaters, shirts or T's (depending on the weather), and one pair of dress shoes will get you through this difficult time away from your closet. Don't worry about wearing the same thing twice—your companion won't hate you for it.

A Long Respite: If you decide that nothing but the full vacation experience is good enough for you and your special friend's first getaway, expect to spend seven to sixteen days in close proximity, and don't act so surprised when the Visa bill comes. These vacations will cost you, but there are ways to cut corners without coming off like a closefisted tightwad.

Traveling at off-peak seasons is the best way to keep your generous image in tact. Airfare is cheap and hotel accommodations plummet, but you still get to take in the same sights as the people who paid too much for their vacation. If you're going to Europe, taking advantage of the strong dollar and the Europeans' difficulty in transferring to the European Currency Unit (ECU) will also save you thousands. When staying in a foreign land, eschew the ATM and opt to use your credit cards for the most favorable exchange rate.

When choosing a hotel, look for those that offer kitchenettes in every room and a complimentary breakfast. Oftentimes, tourists are forced to go out for breakfast, lunch, and dinner simply for lack of alternatives. If your room features a good-sized refrigerator, you can feign interest in the local markets, fill up your shopping cart with every imaginable delicacy, and save yourself a bundle in lunch

What's Your Sign? Romance According to the Zodiac

Pisces

Through the heart, sensitive Pisces experiences his subjective reality as real, solid, perhaps even more tangible than the external world. For some Pisces, romance can be the point of transcendence, the source where he penetrates to the larger mysteries that have concerned him most of his life. To be romantically involved with a Pisces is to be introduced to many levels of consciousness and awareness. If you're not up to it, then get out now because your Pisces isn't going to change.

checks. Your opportunity to appear freehanded will come at dinner time, but going all out on just one meal per day isn't likely to put you in the poor house.

All-inclusive resorts, providing you with three squares per day and all the homespun entertainment you can handle, can also cut down on spending. Many people looking to relax prefer to stay at such places just to avoid having to pick out restaurants and think up new itineraries day in and day out. Of course, these resorts will cost more than those boasting only the basic amenities, but if you don't mind staying put for the duration of your visit, you'll find that you get a great return on your initial investment.

Ocean Liners: Pay no mind to the fashion industry's hype—there is no such thing as cruise wear. For tropical cruises, your summer clothes will suit you just fine. Neither will you stick out like a sore thumb when sailing through the colder regions in your autumnal best.

Come aboard any pleasure cruise, and you'll most certainly find a social calendar chock full of gala-like evenings. You'll need a few outfits of the casually dressy if you plan to attend these functions. If your cruise coincides with New Year's Eve, plan on taking a cocktail dress or a good suit.

The best thing about cruises, aside from their Love Boat-inspired mystique, is the pricing. Since all your meals are included in the cost, and buffets are set up round the clock, you shouldn't have to spend a dime on victuals—unless, of course, you decide to sample some regional cuisine at one of the docking stations. The social director will inundate you with enough charades, bingo, dance lessons, and stage shows to last a lifetime, so your recreation is also taken care of. In short, a cruise, much like all-inclusive resorts, will allow you to calculate the exact cost of your great escape months in advance.

The very quality that makes a cruise great, however, is also the one that can leave you with that sinking feeling. Unlike short vacations or urban travels, a ship gives people little opportunity to go their separate ways. When in you're in the same boat, all attempts to spend time apart may seem forced and unnatural. After all, it's not as if one of you can go shopping while the other hits the slopes or the museums. To get some breathing room, your best bet is to affect a sudden interest in the Conga line class when your companion is intent on getting a tan. Even then, you run the risk of hurting your travel companion's feelings, so tread carefully.

Road Trips: Forget what you've heard about the four directions, a road trip can only go in one of two ways—beautifully or hideously. To survive the paired road trip with your bond in tact, your relationship will have to have weathered a great deal of trials and tribulations already. Otherwise, you two had better be two of the best natured people since Adam and Eve, or, at the very least, Donny and Marie.

Aside from the time you spend in motel bathrooms, you and your s.o. will not have one moment apart. Driving for long stretches will require that you plan ahead. Think of games that you two can play to pass the hours, pack a cooler full of snacks and drinks to enjoy between pitstops, choose music that both you and your companion can sing along with, and bring an assortment of books and/or magazines that will help you to escape into another world—a world where external stimuli are not limited to a neverending stretch of highway.

Before you leave for your trip, you'll have to pack some comfortable traveling clothes. If it's summer time and the weather if fine, bring an excess of T-shirts and shorts (since sitting in a hot car can give you that not-so-fresh feeling, you'll want to change your outfits often). In winter, stay warm and cozy with coats and sweaters—but keep in mind that winter road trips are not recommended due to potentially hazardouz road conditions.

Most importantly, don't forget to discuss the driving arrangements. It would be a shame if one of you had to do all the driving simply because the other couldn't handle a stick-shift.

Chapter 12

Romantic Dining:
Food for Thought

ood and romance have gone together for thousands of years—since the first man came home to the cave from a successful hunt!

Whether it's sharing a pizza delivered by the local pizzeria or grilling a sirloin steak on a hibachi there is no better way to get to know someone than to share a meal at home. You can both dress as you choose, relax, play background music of your choice, and linger over your meal as no waitperson will hover with a check. Your dining table might not be mahogany Chippendale, (and in fact you might have to set up the dinning table in your living room) and your dishes not English bone china, but nothing is more romantic than dinner for two at home.

When planning dinner-for-two at home, don't forget that attention to small details can often set the mood for the evening. You should think about the lighting in the room where you are going to eat. Is it too bright or too dim? What about candles—will that make it too obviously romantic and your date make jokes about not being able to see the food on the table? Or will it add just the "right" touch and set a comfortable mood.

For the table, think about using a real table cloth instead of placemats. It does add a bit of elegance. You can also go all the way and use cloth napkins!

A bunch of flowers in a vase or pitcher placed in the room is a nice addition. You could even put the vase of flowers on the dinner table, assuming they will not block your view of your date.

Make sure any animals you might have, such as a cat or dog are not going to interfere in your dinner for two. It really will not impress your date if your cat jumps up on the table and starts eating from your plate, or the dog suddenly barks to be walked when your serving the appetizer.

And do clean before your dinner-for-two. We're not suggesting clean as if your mother and grandmother were coming to visit. But think about the message you want your pad to convey to your date and tidy up.

Last, but not least, after making all the preparations for your dinner-for-two, be sure to leave some time for yourself before your date arrives. There's no sense in going to all that trouble and then your date arrives to find you hassled.

Wine with Dinner

Wine can enhance any meal and if you want to serve wine with your dinner, give some thought to the wine you will serve.

Remember you and your date need not feel the need to finish a bottle of wine. And if you have plans to go out after your dinner, think about serving lower-alcohol wine.

Since your date probably has only a causal interest in wine (most people do) and is going to drink the wine with a meal, you should serve a wine that is easy to like.

White Wine

If your date likes white wine and likes things that are familiar, then a California Chardonnay is a good choice. The wine is probably going to taste good, assuming you don't look for the cheapest California Chardonnay in the store. Also, there I nothing more familiar to the casual white-wine drinker than "California" and "Chardonnay." If there is a knowledgeable salesperson in the store, ask for a bottle that isn't too acidic or oaky; a $12 Chardonnay from California is a very safe bet. An Italian Pinot Grigio costing $10-$12 is a good choice for a lighter white wine. These wines are excellent with food.

The Semillon/Chardonnay blends from Australia are also usually very good and fairly priced at $8-$10. You could also track down a bottle of wine from your home state. The majority of states have a commercial wine industry that produces accessible wines, although they tend to be a couple of dollars overprices.

Red Wine

When it comes to red wine, there is no sure thing equivalent to the white California Cahrdonnays. If you are trying to buy a red wine, you might try a Chianti from Italy, which matches very well with food. Chianti, thanks in part to the American jug wine named Chianti, has a lot of name recognition. Although decent $8 bottles are out there, you may want to improve your odds of getting a good bottle and spend $10.

A Canadian Baco Noir is a very drinkable red wine. It's quite compatible with food but boring without it. A price of $8-$10 will usually get you a good-tasting, unassuming Canadian red. French Beaujolais (Nouveau or not) wines from the Gamay grape are easy to buy ($8-$10) and easy to drink. Many of the Beaujolais Nouveaus also come with a festive wine label.

If you are interested in spending upward of $20 for a red, a California, celebrity-free Pinot Noir may be your best option. These wines are rich and fruity and go well with food.

Wine and the Internet

The Internet is a great resource. Why? Because in addition to the advertisements from various producers of wine, there is an amazing amount of free, specific, and accurate information.

Web pages come and go, but it looks like www.winevin.com, a computer industry Web-site award winner, will be around for awhile. This is a good place to start in your on-line wine odyssey.

The Internet may become the first place the wine industry ever seriously attempts to target younger adults. The Internet is cheap, hip, and unstuffy—adjectives people don't usually use to describe the wine world.

We don't recommend you order wine on-line and have it shipped, because of the cost of shipping and the uncertainties of temperature and handling of your wine. You may also encounter some unpleasant legal consequences if the wine is shipped across a state line. What you can do is to find a review of a good wine on-line, and then go out and buy it.

WHITES
at a glance...

	CHEAP	BETTER	GREAT	OFF DRY	DRY	WITH FOOD	WITHOUT FOOD
Chardonnay	🍷	🍷	🍷🍷		🍷	🍷	🍷
Riesling	🍷	🍷	🍷🍷	🍷	🍷	🍷	🍷
Sauvignon Blanc	🍷	🍷	🍷		🍷	🍷	
Chenin Blanc	🍷	🍷		🍷	🍷	🍷	
Pinot Blanc		🍷			🍷	🍷	
Pinot Grigio (Gris)	🍷	🍷			🍷	🍷	
Gewürztraminer			🍷	🍷			
Semillon		🍷	🍷	🍷		🍷	
Trebbiano (Ugni Blanc)	🍷				🍷	🍷	

Cheap: Under $10 *Better:* $10–$19 *Great:* $50 and up Extrodinary performance within category

White wine generally isn't as complex as red wine. This is why we have so few in the *Without Food* category. On the flip side, it tends to be acidic (in a good way), which gives it a thirst-quenching quality. That is why whites go so well with food.

REDS
at a glance...

There are good wine values in all price ranges for almost all varietals. This chart is meant to be a general guide of what to look for. It reflects general quality and quantity of wines available at the various price levels.

	CHEAP	BETTER	GREAT	LESS DRY	DRY	WITH FOOD	WITHOUT FOOD
Cabernet Sauvignon		🍷	🍷🍷	🍷	🍷	🍷	🍷
Merlot		🍷		🍷	🍷	🍷	🍷
Gamay	🍷🍷	🍷		🍷		🍷	🍷
Pinot Noir		🍷	🍷🍷	🍷		🍷	🍷
Syrah (Shiraz)	🍷🍷	🍷	🍷	🍷	🍷		🍷
Petit Sirah		🍷			🍷	🍷	
Grenache	🍷				🍷	🍷	
Nebbiolo		🍷	🍷🍷		🍷	🍷	
Sangiovese	🍷	🍷	🍷		🍷	🍷	
Zinfandel		🍷		🍷			🍷
Tempranillo	🍷	🍷			🍷	🍷	

Romantic Menus

Here are five different menus you might want to follow for a fabulous, romantic evening. Always try out a recipe a couple of days before you make it for your BIG DATE DINNER-FOR-TWO, though. You don't want the evening ruined because you made the recipes for the first time that evening and forgot, in your excitement, a major ingredient. Become familiar with the recipes before making them for the big night.

The receipts give you ample leftovers for two, so you two can really indulge yourselves. They range from pasta to fish to a roast to a vegetarian meal. The desserts are particularly elegant! Enjoy!

Dinner #1

Appetizer

Cajun Chicken Fingers

2 cloves garlic, minced
1/4 cup dried bread crumbs
1 tablespoon grated Parmesan cheese
1 tablespoon minced fresh parsley
1/2 teaspoon paprika
1/2 teaspoon dried oregano, crumbled
black pepper to taste
1/2 pound boneless, skinless chicken breasts, cut into long, narrow strips
1/4 cup milk

Preheat oven to 425 F. Spray a banking sheet with nonstick baking spray.

In a shallow dish, mix together the garlic, bread crumbs, Parmesan cheese, parsley, paprika, oregano, and pepper. Dip the chicken strips in the milk, then roll in the crumb mixture and arrange on the prepared baking sheet.

Bake for 5 minutes; turn and bake for 5 more minutes, or until the chicken is done. Serve hot.

You will have plenty of chicken fingers for this appetizer as this makes enough for 6 people.

Main Course

Herbed Rice Pilaf

1 tablespoon olive oil
1 onion, chopped
2 celery stalks, chopped
1 clove garlic, minced
1 teaspoon dried thyme, crumbled
1 bay leaf
2 1/2 cups water
1 cup long-grain white rice
1 fresh thyme sprig

In a medium saucepan, heat the oil over medium heat. Add the onion, celery, garlic, and thyme and sauté until the onion is translucent, about 5 minutes. Add the bay leaf and water, bring to a boil, and add the rice. Cover, reduce the heat to low, and simmer until all the water is absorbed and rice is tender, about 20 minutes.

Remove and discard the bay leaf. Spoon pilaf into a serving bowl. Garnish with the thyme sprig.

Quick-Sole Florentine in the Microwave

1 pound sole fillets
salt and pepper to taste
1/2 teaspoon paprika
2 cups stemmed spinach leaves

On a large microwave-safe plate, arrange the fillets. Season the fillets with salt, pepper, and paprika. Cover the plate with plastic wrap. Cut a small slit in the plastic wrap. Microwave on high for 5 minutes. Remove the plastic wrap. Drain off the juices and sprinkle spinach leaves over fillets. Serve at once.

Summer vegetable Paella

1 teaspoon olive oil
3 cups broccoli florets
2 zucchini, sliced on the diagonal
1 tomato, diced
2 nectarines, pitted and sliced

In a large nonstick skillet, heat the oil over high heat. Add the broccoli and zucchini and cook, stirring often, for 5 minutes. Add the tomato and nectarines, cover, lower heat to medium, and cook until the vegetables are crisp-tender, 2 to 3 minutes longer.

Dessert

Chocolate Fondue
Serves 4

6 ounces milk chocolate
1/4 cup whipping cream
1 1/2 tablespoons orange-flavored liqueur
1/4 cup almonds, toasted and chopped
1 teaspoon honey
angel food cake squares
canned pineapple chunks, drained and chilled
canned mandarin oranges, drained and chilled
sliced bananas, chilled
strawberries, chilled

Combine the chocolate, cream, liqueur, almonds and honey in a saucepan. Heat slowly until the chocolate is melted, stirring well. Pour the chocolate into a fondue pot placed over a low flame.

Arrange the cake squares, pineapple, oranges, bananas (dip in sugar water to prevent browning), and strawberries on a platter or in small bowls. Spear pieces of fruit and cake onto fondue forks and dip into the warm mixture.

Dinner #2

Appetizer

Chilled Yogurt Dip
Yields 1 1/2 cups

1 cup (8 ounces) nonfat plain yogurt
1/2 cup shredded cucumber
1/3 teaspoon dried dill, crumbled

Combine all the ingredients in a bowl and mix well. Serve with carrots, broccoli, celery, cauliflower, sliced peppers for dipping.

Main Course

California Fettuccine

1/2 pound eggless fettuccine
1/2 avocado, pitted, peeled, and cut into chunks
1 can (8 ounces) marinated artichoke hearts, drained
1 large tomato, diced
2 cloves garlic, minced
1 tablespoon olive oil
2 scallions, thinly sliced
1/2 bound cooked shrimp
2 tablespoons grated Parmesan cheese

Cook the fettuccine in boiling salted water until al dente. Drain and place in a bowl. Add all the remaining ingredients except the Parmesan cheese and toss well. Serve warm or chilled. top with the Parmesan just before serving.

Variations: Chopped fresh basil or coriander or toasted sesame seeds are nice additions to this dish.

Stuffed Tomatoes
Serves 2

2 large tomatoes
2 tablespoons chopped fresh parsley
2 tablespoons chopped onion
2 cloves garlic, minced
1/4 teaspoon dried thyme, crumbled
1 tablespoon dried basil
1/4 cup seasoned dried bread crumbs
salt and pepper to taste
1 teaspoon olive oil

Preheat oven to 350 F. slice the top of each tomato, reserving the "lids." Scoop out the pulp and reserve in a bowl. To the tomato pulp, add the parsley, onion, garlic, thyme, and basil and blend. Add the bread crumbs, salt, pepper, and oil and mix well. fill the tomato shells with this mixture. replace the lids.

Bake until mixture is heated through. Serve immediately.

Dessert

Died and Went to Heaven Chocolate Cake
This cake serves 12, so you will have plenty left over.

1 3/4 cups flour
1 cup granulated sugar
3/4 cup unsweetened cocoa powder
1 1/2 teaspoons baking soda
1 1/2 teaspoons baking powder
1 teaspoon salt

1 1/4 cups buttermilk
1 cup packed brown sugar
2 eggs, lightly beaten
1/4 cup vegetable oil, preferable canola oil
2 teaspoons vanilla extract
1 cup hot strong brewed coffee

Frosting:
1 1/2 cups confectioners' sugar
1/2 teaspoon vanilla extract
1 to 2 tablespoons buttermilk

Preheat an oven to 350 F. Lightly oil a 12-cup bundt pan.

In a bowl, stir together the flour, granulated sugar, cocoa, baking soda, baking powder, and salt. Add the buttermilk, brown sugar, eggs, oil, and vanilla and beat for 2 minutes until well incorporated. Stir in the hot coffee until completely incorporated. (The batter will be thin.) Pour into the prepared bundt pan.

Bake for 35 to 40 minutes, or until a knife comes out clean. Let cool in the pan on a rack for 10 minutes, then turn out onto the rack and let cool completely.

To make the frosting, in a bowl, beat together the confectioners'; sugar, vanilla, and enough butter-milk to make a thick but pourable frosting. Drizzle the frosting evenly over the tope of the cake.

Dinner #3

Appetizers

Melted Cheese Triangles
Makes 20 to 30 pieces

1/4 pound mozzarella, Brie, Camembert, or
*   other melting cheese*
2 cups fresh dill, packed
20 to 30 wonton skins
1 egg, beaten
Vegetable oil for deep-frying

Slice the cheese into about 30 strips, each 1 inch long and $\frac{1}{4}$ inch thick. Cut dill into 1-inch pieces.

Work with a few wonton skins at a time. Keep others covered with a damp cloth to prevent drying. Brush edges with beaten egg. Place 1 strip of cheese and 1 piece of dill in the middle and fold to form a triangle. press edges firmly to seal. Place the triangles on a lightly oiled surface and cover with a kitchen towel to keep from drying out.

In a 5-quart saucepan or a deep fryer, heat 2 inchs of oil to 370. Fry the triangles, 5 at a time, until golden brown on both sides. Remove and drain on paper towels. Serve hot.

Main Course

Steak Stroganoff
Enough for 4

1 pound boneless round steak
3 tablespoons margarine
$\frac{1}{2}$ cup chopped onions
$\frac{1}{2}$ pound mushrooms, sliced
2 tablespoons tomato paste
2 tablespoons water
$\frac{1}{2}$ teaspoon dried basil, crumbled
1 tablespoon cornstarch
1 cup lain yogurt
$\frac{1}{4}$ cup sherry or beef broth
3 cups hot cooked noodles

Trim off any visible fat from the beef, then slice the beef into narrow strips.

In a skillet, melt 2 tablespoons of the margarine over medium heat. Add the onion and sauté until soft about 5 minutes. Add the beef and cook, stirring occasionally, until browned, about 5 minutes. Remove the beef to a plate and keep warm. Add the remaining 1 tablespoon margarine to the skillet, melt over medium heat, and add the mushrooms. sauté

until mushrooms are soft, about 8 minutes. Stir in the tomato paste, water, and basil. Return the meat the skillet and simmer briefly.

In a small saucepan, mix together the cornstarch with 1 tablespoon of the yogurt until thoroughly combined. Then stir in the remaining yogurt and cook over medium heat until thickened, about 10 minutes. Add to the meat mixture and heat through. Thin the sauce with the sherry or broth. Serve over cooked noodles.

St. Tropez Vegetables

2 pounds summer squash, cut into $\frac{1}{4}$-inch-thick
*   slices*
2 pounds tomatoes, cut into wedges
1 onion very thinly sliced
2 teaspoons dried basil
$\frac{1}{4}$ teaspoon pepper
4 teaspoons minced garlic
3 tablespoons pistachio nuts, chopped

Preheat oven to 400 F.

Cut six 15-inch squares of parchment paper or foil. Place on a work surface. Divide the squash, tomatoes, and onion evenly among the squares, stacking the ingredients. Sprinkle with the basil, pepper, and garlic. Bring together the opposite sides of the square and fold down tightly. Next, fold the ends under to seal in any juices. Place in a shallow baking pan. Bake until the vegetables are tender, about 40 minutes. To test for doneness, open 1 packet and check for firmness and temperature. (Be careful of steam.) Sprinkle the vegetables wit the pistachios just before serving.

Roasted Potatoes with Rosemary and Garlic

2 pounds red new potatoes, sliced
2 tablespoons olive oil
3 cloves garlic, minced
2 teaspoons dried rosemary
salt and pepper to taste

Preheat oven to 325 F.

In a large banking dish, toss the potatoes with the oil, garlic, rosemary, salt, and pepper. Bake until the potatoes are tender when pierced with a fork, about 1 hour. Serve at once.

Dessert

Peach Melba

Serves 4

Melba Sauce:

1 package (10 ounces) frozen raspberries, thawed
1/2 cup currant jelly
1 1/2 teaspoons cornstarch
1 tablespoon water
1 pint vanilla ice cream
4 peach halves
sweetened whipped cream (optional)

To make the Melba sauce, combine the raspberries and jelly in a saucepan and bring to a boil. In a small cup, stir together the cornstarch and water, and then stir into the raspberry mixture. cook for 15 minutes, or until thickened, stirring constantly. Strain, let cool, cover, and chill before serving.

Scoop out (or slice) one-fourth of the ice cream onto each of 4 dessert plates. Top each with a peach half, cut side down. Spoon the sauce over the peaches and top with whipped cream, if desired.

Dinner #4: Light Dinner

Appetizer

Shells stuffed with Chicken and Fennel

Makes about 36

$3/4$ pound jumbo shells
1 tablespoon salt

Filling

$3/4$ pound ground chicken, white meat only
1 tablespoon ground fennel seeds
1 egg white
$1^{1}/_{4}$ cups cold heavy cream plus 1 teaspoon
1 teaspoon oilive oil
2 dashed Tabasco

Sauce

$2^{1}/_{2}$ cups heavy cream
$1/_{2}$ cup freshly grated parmesan cheese
1 teaspoon salt
$1/_{2}$ teaspoon pepper
2 tablespoons chopped scallions

Preheat the oven to 400 f.

In a large pot, bring at least 4 quarts of water to a rolling boil. Add the tablespoon salt. Add the shells and stir to prevent sticking. cook until al dente. Drain. Transfer to a bowl and toss lightly with olive oil.

Make the filling: Puree the chicken, fennel and egg white in a food processor until smooth. Transfer to a bowl, then set in a larger bowl containing ice water to chill. Add the cream, $1/4$ cup at a time, stirring after each addition. Stir in the teaspoon salt and Tabasco. When thoroughly chilled, fill shells with the filling, using a pastry bag with a plain tube tip or a spoon.

Make the sauce: Combine all the sauce ingredients in a saucepan and bring to a boil over low heat.

Place a single layer of filled shells in a baking dish, keeping them separated, and pour the sauce over them. Bake until the sauce is thick and bubbly, about 15 minutes. Arrange attractively on a warm serving tray and place a toothpick in each shell.

Main Course

Strawberry Chicken Salad

1/2 cup mayonnaise
2 tablespoons chutney
1 tablespoon lemon juice
1 teaspoon grated lemon zest
1 teaspoon salt
1 teaspoon curry powder
2 cups diced cooked chicken
1 cup sliced celery
1/4 cur chopped red onion
4 lettuce leaves
1 1/2 pints strawberries, stemmed
fresh mint sprigs

In a large bowl, stir together the mayonnaise, chutney, lemon juice and zest, salt, and curry powder, mixing well. Add the chicken, celery, and onion. Toss well, cover and chill.

Just before serving, slice 1 pint of the strawberries. Add to the chicken mixture and toss gently. Line a platter of individual serving plates with the lettuce leaves. Mound the chicken mixture on the lettuce. Garnish with the whole strawberries and mint. Serve at once.

Dessert

Cherries Jubilee

1 can (16 ounces) pitted sweet cherries
1/3 cup sugar
2 tablespoons cornstarch
1 tablespoon lemon juice
1/3 cup brandy (optional)
ice cream or cake a la mode

Drain the cherries, reserving the juice in a measuring cup. Add enough eater to the juice to make 1 cup liquid. In a small saucepan, mix together the sugar and cornstarch. Gradually stir in the dilutes cherry juice until smooth. Bring to a boil over medium heat, stirring constantly. Boil for 1 minutes. Add the cherries and lemon juice, remove from the heat, and keep warm.

Just before serving, add the brandy, if desired, and ignite. After the flame dies down, spoon the cherries over ice cream or cake a la mode.

Dinner #5: Vegetarian

Appetizer

Stuffed Celery Stalks

12 long celery stalks with leaves attached
6 ounces cream cheese, at room temperature
1/2 cut cottage cheese
1/4 onion, cut up (optional)
2 tablespoons milk (if needed)
12 large pimiento-stuffed green olives, cut into
    1/4 inch-thick slices
several shakes of paprika

Set the celery stalks on a cutting board, hollow side up. In small blender or food processor, combine the cream cheese, cottage cheese, and the

Superstitions About Dating

If you have tried a computer dating service, astrology, singles clubs, volunteered and gone on many blind dates and still haven't found the "right" mate for you, take some tips from our ancestors. Here are some old superstitions and rituals that might be helpful.

If you are a young woman, make a pie. That's a tall order these days. How many women, even middle-aged, make pies? But if you're desperate to know when you'll marry, it's worth it. While trimming the pie crust, if it falls over your hand, that is a sign you will marry young.

If a man dreams of the same woman three nights in a row, then she is the woman he is to marry. If a man dreams ofthe same woman three nights in a row, find out what perfume she was wearing!

For eons four-leaf clovers have meant good luck. One of these suggestions using a four-leaf clover might help you find the right mate. But first, you have to find a four-leaf clover. Four-leave clovers grow best in unkempt lawns. Be sure the clover hasn't been sprayed with pesticides, our modern-day equivalent of evil spirits.

For women: Take your newly-found four-leave clover and pin it over the door to your house or apartment. Don't use tape, that might break the charm. There's something about the clover's touching metal that makes the charm work. And besides, the ancients didn't have tape. The first unmarried man who walks through your door after you've hung the clover is the man you will marry.

For men: In the morning, put the newly-found four-leaf clover in one of your shoes you are going to wear that day. The first unmarried woman you meet that day is the woman you will marry. And besides, fresh clover is better than Odor-Eaters!

onion, if using. Process at high speed for 4 minutes until smooth. If the mixture is very thick, add the milk, a few drops at a time, to thin to spreading consistency.

Using a knife, spread the mixture in the hollows of the celery stalks, dividing it evenly among the stalks. Push olive slices into the spread along with the entire length of each stalk. Wrap in plastic wrap and chill well. Just before serving, unwrap and sprinkle with paprika.

Main Course

Pad Thai

1/4 pound dried rice noodles
2 teaspoons peanut oil
3 cloves garlic, minced
1 egg, lightly beaten
1/2 pound small shrimp, peeled and deveined
2 cups mung bean sprouts
1/2 cup sliced scallion greens
3 tablespoons rice vinegar
2 1/2 tablespoons fish sauce
2 tablespoons sugar
1 teaspoon Chinese chile paste with garlic
3 tablespoons chopped dry-roasted peanuts

In a large bowl, soak rice noodles in warm water to cover until they are limp and white, about 20 minutes. In a wok or large deep skillet, heat oil over high heat until very hot. Add the garlic and stir-fry until golden, about 10 seconds. Add the egg and cook, stirring, until scrambled, about 30 seconds. Add shrimp and stir-fry until they curl and turn pink, about 2 minutes.

Drain the noodles and add to the wok, tossing with tongs until they soften and curl, about 1 minutes. Add bean sprouts, scallion greens, vinegar, fish sauce, sugar and Chile paste. Toss until the shrimp are fully cooked and noodles are heated through, 1 to 2 minutes. Sprinkle with peanuts and serve immediately.

Dessert

Strawberry whip

1 egg white
1 1/4 cups strawberries, sliced
1/4 cup sugar
a few drops of lemon juice

In a bowl, using an electric mixer, whip together the egg white and strawberries. When the mixture begins to thicken, gradually add the sugar. Continue to beat until the mixture holds soft peaks. Stir in a few drops of lemon juice. Chill before serving.

Last Words: May The Dating Force Be With You

Congratulations! You have earned a degree from our very own dating school. You are now prepared to enter the world of dating with full force and vigor. It's not everyday you learn the ins and outs of the dating world, and you have done precisely that. You've acquired crucial skills and strategies that will help you make every date better than the last. From the first impression to the first joint purchase, you now have the power to call the shots and have a great time doing it.

Whether you were utterly confused or already in the know when it came to the opposite sex, we hope you've gained the added insight you'll need to forge lasting and durable relationships with anyone you choose. But even though you have earned your dating stripes, you will probably have to keep learning and growing as you make your way through life's tunnel of love.

One of the best things about the world of dating, is that you will be continuously challenged, amused, and surprised. One day you may be composing depressing poems about solitude and feeling like you'll never find someone who cares, and the next, you'll be wearing rose-colored glasses and riding cloud nine all the way into the sunset with someone you love. It's that unpredictable.

So we urge you to take things slow. Once you've read this book, try to digest the contents. Decide which rules apply to you, and how you can best use them to bring love into your life. It may take some time to get what you want, but remember to enjoy the process. Because if you only learned one thing, it's that the journey toward love can be as much fun as the destination. Good luck—not that you need it.

Index

EVERYTHING

The Everything Wedding® Book

by Janet Anastasio and Michelle Bevilacqua

Setting the date. Registering for gifts. Hiring the caterer. Arranging the reception. Finding the right photographer. Selecting the attire for the bridal party. The list goes on and on. There are hundreds of details to be attended to when it comes to planning the most special day of your life. Wedding experts Janet Anastasio and Michelle Bevilacqua offer insights, advice, menu plans, ceremony suggestions, and dozens of detailed charts and lists—in short, everything needed to plan the perfect wedding. For anyone planning a wedding—or anyone planning to make life easier for anyone planning a wedding—*The Everything Wedding Book*® is the A-Z resource to use.

Trade paperback, $12.95
1-58062-190-2, 320 pages

The Everything Wine Book

by Danny May and Andy Sharpe

It used to be that the world of wine was a closed door to all except for the cultural elite. Well, not any more! *The Everything Wine Book* is the perfect primer for anyone with even the slightest interest in wine, whether you are planning to spend $5 a bottle or $50. This is the complete wine resource that's easily accessible and authoritatively written. This friendly, informative book covers everything you need to know. *The Everything Wine Book* takes the mystery out of ordering the perfect bottle of wine.

Trade paperback, $12.95
1-55850-808-2, 304 pages

Available Wherever Books Are Sold

If you cannot find these titles at your favorite retail outlet, you may order them directly from the publisher. BY PHONE: Call 1-800-872-5627. We accept Visa, MasterCard, and American Express. $4.95 will be added to your total order for shipping and handling. BY MAIL: Write out the full titles of the books you'd like to order and send payment, including $4.95 for shipping and handling, to: Adams Media Corporation, 260 Center Street, Holbrook, MA 02343. 30-day money-back guarantee.

We Have EVERYTHING

More bestselling Everything titles available from your local bookseller:

Everything **After College Book**
Everything **Astrology Book**
Everything **Baby Names Book**
Everything® **Bartender's Book**
Everything **Bedtime Story Book**
Everything **Beer Book**
Everything **Bicycle Book**
Everything **Bird Book**
Everything **Casino Gambling Book**
Everything **Cat Book**
Everything® **Christmas Book**
Everything **College Survival Book**
Everything **Crossword and Puzzle Book**
Everything **Dating Book**
Everything **Dessert Book**
Everything **Dog Book**
Everything **Dreams Book**
Everything **Etiquette Book**
Everything **Family Tree Book**
Everything **Fly-Fishing Book**
Everything **Games Book**
Everything **Get-a-Job Book**
Everything **Get Ready For Baby Book**
Everything **Golf Book**

Everything **Guide to Walt Disney World®, Universal Studios®, and Greater Orlando**
Everything **Home Buying Book**
Everything **Home Improvement Book**
Everything **Internet Book**
Everything **Investing Book**
Everything **Jewish Wedding Book**
Everything **Low-Fat High-Flavor Cookbook**
Everything **Money Book**
Everything **One-Pot Cookbook**
Everything **Pasta Book**
Everything **Pregnancy Book**
Everything **Sailing Book**
Everything **Study Book**
Everything **Tarot Book**
Everything **Toasts Book**
Everything **Trivia Book**
Everything® **Wedding Book**
Everything® **Wedding Checklist**
Everything® **Wedding Etiquette Book**
Everything® **Wedding Organizer**
Everything® **Wedding Shower Book**
Everything® **Wedding Vows Book**
Everything **Wine Book**